Machiavellian Ontology

Incitements

Series editors: Peg Birmingham, DePaul University and
Dimitris Vardoulakis, Western Sydney University

Editorial Advisory Board

Étienne Balibar, Andrew Benjamin, Jay M. Bernstein, Rosi Braidotti, Wendy Brown, Judith Butler, Timothy Campbell, Adriana Cavarero, Howard Caygill, Rebecca Comay, Joan Copjec, Simon Critchley, Filippo Del Lucchese, Costas Douzinas, Peter Fenves, Christopher Fynsk, Moira Gatens, Gregg Lambert, Leonard Lawlor, Genevieve Lloyd, Catherine Malabou, James Martel, Christoph Menke, Warren Montag, Michael Naas, Antonio Negri, Kelly Oliver, Paul Patton, Anson Rabinbach, Gerhard Richter, Martin Saar, Miguel Vatter, Gianni Vattimo, Santiago Zabala

Available

Return Statements: The Return of Religion in Contemporary Philosophy
Gregg Lambert

The Refusal of Politics
Laurent Dubreuil, translated by Cory Browning

Plastic Sovereignties: Agamben and the Politics of Aesthetics
Arne De Boever

From Violence to Speaking Out: Apocalypse and Expression in Foucault, Derrida and Deleuze
Leonard Lawlor

Agonistic Mourning: Political Dissidence and the Women in Black
Athena Athanasiou

Interpassivity: The Aesthetics of Delegated Enjoyment
Robert Pfaller

Derrida's Secret: Perjury, Testimony, Oath
Charles Barbour

Resistance and Psychoanalysis: Impossible Divisions
Simon Morgan Wortham

Reclaiming Wonder: After the Sublime
Genevieve Lloyd

Arendt, Natality and Biopolitics: Towards Democratic Plurality and Reproductive Justice
Rosalyn Diprose and Ewa Plonowska Ziarek

Worldlessness After Heidegger: Phenomenology, Psychoanalysis, Deconstruction
Roland Végső

Homo Natura: Nietzsche, Philosophical Anthropology and Biopolitics
Vanessa Lemm

Spinoza, The Transindividual
Étienne Balibar, translated by Mark G. E. Kelly

Uncontainable Legacies: Theses on Intellectual, Cultural, and Political Inheritance
Gerhard Richter

The Trial of Hatred: An Essay on the Refusal of Violence
Marc Crépon, translated by D. J. S Cross and Tyler M. Williams

Machiavellian Ontology: Political Conflict and Philosophy
Francesco Marchesi, translated by Dave Mesing

Visit the series web page at: edinburghuniversitypress.com/series/incite

Machiavellian Ontology

Political Conflict and Philosophy

Francesco Marchesi

Translated by Dave Mesing

EDINBURGH
University Press

Edinburgh University Press is one of the leading university presses in the UK.
We publish academic books and journals in our selected subject areas across
the humanities and social sciences, combining cutting-edge scholarship with
high editorial and production values to produce academic works of lasting
importance. For more information visit our website: edinburghuniversity
press.com

© Francesco Marchesi, 2024
English Translation © Dave Mesing, 2024

Edinburgh University Press Ltd
13 Infirmary Street
Edinburgh EH1 1LT

Typeset in 11/14pt Bembo
by Cheshire Typesetting Ltd, Cuddington, Cheshire, and
printed and bound in Great Britain

A CIP record for this book is available from the British Library

ISBN 978 1 3995 2045 4 (hardback)
ISBN 978 1 3995 2047 8 (webready PDF)
ISBN 978 1 3995 2048 5 (epub)

The right of Francesco Marchesi to be identified as the author of this work
has been asserted in accordance with the Copyright, Designs and Patents Act
1988, and the Copyright and Related Rights Regulations 2003
(SI No. 2498).

The baby boomers have tyrannised the Left's imagination – bequeathing tremendous capacities to deconstruct and critique authority but feeble capacities to construct and compose.

Perhaps the '68 generation's last revenge upon those who inherit their messes, is the intellectual axiom that structure is always more suspicious than its dismantling and composition more problematic than resistance, not just as political strategies but as metaphysical norms.

Their project was and remains the horizontal multiplication of conditional viewpoints as both means and ends, via the imaginary dismantling of public reason, decision and structuration.

I grew up in this tradition, but the world works very differently than the one imagined by *soixante-huitards* and their secretaries. I hope that philosophy will not continue to fail those who must create, compose and give enforceable structure to another world than this one.

Benjamin Bratton

Machiavelli's conception of *governo popolare* is just that: the people participating in government through the workings of institutions such as the Roman tribunes of the plebs; assemblies in which the people propose and discuss, affirm, or reject laws; and public trials in which the people serve as ultimate judges of citizens accused of political crimes [. . .].

Machiavelli did not simply want the people, through public demonstrations, to protest against the power of oligarchy manifested by 'the State' from the outside. He also wanted them to perpetually contest the power of oligarchy *within* the workings of the state—that is, from the inside.

Only by getting their hands dirty through political practice exercised without and within institutions could they effectively combat oligarchy and exercise self-government.

John P. McCormick

What distinguishes Machiavelli from Hobbes is not the stark choice between order and conflict: it is the acceptance, or not, of their coexistence at the same time.

Roberto Esposito

Contents

Acknowledgements	vii
Introduction: Geometry of Conflict	1

Part 1: Symmetrical Conflict – The Military Model

1 Foucault's Genealogy	15
2 Schmitt: Conflict as Enmity	45
3 Arendt: Competition and Distinction	71

Part 2: Asymmetrical Conflict – The Psychic Model

4 Lacanian Suture	101
5 Althusser's Overdetermination	125
6 Laclau and Mouffe: Antagonism and Equivalence	152

Part 3: Machiavellian Ontology

7 Three 'Ontologically Oriented' Concepts: *Inimicizie, Ordini, Riscontro*	181
8 Neither Monistic, nor Dualistic, nor Pluralistic: A Mixed Ontology	215
9 Machiavellian Ontology and Us: Philosophical Lineages of the Twenty-First Century	229
Index	235

Acknowledgements

This book is truly indebted to the work, the friendship, and the love of Roberto Esposito and Francesca Monateri.

I want to give special thanks to Dimitris Vardoulakis and Peg Birmingham, editors of the Incitements series, to Carol Macdonald, the philosophy publisher at Edinburgh University Press, and to Dave Mesing, much more than a translator, all of whom followed the journey of the book with passion and patience. Timothy Campbell also supported this book from the beginning. Without the generosity of each of them, the book would not exist.

I would also like to thank Mattia Di Pierro, Giuseppe Duso, Simona Forti, Paolo Gerbaudo, Alfonso Maurizio Iacono, Enrica Lisciani-Petrini, Oliver Marchart, John P. McCormick, Valentina Monateri, Tommaso Nencioni, Giovanni Paoletti, Gabriele Pedullà, Miguel Vatter, and the Seminar in Political Philosophy of the Scuola Normale Superiore di Pisa.

Introduction: Geometry of Conflict

1. A New Philosophical Situation

The events of the first twenty years of the twenty-first century alone have put an end to the philosophical twentieth century. From the 2008 financial crisis to the shock of the pandemic, the transformations that took place during this period have made the philosophical demands that animated the previous century, particularly its final portion, obsolete.

The deconstruction of all absolutes promoted by Heidegger and Wittgenstein, as well as their parcelling into the flow of differences by Deleuze and Foucault, now appear as residues of an era that dedicated most of its energy to the critique of every order of experience, history, and even politics. This terminated with the end of the privileged terrain that these theories found in the final thirty years of the century, the neoliberal *belle époque*, which exalted the rejection of order, the conception of freedom as individual difference, and the suspicion of every form of structuring. And to this, we should of course add their necessary correlate: the equivalence of all absolutes (from systems of thought to economic regulation, to state sovereignty), understood as sources of totalitarian repression and closure.

The periodic economic, political, environmental, and health crises, which have returned to pass through the industrialised West, have on the contrary emphasised the importance of structuring, regulation, and order.[1] Indeed, if economic depressions have returned to show the despotism that the deregulated market exercises on our lives and the need to collectively control it, the pandemic event represented a sort of global comparison of the different forms of *governance*. Those that were more regulated, and had greater availability of public goods, reacted promptly and with better results, while those that were more destructured and privatised reacted with difficulty and paid a much higher price.[2]

These episodes and trends call philosophy into question in two main ways. On the one hand, they speak to the need for structuring, and on the other, they speak to the difference between various forms of order, which are traversed by divergent interests and perspectives. In short, now is no longer the time to think how repressive a collective structure might be for our individuality, but instead how much it could defend us from the risks and uncertainties of the market, and how the power relations within each order determine its orientation in favour of one social part or another.

There is also more to add. Behind the image of the widespread philosophical space in the final thirty years of the twentieth century – smooth, repetitive, devoid of material needs and striations that are not subjective and isolated singular differences – a real, clear reference leaps out: the figure of neoliberal globalisation in its widespread version within the discourse of the social sciences beginning in the 1990s.[3] An open and uniform space, lacking borders and conflicts, this image had already been anticipated by poststructuralist philosophy in the 1970s, to the point of generalising itself as transcendental for any possible reflection. This rendered any limitation and definition of such a space tendentially totalitarian, and any rationalisation of experience, including the political, fatally dogmatic.

Today, such a theoretical horizon appears obsolete. The thrust towards public interventions of a social and infrastructural nature that the West is drawing from its own decline – as respectively shown in the European and US administrations' plans drawn up after the pandemic – the affirmation of an eastern model in which regulation and planning play an essential role, and the necessary collective control of the climate crisis are just some of the social and economic factors that reverse the tasks of philosophy.

It is no longer a matter, in other words, of opposing conflict to form, freedom to control, or biological life to its public protection, but instead of analysing the conflicts within such structures which orient and define their sign. Among these, three politico-institutional forms in particular emerge as places of contemporary conflict: the plan, the state, and globalisation as a whole. In short, what matters is to define which subjects and social classes are the privileged recipients of public plans, how different external impulses guide the work of state intervention in a conservative or progressive sense, and which guise is assumed by a global space which, no longer smooth, appears animated not so much by individual state actors but rather by various globalisation projects between East and West.[4]

Structuring and conflict within order – these seem to be the new objects of philosophy. In order to think them, we have often turned to what could be called the philosophical counter-conduct of the twentieth century. Recently, there has been talk of the 'Polanyi moment', after the author who described the request for order and control that occurred after the 1929 crisis, or the 'Poulantzas moment', from the name of the theorist of the state (and thus political form) as social relation and conflictual space. More generally, the twentieth century saw, in opposition to the crisis of bourgeois philosophy described by Heidegger and Wittgenstein, Lukács and Gramsci's attempt to renew the dialectic, projected towards the new order established by the October Revolution. Similarly, it has registered among its main events – prior to the philosophies of modernisation and difference of Deleuze and Foucault among others – the rationalist reflection on new forms of mediation by means of the structuralism of Lévi-Strauss, Lacan, and Althusser, in harmony with the spread of collective planning after the Second World War.

However, the feeling is that today a deeper discontinuity is at stake, and that only a rereading of the classics can lead to what the new philosophical situation requires us to at least begin thinking: a different political ontology.

2. Machiavellian Ontology

Despite the distance that separates us from his work, the name Niccolò Machiavelli immediately recalls the notion of political conflict. Indeed, conflict was a key concept in the political ontologies spanning the twentieth century, and it was the theoretical instrument through which the tendency of the deconstruction of order towards the equivalence of absolutes manifested itself in this field. This tendency remains the prevailing philosophical legacy of the century.

Conflict has been described as a fundamental duality which precedes every structure. No order is possible in the presence of conflict: either order, or conflict. But this antagonism, which is never resolved in the construction of a political form, fundamentally describes a static plurality opposed to any structuring and, therefore, to historical transformation. This is not unlike, in fact, a completely homogeneous order.

By analysing the theories of Carl Schmitt, Hannah Arendt, and Michel Foucault in the first part of this book, we will call this mode of thinking *symmetrical conflict*: a struggle that takes place between similar actors, for the same objectives and with comparable tools. Such a notion of conflict, by rejecting all organisation and order, resolves conflict into its flat repetition or an equally stable disorder. On the one hand, there is the continuous shifting of relations within the same conflict: between the poles of enmity for Schmitt, among the few citizens endowed with political rights in Arendt's *polis*, and between power and resistance according to Foucault. What never changes is the relation itself. On the other hand, there is the dispersion of multiple conflicts. No order, as in Foucault's case, is not fundamentally different from an unchanging order, as in Schmitt and Arendt.[5]

The models of these authors are *competition* or *war*: two types of conflict that reject structuring and change insofar as they are thought within that homogeneity of actors, tools, and ends. In competition, there is indeed a divergence of means just as there is a convergence of ends, whereas in war, a shift in relations of force is observed but never a change in terrain. In short, it is a question of winning the same battle or prevailing in the conquest of the same objective.[6] On the ideological level, this resolution of conflict into competition or disorder has contributed to the establishment and legitimation of both the liberal democracies that are widespread in the West, and an image of global space as flat and inert plurality.

In the second part of the book, we will analyse instead theories of what we might call *asymmetrical conflict*. These originate from the Lacanian and Althusserian schools and today are quite influential through authors such as Alain Badiou, Ernesto Laclau, Chantal Mouffe, and Slavoj Žižek, among others. These theories relate conflict and order through a *psychic* model, or in other words, by thinking antagonism within political form as the *return of the repressed*. Here there is a difference, and precisely an asymmetry, between conflict and order, but both appear as anonymous and undifferentiated, no longer capable of thinking the specificity of individual political forms, and thus, their specific partiality and difference. Conflict always attacks order from within but never changes its structure, and rather sometimes causes its complete dissolution. Event, antagonism, lack are only the names of a conflict that is thought against the background of structure but incapable of distinguishing between order and order and between conflict and conflict.[7]

Overall, both theoretical areas have attempted to valorise difference and movement, perhaps the task that was pursued most obstinately by the philosophy of the century, in opposition to the alleged homogeneity and static nature of the systems of the preceding century. The late outcomes of these attempts perhaps suggest that they have incurred a different type of inertia and indifference: one of plurality without relation and repetition without history.

A Machiavellian ontology, to which the third part of the book is dedicated, is constructed against this context, by first of all elaborating a different idea of conflict. Attempting to distil some ontological assumptions from the work of an author of the past naturally brings with it risks of anachronism or abuse from which only historicisation, here and elsewhere,[8] can protect.

Moreover, philosophy has often let itself be inspired by classics in order to respond to contemporary problems.

Machiavellian conflict is not opposed to structuring as duality or multiplicity, but instead mediates between the absolute plurality of individuals and social groups and the unity of order as such. Machiavelli, by re-elaborating the mixed Roman order and the conflict between its institutions, especially the senate on the aristocratic side and the tribunate on the plebeian side, suggests the elaboration of a *mixed, or triadic, ontology.* Here conflict is the intermediate element between one and many that overcomes the aporias of binary structures noted above. Conflict organises plurality within institutions on the one hand, while on the other it is precisely the prevalence of this conflict between institutions which decides the overall character of order. In short, it decides whether it is in favour of one part or the other.

An ontology with Machiavellian characteristics therefore grasps conflict first of all as an *instrument of organisation* for plurality and as *degree zero of mediation*: no longer flat repetition or irrational nucleus within order, conflict articulates multiplicity by tracing a line of demarcation with the adversary – here, to separate means to organise the parts, and to do it at a sort of degree zero, through a simple division into parts, without the qualitative leap of rationalist or dialectical mediations. It is an organisation of plurality that is only the first step in an overall *instituting procedure*, which is made up of this first step and a second one constituted by the conflict between institutions and for hegemony over order. From this, *a geometry of conflict* derives, that is, a non-neutral concept of structuring that is traversed by a struggle between parts for prevalence within it. This struggle is not only a means for the generation of order, but also an instrument for measuring its specific quality: the geometry of each structure, its distinctive sign, its form, in fact derives here from the state of the relations of force between the organised parts that compose it. In short, only relation between conflictual parts allows for difference and historicity to be saved, as a coexistence in a whole and through the recombination of their articulation.

Neither monistic, nor dualistic, nor pluralistic, a Machiavellian ontology has a mixed or triadic structure. It can allow, at least in part, for thinking the two needs which traverse the new philosophical situation: the modalities of structuring and the conflictual orientation of this same ordering act.

3. Conflict, Competition, Cooperation: Ontology as Strategy

The final decades of the twentieth century were also those of the proclamation of the end of philosophy, of its function and, at times, its very possibility. In this case as well, there was a trend reaching its maturation and, with it, a counter-conduct that emerged as Alain Badiou's Platonism,[9] in opposition to the self-dissolving temptations of post-Heideggerian deconstruction, or more recently, the multiple rediscoveries of philosophical realism in the crisis of so-called postmodernism.[10]

And yet these reactions, while rediscovering several classical vocations of philosophy, have not identified a specific or, at least in part, new task. Perhaps only the contemporary discussion around political ontology can at least broach the problem. For our part, through proposing a Machiavellian ontology, we also suggest a task for philosophy that rediscovers its materialist

INTRODUCTION

attitude: political ontology, indeed, using conceptual depth, sets for itself the task of focusing on and filtering the properly onto-logical coordinates that are inscribed in one's own time, with the objective of isolating the fundamental characteristics of the ongoing process, in order to respond to them philosophically.[11]

In this way, by renewing the maxims of all historicisms, apprehending one's own time in thought, and out of all struc-turalisms, making a theory of practices – political ontology can perhaps merge philosophical analysis and strategic proposal. It is certainly not a question of new tasks – separating appearance and reality, event and process, conjuncture and structure – but the so-called end of the philosophy of the late twentieth cen-tury distanced itself from them in the name of the appearance of every reality, the priority of the event over process, and the primacy of deconstruction over affirmation. And this can be done, of course, by recognising the reasons for such critiques, and assuming that reality always produces its own representation, that the process is nothing more than the weave of events, and that structures are fully oriented and historical.

What, then, is the strategic horizon indicated by Machiavellian ontology? As noted, it presents itself primarily as an ontology of conflict, but one that is elaborated as an instru-ment of organisation and inclusion. It organises plurality by dividing it up and constructs order by rendering it necessarily partial. The Western tradition has often brought conflict closer to competition, accentuating its agonistic character but dilut-ing its capacity for social inclusion and historical transforma-tion. The contemporary conjuncture, which we have invoked, and its philosophers, which we will analyse in the pages that follow, are but one case of a more general tendency: from the Greek negation of division (*stásis*, *diástasis*), transformed into

9

regulated competition and temporal succession (*metástasis*),[12] to the recent experiences of procedural and elite democracies, passing through the formulations of the *concordia ordinum* and the Renaissance *similitudines*.[13] At the opposite extreme, this same tradition has always treated conflict and cooperation separately, thereby encountering numerous difficulties in articulating the role occupied by both notions, from Aristotle to Marx. On the one hand, conflict as a social pathology or historical constant, and on the other, cooperation as a natural faculty of the species or ambivalent instrument of coexistence.[14]

Today, in Western societies that for decades have been dominated by internal and external competition, and in a world in which cooperative tendencies are re-emerging that seemed to have experienced an overall retreat, it is probably a matter of constructing a connection between conflict and cooperation which has perhaps never fully been accomplished in philosophy. And if a Machiavellian ontology – as a theory of conflict as organisation and institution as conflictual order – in many ways opposes the dominant sceptical tendencies of the philosophical twentieth century, bridging the gap between conflict and cooperation can address an enigma that this same century often tried to resolve.

Notes

1　Two books by Adam Tooze have recently focused on these transformations: *Crashed: How a Decade of Financial Crises Changed the World* (London: Allen Lane, 2018) and *Shutdown: How Covid Shook the World's Economy* (London: Allen Lane, 2021).

2　Cf. Benjamin Bratton, *The Revenge of the Real: Politics for a Post-Pandemic World* (London: Verso, 2021).

INTRODUCTION

3 Cf., for example, Thomas Friedman, *The World Is Flat: A Brief History of the Twenty-First Century* (New York: Farrar, Straus and Giroux, 2005).

4 Cf. Paolo Gerbaudo, *The Great Recoil: Politics After Populism and Pandemics* (London: Verso, 2021).

5 The triad of Schmitt, Arendt, and Foucault, who are different in many respects, has, for example, been defined as the canon of the entire contemporary discussion about biopolitics. Cf. Sandro Chignola, 'La vita, il lavoro, il linguaggio: Biopolitica e biocapitalismo', in Pietro Maltese and Danilo Mariscalco (eds), *Vita, politica, rappresentazione: A partire dall'Italian Theory* (Verona: Ombre Corte, 2016), pp. 25–42.

6 The effects of this transformation of conflict into competition or war have been noted in Étienne Balibar, *Cinq études du matérialisme historique* (Paris: Maspero, 1974), pp. 191–2; Jacques Rancière, *Disagreement* (Minneapolis: University of Minnesota Press, 1999); Jacques Rancière, *Hatred of Democracy* (London: Verso, 2007).

7 Cf. Yannis Stavrakakis, *The Lacanian Left* (Albany, NY: SUNY Press, 2007).

8 I refer here to the third part of this book, as well as to Francesco Marchesi, *Riscontro: Pratica politica e congiuntura storica in Niccolò Machiavelli* (Macerata: Quodlibet, 2017); Francesco Marchesi, *Cartografia politica: Spazi e soggetti del conflitto in Niccolò Machiavelli* (Florence: Olschki, 2018).

9 The latest response is Alain Badiou, *L'immanence des vérités: L'être et l'événement 3* (Paris: Fayard, 2018).

10 Cf., for example, Quentin Meillasoux, *After Finitude: An Essay on the Necessity of Contingency* (London: Continuum, 2006); Bruno Latour, *Reassembling the Social: An Introduction to Actor-Network-Theory* (Oxford: Oxford University Press, 2007).

11 Regarding the debate on political ontology, cf. at least Mihaela Mihai et al., 'Democracy, Critique, and the Ontological Turn', *Contemporary Political Theory* 4 (2017), pp. 501–31; Oliver Marchart, *Thinking Antagonism: Political Ontology After Laclau* (Edinburgh: Edinburgh University Press, 2018); Roberto Esposito, *Pensiero istituente: Tre paradigmi di ontologia politica* (Turin: Einaudi, 2020).

12 Cf. at least Nicole Loraux, *The Divided City* (New York: Zone Books, 2002); Paula Botteri, 'Stasis: le mot greg, la chose romaine', *Metis* 4 (1989), pp. 87–100; Ninon Grangé, *De la guerre civile* (Paris: Armand Colin, 2009); Ninon Grangé, *Oublier la guerre civile? Stasis, chronique d'une dispartition* (Paris: Vrin, 2015); Dimitris Vardoulakis, *Stasis Before the State* (New York: Fordham University Press, 2017).

MACHIAVELLIAN ONTOLOGY

13 Cf. Roberto Esposito, *Ordine e conflitto: Machiavelli e la letteratura politica del Rinascimento italiano* (Naples: Liguori, 1984).

14 Cf. Alfonso Maurizio Iacono, 'The Ambivalence of Cooperation', in Marcello Musto (ed.), *Marx's* Capital *150 Years After* (Abingdon: Routledge, 2019).

Part 1

Symmetrical Conflict – The Military Model

1

Foucault's Genealogy

Self-commentary is never the literary genre of transparency. Despite numerous reworkings and corrections – among the well-known, for example, is the status of madness between *Folie et déraison* and the early 1970s lecture courses – Michel Foucault tried to restore a particularly unitary profile to his conceptual itinerary at the end of his life.[1] This unity is first of all thematic:

> I would like to say, first of all, what has been the goal of my work during the last twenty years. It has not been to analyze the phenomena of power, nor to elaborate the foundations of such an analysis. My objective, instead, has been to create a history of the different modes by which, in our culture, human beings are made subjects.[2]

This is an autobiographical reflection that throws itself into a relation between the moments of one's own intellectual work or the type of temporal scanning, and the postulation of a complementarity always-already inscribed within them.

> In that sense, this criticism is not transcendental, and its goal is not that of making a metaphysics possible: it is genealogical in its design and archaeological in its method. Archeological—and not transcendental—in the sense that it will not seek to identify

15

the universal structures of all knowledge or of all possible moral action, but will seek to treat the instances of discourse that articulate what we think, say, and do as so many historical events. And this critique will be genealogical in the sense that it will not deduce from the form of what we are what it impossible for us to do and to know; but it will separate out, from the contingency that has made us what we are, the possibility of no longer being, doing, or thinking what we are, do, or think.[3]

However, from the perspective of the nexus between conflict and history, these aspects of Foucault's mediation take on trajectories which are not entirely overlapping. Thus, it is not possible to closely examine the elaboration of the genealogical paradigm and its correlated 'microphysical' analysis of power – the theory of history and the theory of conflict – which emerge fully in Foucault's thought after the Parisian May of 1968, without at least partially lingering over what this frame of reference intends to depart from: an archaeological approach to historiography and a positive analysis of the systems of discourse and knowledge. These frames of reference are not only, and not precisely, arranged in order of temporal succession, but often in relation to contemporaneity, if not setback (also considering the short range of years), yet nevertheless they are strictly separable. *Episteme* (and archaeology) and *dispositif* (and genealogy) will therefore be the fundamental structures of order that incorporate this transition, whose link must be observed exactly by starting from the point of rupture between the two, in order to then fully examine the doctrine of conflict, and the primacy of disorder, before finally attempting to show the concept of history (genealogically understood) which results from such an overall problematic.

1. Outside of the System

Rodolphe Gasché has argued that the most important service of Derridean deconstruction consists in a formal transformation of the fundamental structures of reality inherited from the tradition, one still substantially influenced by the perspective of the so-called structuralists: by substituting the duplication of the beginning of the *arche-trace* for the monism of origin, the posteriority of the *supplement* for the primacy of foundation, the difference of *différance* for the permanence of order, the iteration of the *remark* for regular transformation, and the disorder of *dissemination* for the closure of the system, deconstruction would thus account for the remains of every totalisation, synchronic and diachronic.[4] As such, it is perhaps not extraneous to observe how the major semantic and conceptual shifts within Foucault's work result from a period of close confrontation with the beginning of the Derridean problematic, among other things. We will see that it is here that the emergence of structures on the surface, their opening and adherence to the real, encounters an epistemology of conflicting forces and a theory of power, proceeding from the connection between immanentisation, immediate politicisation, and the deconstructing [*destrutturazione*] of every form of knowledge, of politics itself, and not only this.

What is at issue in the dialogue between Derrida and Foucault is the morphology of a reason that is more or less capable of describing what lies at its margin, namely non-reason.[5] And thus what is at stake is also the status of the universality and neutrality of this rational instrument of comprehension, which under certain conditions – here is where politics creeps in – intends to colonise areas of experience and knowledge that present other logics which do not fall under the domain of possible rationalisation.

Already here there are elements that will be noted in a number of Foucault's texts from this period, such as the condemnation of any external, neutral, or third viewpoint – a comprehensive reason situated outside of the object of knowledge, such that it is able to embrace it entirely and without remainder. But there is also, in this complete horizontality of discourse, the irreducibility, instead, of the parts between them: the equivalence on the axiological level does not in fact correspond to an equal dialogue, as is the case in mature deconstructionist results, but rather to a battle for power over knowledge and in knowledge. Deconstruction and therefore conflict, in the Foucauldian horizon, deconstruction and thus dialogue, in the Derridean. For the moment, it is worth quickly observing the well-known knots of this discussion before analysing some of the important Foucauldian texts in this period, where his specific geometry of conflict takes shape.

> The language of everything that has participated, from near or far, in the adventure of Western reason—all this is the immense delegation of the project defined by Foucault under the rubric of the capture or objectification of madness. *Nothing* within this language, and *no one* among those who speak it, can escape the historical guilt [. . .] which Foucault apparently wishes to put on trial. But such a trial may be impossible, for by the simple fact of their articulation the proceedings and the verdict unceasingly reiterate the crime. If the *Order* of which we are speaking is so powerful [. . .] this is so precisely by virtue of the [. . .] universal, and infinite complicity in which it compromises all those who understand it in its own language.[6]

As is known of Foucault's attempt to give voice to the silence of madness understood as a language and logic wholly different from the entirety of Western reason, Derrida above all opposes an objection which Carlo Ginzburg has defined as 'easily skeptical':[7]

every form of rationalisation involves a violence against its own object, but using the language of reason to relativise reason itself by giving voice to its opposite, to the secular silence of madness, is an excessive claim. In this crucial passage, the loss of a third and external position emerges, as anticipated: on an epistemological terrain, in fact, by identifying a target that is so high and comprehensive, Foucault condemns himself to eternally repeat the gesture, conceding again and again to madness through the language of reason, the power that oppresses it.

And yet, precisely at the Derridean point of attack, something else also appears. By focusing on the subordination of madness to reason, and not for example simply delimiting its boundaries, Foucault opens himself up to this objection, which would indeed be easy were it not for the explicit political tone of his speech. In other words, when the aim of the research is no longer descriptive, delimiting and describing the formal structures of reason and madness and, at the limit, signalling the intrusiveness of one into the other, but instead performative, so to speak, or giving voice to the cries of pain in subordination, then structural epistemology can present itself as a totalisation and a linear determination of its parts by the whole. This also happens when the posing of a further external point of view is considered, even with respect to the most general categories such as reason and madness. Here the breach is generated which leads to the equivalence of all points of observation, to the implication of the observer in the object observed, and hence to the impossibility of any comprehensive paradigm.

And this is not all:

the attempt to write the history of the decision, division, difference runs the risk of construing the division as an event or a structure subsequent to the unity of an originary presence

[. . .] [and] it must be assumed *in general* that reason can have a contrary, that there can be an other of reason, that reason itself can construct or discover, and that the opposition of reason to its other is *symmetrical*.[8]

The choice of the object, in short, and its political tension compromise the historicity of the investigation, which leads the critic to ask whether such a decisive and general contrast has not always been incarnated in the frameworks of knowledge, rather than inscribed in the systematic that is specific to the classical age. The fundamental opposition between reason and non-reason hence seems to be located in the original structure of every discourse, being its condition of possibility, establishing a deferred beginning that hinges exactly on this ambivalence, rather than on the succession of one element by the other. Finally, the relativisation and dehistoricisation of the point of observation make the internal differences identified in the temporal segment that Foucault considers vanish; in other words, the cause–effect relations between the parts allow for the system to be opened up to a supplementary dissemination of any nexus of dependency. Again, the equivalence between all of the elements in principle prevents the construction of a hierarchy among the factors and the identification of their specific position. This is a trait that will be accentuated in Foucault after this dialogue.[9]

However, it could be said that for Foucault the question does not arise so much from the objections as in the answers. The knot Foucault grasps here in order to discuss and overcome Derrida's critique, as has been often emphasised, is that of the *outside*, what is external to the concept and to discourse. And yet this extrinsic quality changes between what Foucault seems to defend in the theoretical apparatus of *Folie et déraison* and the new approach in 1972, which equally attempts to answer

Derrida. Indeed, this shift seems to allow for an effective replication, but – considering the difference in time between Derrida's remarks and Foucault's response – also appears to be the result of an intellectual transition that is not brief.

Thus, the question of the *outside*: in *Folie et déraison*, madness is presented as external to reason, the result of a historically determined division (namely, that typical of the classical age) that the author wants to bring back to a more general binary opposition, which is precisely between reason and madness, within which we can trace the emergence of a specific configuration of reason itself. Certainly, madness as external, but included in a fundamental binary structure that is capable of accounting for the reciprocal transformations of its poles, as well as, undoubtedly, the implicit violence that culture entails in constituting itself as such.

It is here that, as we noted above, Derrida attacks with sceptical arguments, resorting to an accusation/assumption of infinite regress in tracing Foucault's historicisation to an atemporal origin, but above all by implementing that critical apparatus which will be extended to the set of variants in a structural epistemology: the arbitrariness of historicisation and thus of the documentable succession between the poles of the binary opposition; the closure of the system and its internal recursivity; foundationalism re-proposed through the universalistic gaze of the one who observes the object and determines its inner logic, which is replaced by resolution in an always double origin; the dissemination of the elements starting from this primary generative machine; an anti-foundationalism that relocates the gaze of the observer within the problematics of the object observed, reducing its possibilities to an ethics as the contestation of the infinite duplication of the beginning. In this context, madness is

MACHIAVELLIAN ONTOLOGY

always internal to the discourse of reason, and moreover, it has always (and not from a specific moment) represented its necessary reversal.

Foucault's reply is well-known and influential, as well as being testimony to an important turning point. If, as Derrida argued, what is gathered in theory and discourse is always subject to the deconstructive movement as the result of the movement of reason, which rather than founding, originates from the additional covering of a primary duplicity, in this way condemning every systematic undertaking, then the authentic that is external to the mechanisms of knowledge (and now power) in the European philosophical tradition will be non-conceptual, that is, that which is outside of the concept. An exteriority that arises not as the remainder of the historical clippings of Western reason, but as reality itself, as a practice no longer necessarily inscribed in a theoretical whole, but existing in its singular individuality irreducible to totality, and thus, together with its deconstruction. Foucault's counter-accusation to Derrida is therefore to demand an overall and general inclusion in the concept, in the theory, in order to demonstrate its original duplicity and to parasitically deconstruct it. The faults of totalisation, of original foundation, of theoretical abstractness, are thus turned back towards the critic, and perceived as a sort of sceptical residue of structuralism and the linguistic turn. The outside of the philosophical as a new horizon, beyond any conceptualisation:

> I am in agreement on one fact at least: that it was not at all on account of their inattentiveness that classical scholars omitted, before Derrida and like him, this passage from Descartes. It is part of a system, a system of which Derrida is today the most decisive representative, in its waning light: a reduction of discursive practices to textual traces; the elision of events that are

FOUCAULT'S GENEALOGY

produced there, leaving only marks for a reason; the invention of voices behind the text, so as not to have to examine the modes of implication of the subject in discourses; the assignation of the originary as said and not-said in the text in order to avoid situating discursive practices in the field of transformation where they are carried out. I would not say that it is a metaphysics [. . .] I would go much further: I would say that it is a historically well-determined little pedagogy, which manifests itself here in a very visible manner. A pedagogy which teaches the student that there is nothing outside the text, but that in it, in its interstices, in its blanks and silences, the reserve of the origin reigns.[10]

Now it is Derrida who is the final representative of the 'System', and one could say of the philosophical in general, in comparison with an external, a concrete real, which is no longer grasped through the mediation and delimitation of the theorist, but firsthand through the direct observation of reality. This is a reality that certainly returns to being historical, but at the cost of separating itself from any theoretical rearrangement, always at risk of being deconstructed. Practice is instead already such, before and without any understanding: it can only be observed and documented, in a singularity that precedes any systematisation and reflection.[11] Not even an empiricism but a mysticism of the *outside*, which actually does not have its own rational voice, but testifies to a presence that has the nature of something crying out: inarticulate but well-perceived. Madness, plebs, biological life will be the incarnations that this peculiar object will assume.[12]

Thus, what is important to note is Foucault's assumption, so to speak, of Derrida's critique, and probably the profound influence that it exercised on a path dense with internal lines that have contributed to such transformations, as well as being inserted into the overall changes of the philosophical horizon after structuralism which produced results in other authors and currents of thought that are not dissimilar.[13] However, Foucault's reflection remains a vector that testifies to this movement in a particular way. To the essentialism, synchronic and diachronic, that deconstruction diagnoses in every overall representation, the only possible answer seems to be to abandon the discussion of how to make these forms of understanding immune from the commitments of the past, rejecting any designation of overall sense as such. The alternative is thus incarnated outside of the philosophical:[14] how to characterise such an external, in which politics plays a primary role, is what we must now turn to observe.

2. Disorder and Conflict

Order is the other of the outside. Put differently, what is other of the outside are the articulations which at the same time unite and divide the factors of a whole: the elements of a discourse, the practices of an institution, the *dispositifs* of a system. In this way, it is possible to describe a movement within the status of the order, system, structure which correlates to change in the status of the exterior. A text such as Foucault's inaugural lecture at the Collège de France, 'The Orders of Discourse', suggests that the reversal Gasché points out can be generally compared, with some essential differences, to Foucault's work in the period of transition after the French May. Order, in short, is no longer simply described and diagnosed, as was predominantly the case in the 1960s, but instead is identified as a cover for something else, as a supplement to a fundamental disorder. Moreover, order results immediately from the presence of a

FOUCAULT'S GENEALOGY

power, whose manifestations are listed in this writing: first of all, in the methods of exclusion, interdiction, partition [*partage*], and rejection, and above all in the opposition between true and false.[15] Alongside these, principles of classification, regulated modes of the distribution of discourses and a filter applied to the ordering of the same: from the practice of the commentary as a unitary restitution of meaning, to inclusion in delimited spaces such as the work attributable to an author or integrable into a discipline. Finally, there are the prescriptive rules of access to a certain status of discourses, the norms of their formation and their implementation: 'what is an educational system, after all, if not a ritualisation of the word [. . .] if not a distribution and an appropriation of discourse, with all its learning and its powers'.[16]

At the end of this classification of the forms of order, the text presents a kind of crossroads. On one side: to remain within a structural (so to speak) horizon and move in search of a different morphology of order, of conceptual and institutional frameworks which, while conferring stability and meaning to the understanding of the object, give it a form that, in short, escapes the commitments of the past. On the other: to pursue instead the hypothesis that strictly speaking there is nothing other than order, but that under it something is hidden,[17] a logic other than order which does nothing but parasitise and regulate. In other words, there is a fundamental disorder before structures, power, and even reason. And from such an absence of rule, or work, a sort of peculiar normativity spreads, one that is naturally external to every determination.[18]

> There is undoubtedly in our society [. . .] a sort of dumb fear of these events, of this mass of spoken things, of everything that could possibly be violent, discontinuous, querulous, disordered

even and perilous in it, of the incessant, disorderly buzzing of discourse.[19]

At this height, Foucault explores both hypotheses, often contrasting them, but it is the second that will be assumed at the end of the transition. However, at that point the two ways are not only disjoined, but in part a compromise solution is sought. On the one hand, it is indeed assumed that the infrastructures of disorder are primary through a declared reversal.[20] The forms of disorder describe everything that lies on this side of regulation: discontinuous movement of discourse, practices overlapping and side-by-side in an at-times chaotic way; traits and aspects endowed with individuality and specificity, which do not respect any law of reflection with the world; and finally, exterior elements which do not reveal a hidden or ultimate meaning lying beneath the surface. The idea of an articulation of order and disorder is in fact something more than a survey in this period of transition, which will conclude in any case with a decisive choice in favour of disorder.[21]

Here a reform is placed on this theme, as from the name of the chair that Foucault took, the epistemology of the history of ideas or systems of thought. In this sense, new forms of order, new categories, are being advanced which were largely borrowed from the *histoire sérielle* of the Annales School during those years. But what matters, above all, is the hypothesis of a specific arrangement between series – that is, structured regularities that are horizontal, so to speak, or without foundation – and the aleatory events of their transformation: 'the fundamental notions now imposed upon us are no longer those of consciousness and continuity [. . .] nor are they those of sign and structure. They are notions, rather, of event and of series, with the group of notions linked to these; regularity, chance, discontinuity, dependence, transformation.'[22]

It is certain, however, that what remains of this writing is the rupture of order and the choice for disorder, for exteriority with respect to form, which can be clarified by observing the specific connotation of this absence of figure.

For a long and durable tradition that Foucault reactivates in a new guise, the complementary inverse of order is conflict. Starting with the genealogical turn of the early 1970s, this peculiar outside is configured explicitly through the image of political antagonism. The path from the globality of the system has led to the duplicity of inclusion and exclusion, to the tendential opposition of order and disorder – this path finds its fulfilment in the contrast between power and resistance, between the covering of the plurality obtained through techniques of domination and the logical primacy of duplicity or discord.

If there is a typical representation of the third element within a conflictualist schema, it is certainly that of the court. It is not by chance that the Foucauldian text in which this aspect is most extensively discussed comes from the debate 'On Popular Justice' held in the pages of *Les Temps Modernes* in 1972. This debate between Foucault and some Maoist positions focuses precisely on the need for a third instance that implies the organisation and tendential resolution of a conflict.

Foucault's starting point is that of the character of artificial concealment that is typical of every third instance: 'there thus sprang up a "judicial" order which had the appearance of the expression of public power: an arbitrator both neutral and with authority, of whom the task was both to "justly" resolve disputes and to exercise "authority" in the maintenance of public order'.[23] Reconstructing a chapter of French history, Foucault shows how the court form is constituted at the same time and in conformity with the modern centralised state, an institution aimed at pacifying conflicts in the name of an abstract universalism that actually conceals a partial viewpoint – an outcome, as we have seen, of struggles and power relations that continue to function within it.[24] The objection to this thesis emphasises, however, how elements of transcendence have historically played the function of defining the boundaries of the actors in the conflict, which do not exist as such, as already given in social reality:

> I would be against people's courts, I would find them completely unnecessary or detrimental if the masses—once set in movement, were a homogenous whole—that is, in short, if there were no need, in order to keep the revolution moving ahead, for institutions which could discipline, centralise and unify the masses.[25]

Beyond the immediately political colouring which is typical of the context of the reference, what can be noted here is the strictly philosophical nature of the response: without an artificial and external instance of the articulation of isolated individuals and groups, no agent of the conflict can be adequately thought and eventually activated.

> Foucault: I identified three elements: (i) a 'third element'; (ii) reference to an idea, a form, a universal rule of justice; (iii) decisions with power of enforcement. It is these three characteristics of the courts which are represented in anecdotal fashion by the table, in our society.
> Victor: The 'third element' in the case of popular justice is a revolutionary state apparatus.[26]

For Foucault, this third element, a universalistic claim that is external to the parts and a legitimacy detached from conflict, is a factor that shields an underlying antagonism, unable to aspire to any consistency and validity, always situated in the field of deception. It is not even a matter of rigour, of neutrality, but of appearances under which the dominion of the part is hidden. Foucault's interlocutor instead tries to show how all forms of order are not identical, but rather reflect the crystallisation of a power that under certain conditions is partisan, even sometimes of the subaltern part. Institution or order, then, as a sort of measure of the power of the part, an instance capable of corroborating, if not constituting, the part itself.

On this ground, Foucault's response attempts to bring every order back to one side of the contrast, to a pole of conflict, thus compromising its exteriority from the dualism.[27] In other words, a court has always been a court, whereas Foucault's interlocutor tries to show how every institution can be many different things, embodying divergent values and orientations. It is not the pure concealment of factional logic but the suspension of partiality, under certain conditions, in the name of a historically determinate and socially defined generality.[28]

But this is not sufficient. Foucault actually describes such conflict, by now the fundamental infrastructure of his thought, through a metaphor that is as precise and traditional as it is demanding on the theoretical level, namely the military model. Taken from Clausewitz, while reversing its sign, this image suggests identifying politics, and with it the etiology of order, with an antagonism that has specific characteristics:

> This does not, however, mean that society, the law, and the State are like armistices that put an end to wars, or that they are products of definitive victories. Law is not pacification, for beneath the law, war continues to rage in all the mechanisms

> of power, even in the most regular [. . .] There is no such thing
> as a neutral subject. We are all inevitably someone's adversary.[29]

This identification is not neutral and not without consequences. Indeed, the overlap between political conflict and war implies that the partition identified at the root of historico-social phenomena offers a number of specific characteristics.

1. Every event and episode must be judged according to a binary and symmetrical schema, through which the dynamic as well as the meaning of the ongoing process are accounted for.[30]
2. A reality that is always comprised of a *relation between forces*, within a polemological schema that looks at the transformations of the object as variations within one same relation of power that remains such. In other words, what can happen is a displacement of the relation, but never its transcendence.[31]
3. What is essential is thus the assumption of a perspective, the taking of sides and choosing a battlefield. Only by way of such a partial position is it possible to act on and know the historical phenomenon, which is never observable by itself, but always from a specific angle.[32]
4. A prospective knowledge that is connected to the truth. It is both the result of a relation between forces and an instrument for altering the balance. If knowledge reflects a specific state of forces, in a circular form, the stability it confers on a state of the relation between forces contributes to its consolidation.[33]
5. An approach that rejects the comprehending, universalising *third* institutionalisations, and the overall, *totalising* orders.[34]

These are the connotations that Foucault attributes to a historical discourse that he seems to take on as his own. Such characteristics bring a certain number of effects on the level of the description of frameworks of conflict. Conflict presents itself here as integrally horizontal, immanent in itself, and above all symmetrical: symmetry, immanence, and 'flatness'[35] observed in the tendential identity of the poles of antagonism, according to the coordinates of the military metaphor: socially anonymous adversaries, because historically interchangeable within a given model; indistinguishable as to the ends pursued in conflict, since the victory is in the same battles; identical relative to means and starting forces; irremediably forced, from time to time, into a relation that cannot be transcended through a change in battlefield and a third view capable of grasping the non-aleatory logic of the process.

As the alternative to order – to whatever order, institution, structure, or totality – Foucault traces (throughout the 1970s) a disorder understood as conflict. On the one hand, his conclusion takes up the thesis that every transcendence of the horizontal plane of conflict re-proposes its covering of reality, a concealment that in the final analysis represents a viewpoint of a party involved in the opposition. The third element is thus always on the point of transforming itself into a monism, of compressing and stabilising antagonism, of reproducing totalisations that stiffen the power of one part. Thus, ultimately the conflict can never be decided, or even undergo a partial stabilisation capable of giving rise to orders that are different than what came before: every order always presents itself as a dissimulation of conflict. The pure immanence of the relation between power and what Foucault will come to call resistance is, then, the terrain in which the figure of undecidability dominates.

3. Neutralising History

In an only apparently peripheral passage from *Les mots et les choses*, Foucault questions the status that must be attributed to the transformations that have taken place between one *episteme* and the next:

> Establishing discontinuities is not an easy task even for history in general. And it is certainly even less so for the history of thought. We may wish to draw a dividing-line; but any limit we set may perhaps be no more than an arbitrary division made in a constantly mobile whole. We may wish to mark off a period; but have we the right to establish symmetrical breaks at two points in time in order to give an appearance of continuity and unity to the system we place between them? Where, in that case, would the cause of its existence lie?[36]

This is an uncertain passage, as we can see. At this level of his reflection, Foucault grasps the event of discontinuity only as a problem, whose object is given by the punctual transformation from one epistemic framework to the other. In other words, between systems there is a rare caesura, which is perhaps identifiable only by comparison. History therefore presents discrete states rather than systems in motion to the eye of the observer: if the microphysical changes can be traced back to the unitary logic of one frame of reference, the rupture of such equilibria only shows the possibility of a dynamic, while remaining external to the regularity of the structures.

The status of history is an index of utmost importance in describing the transformations that took place in Foucault's thought, starting from its analysis of long-lasting *epistemes* and arriving at a dimension strictly related to political conflict. But if the former seems to assume historicity only in the form of interrogation – of the empty, non-theoretical space that is only attainable indirectly or by comparison – the latter appears to fix the centre of gravity of the genealogical examination in the permanent succession of discontinuities, the authentic hinge between the diachronic dimension and conflictualist politics (civil war, microphysics of power, the power–resistance nexus).[37] At the heart of this transition, what can be traced is an intermediate degree between the two polarities which, analogous to what we saw for the dimension of order and conflict, is situated in the immediate vicinity of May 1968, between the end of the 1960s and the beginning of the 1970s. This is an analysis that has the notions of series and event at its centre:[38]

> To be schematic, we could say that history, and in a general way, historical disciplines have ceased to be the reconstitution of the concatenations behind the apparent sequences; they now practice the systematic introduction of discontinuity. The great change that characterizes them in our epoch [. . .] is the transformation of discontinuity: its transition from obstacle to practice.[39]

In his response to the *Cercle d'épistemologie* published in the *Cahiers pour l'analyse* in 1968, and especially in the 1970 Japanese lecture 'Returning to History', Foucault fully develops these theses that place the event and the discontinuous at their centre. He tries first of all to emphasise how the Annales School instruments – in the period of Braudel, Labrousse, and Chanu in particular[40] – did not decentralise the function of the event on the whole, but rather subverted its role and status. According to Foucault, beyond the appearance of this so-called serial approach, discontinuity is found at the centre and not at the margins of the historical work of the period: 'the two fundamental notions of

MACHIAVELLIAN ONTOLOGY

history as it is practiced today are no longer time and the past but change and the event'.[41]

By relativising periodisations and geographical sectors, serial history works to construct relations between elements, statistically detecting fluctuations, cycles, evolutions, progress, and ruptures.[42] Foucault describes the result as follows:

> In traditional history [. . .] the cause or meaning was essentially hidden. The event, on the other hand, was essentially visible, even if one sometimes lacked the documents to establish it with certainty. Serial history makes it possible to bring out different layers of events as it were, some being visible, even immediately knowable by the contemporaries, and then, beneath these events that form the froth of history, so to speak, there are other events that are invisible, imperceptible for the contemporaries, and are of completely different form.[43]

Foucault notes how aspects such as the exchange of commodities in a port can certainly be observed by contemporaries, but the events that serial history traces take place at deeper levels, and are thus invisible to their contemporaries. It is a matter of the inversion of a statistical curve, the change of a commercial flow, the growth of a population, 'for it is quite clear to us now that the reversal of an economic trend is much more important than the death of a king'.[44] Focusing on these kinds of events produces the emergence of some important traits: the forms of discontinuity tend to multiply, because an economic curve and the increase of a population can affect the same field but take place over non-homogeneous temporalities, in contradiction of the great traditional periodisations that capture the index of a series of contemporary variations within an event (the discovery of America, for example).[45] This history, moreover, substantially reforms the category of time.

FOUCAULT'S GENEALOGY

> So the old notion of time should be replaced by the notion of multiple time spans, and when the structuralists' adversaries tell them, 'You're neglecting time,' these adversaries do not seem to realize that it's been a long time, if I may say so, since history got rid of time.[46]

Serial or structural historiography aims to outline the network of the internal and external relations of the object selected, thus describing a horizontal systematic, a whole without an ultimate foundation or overall illustration. Only the topic of structure and the order of the series can inform us about the nature of the phenomena. Serial and structural history impose a model of understanding which alternates between secular and almost synchronic frameworks of civilisations, an epistemology of the event that avoids the double alternative of the superficial, event-based frequency typical of political history and the complete absence of these that can be registered in evolutionary hypotheses (such as in certain forms of structuralism).[47] Structure and series thus not as the negation of historicity, but as a complementary reversal of the institution of the event.

However, such a direction suffers from some theoretical limits. Indeed, if serial and structural epistemologies left the status of the singular event in the background, it was precisely because of a conceptual difficulty in defining its status. In Foucault's talk, this difficulty seems to place itself beyond the pure void between one system and the other, which is only describable by means of comparison. In fact, it is clear that a singular event, in a philosophical framework of this kind, requires insertion within the whole in order to emerge at the level of the visible.[48] Similarly, such options have often been attributed to re-proposing a sort of foundation in the closure of the overall system or in the identification of a third point of view that is external to the

MACHIAVELLIAN ONTOLOGY

conflictual polarity, of which the elements would end up constituting nothing more than effects. Foucault, among many others in this period, is not insensitive to such questions, and ends up articulating the event-based character of his historical epistemology. The work which takes up these problems at their root is the essay 'Nietzsche, Genealogy, and History', published in 1971.

'Genealogy is gray, meticulous, and patiently documentary. It operates on a field of entangled and confused parchments, on documents that have been scratched over and recopied many times [. . .] It opposes itself to the search for "origins".'[49] Foucault's analysis begins from the term origin [*Ursprung*]: after comparing it to other terms in Nietzsche's lexicon such as *Herkunft*, *Enstehung*, or *Geburt*, Foucault notes how the Nietzsche of the *Genealogy of Morality* seems to contrast *Ursprung* and *Herkunft* (which in addition to origin, he translates as 'descent') in at least some passages, which thus alters the meaning of the term origin, questioning its entire role.

> Why does Nietzsche challenge the pursuit of the origin [*Ursprung*], at least on those occasions when he is truly a genealogist? First, because it is an attempt to capture the exact essence of things, their purest possibilities, and their carefully protected identities; because this search assumes the existence of immobile forms that precede the external world of accident and succession.

In this way, it is possible to tear off every veil and discover true essences. And yet, from a Nietzschean perspective, the secret of things is not their origin, their intrinsic nature, but rather the fact that they are precisely 'without essence'. For Foucault, the lesson of Nietzschean genealogy is thus the denial of the stability and primacy of the beginning, in the direction of a properly historical research that, 'excavating in the depths', places *Herkunft* and *Enstehung*, descent and emergence, at the centre of reflection.

In Nietzsche's lexicon, according to Foucault, *Herkunft* designates lineage, belonging to a group, blood, and tradition, and it often concerns race or social type. It plays a genealogical role insofar as it allows for the dissociation of unity, for seeing the multiple below the unique.[50] With the term *Enstehung*, he instead indicates emergence as birth, beginning, appearance: something that is thus unexpected, which breaks linear continuity and takes randomness into account, against the endowment of meaning that is provided by the destination. It 'is always produced through a particular stage of forces', in a particular moment of struggle, in definite circumstances: if descent describes the space of the event, emergence designates its time.

> In a sense, only a single drama is ever staged in this 'non-place,' the endlessly repeated play of dominations [. . .] Humanity does not gradually progress from combat to combat until it arrives at universal reciprocity [. . .] Rules are empty in themselves, violent and unfinalized; they are impersonal and can be bent to any purpose.[51]

After outlining the characteristics of genealogy, and its objects *Herkunft* and *Enstehung* as well as the main lines of development which start from them, Foucault attempts an analysis of the relation between genealogy and traditional history. In this sense, Nietzsche defines the figure of a historical spirit or sense for Foucault. Such a historical sense first has a role of critique towards 'the historian's history [which] finds its support outside of time and pretends to base its judgments on an apocalyptic objectivity. This is only possible, however, because of its belief in

MACHIAVELLIAN ONTOLOGY

an eternal truth.'[52] Against this, the historical sense has the task of rejecting any absolute through a 'dissociating view'. Second, it must reintroduce becoming into what appears unchangeable or eternal, grasping the multiple and the discontinuous. Third, history that is effective must be capable of 'reviving the event', the rupture of the event with continuity. It is not the causes, therefore, but the inversion of forces, the randomness of struggle, or the genealogy that overturns the relation between proximity and distance that is typical of historical analysis, re-evaluating what is humble and close against what appears high and distant. Finally, historical sense is a perspectival knowledge – it does not hide its position, the side that it takes, and the moment in which it is elaborated. It does not conceal its own lineage with the pretence of universalising a point of view through the idea of a necessary movement and a foregone conclusion.[53]

The relationship between conflict and event, antagonism and history, is now clear. Thus, the oppositions: it is no longer a question of grasping the ambivalences and opportunities of structural or serial methodologies, of new practices and epistemologies, but of rigidly opposing the nineteenth-century philosophies of history (reduced to an elementary skeleton) with a set of deconstructed polemical notions that, through a very selective interpretation of Nietzsche, overcome the shortcomings and opportunities of historiography and the most recent historiographical theories in a single moment. In short, either Nietzsche or 'traditional' metaphysics.

As such, every idea of overall systematisation is immediately superimposed on to idealistic and historicist totalisations and contrasted with an idea of the dispersion of elements.[54] Now the discovery of an epochal transformation is assimilated to the postulation of a destiny or the identification of an overall historical logic, and without mediation, a teleological form. The alternative: pure randomness of the fact, of the evental – no longer rare, discrete, and, strictly speaking, describable – the immediacy of chance that annuls any possibility of the restitution not only of meaning but of any motivation for the discontinuous. 'An event, consequently, is not a decision, a treaty, a reign, or a battle, but the reversal of a relationship of forces [. . .] The forces operating in history are not controlled by destiny or regulative mechanisms, but respond to haphazard conflicts.'[55]

Finally, the discontinuous is described as conflict, which divides temporal segments that are now infinitesimal, instants between one conflict and the next which do not produce any concept or logic but register only the spatial and temporal dispersion of identity and order. Antagonism is now not subject to order, nor is it articulated diachronically, but instead occupies the entire space of the visible and in itself sums up history as such. History, in the last instance, is the infinite story of a conflict that always recurs in the same way, symmetrical because socially and historically anonymous, identical because it is metaphorised through the military, and inert because the indefinite succession of events of rupture does not reach anywhere to a structure that can be accounted for.[56]

The historical theory of civil war, of the microphysics of power and genealogy, thus seems to produce two convergent outcomes: a *synchronic undecidability*, configured by the functional equivalence of the forces on the battlefield, accompanied by a *diachronic neutralisation*, evident in the form of a substantial logical disappearance of historical rupture, impossible in a context that is marked by the interminable and indeterminable presence of conflict itself.

Notes

1 Cf. Judith Revel, *Foucault: La parola e i poteri* (Rome: Manifestolibri, 1996); Judith Revel, 'Foucault e la letteratura: storia di una scomparsa', in Judith Revel (ed.), *Archivio Foucault* 1 (Milan: Feltrinelli, 1996), pp. 13–24.

2 Michel Foucault, 'The Subject and Power', in James D. Faubion (ed.), *Essential Works of Michel Foucault (1954–1984), Volume Three: Power* (New York: The New Press, 2000), p. 326. Cf. Michel Foucault, 'On the Genealogy of Ethics: An Overview of Work in Progress', in Paul Rabinow (ed.), *The Foucault Reader* (New York: Pantheon Books, 1984), pp. 351–2.

3 Michel Foucault, 'What Is Enlightenment?', in Rabinow (ed.), *The Foucault Reader*, p. 46.

4 Cf. Rodolphe Gasché, *The Tain of the Mirror: Derrida and the Philosophy of Reflection* (Cambridge, MA: Harvard University Press, 1988), pp. 142–63. See also the reprisal of this theme in Aletta Norval, 'Hegemony After Deconstruction: The Consequences of Undecidability', *Journal of Political Ideologies* 9 (2004), p. 14.

5 On this dialogue, see Ray Boyne, *Foucault and Derrida: The Other Side of Reason* (London: Unwin Hyman, 1990); Cook 1990; Robert D'Amico, 'Text and Context: Derrida and Foucault in Descartes', in John Fekete (ed.), *The Structural Allegory: Reconstructive Encounters with the New French Thought* (Minneapolis: University of Minnesota Press, 1984), pp. 164–82; Bernard Flynn, 'Derrida and Foucault: Madness and Writing', in Hugh Silverman (ed.), *Derrida and Deconstruction* (London: Routledge, 1989), pp. 201–18; Olivia Custer, Penelope Deutscher, and Samir Haddad (eds), *Foucault/Derrida Fifty Years Later: The Futures of Genealogy, Deconstruction, and Politics* (New York: Columbia University Press, 2016).

6 Jacques Derrida, *Writing and Difference* (Chicago: University of Chicago Press, 1978), pp. 41–2. Derrida's emphasis.

7 Carlo Ginsburg, *Il formaggio e i vermi: Il cosmo di un mugnaio del '500* (Turin: Einaudi, 1999), p. xvi.

8 Derrida, *Writing and Difference*, p. 48. Derrida's emphasis.

9 Ibid., p. 52.

10 Michel Foucault, 'My Body, This Paper, This Fire', in Yubraj Aryal, Vernon W. Cisney, Nicolae Morar, and Christopher Penfield (eds), *Between Foucault and Derrida* (Edinburgh: Edinburgh University Press, 2016), p. 79

11 Cf. Richard Macksey and Eugenio Donato (eds), *La controversia sullo*

strutturalismo (Naples: Liguori, 1975). More generally, cf. François Cusset, *French Theory: Foucault, Derrida, Deleuze & Co.* (Minneapolis: University of Minnesota Press, 2008).

12 Cf. Michel Foucault, 'Poteri e strategie', *Aut aut* 164 (1978), p. 25. My emphasis. In a more critical key, see also Gianna Pomata, 'Storie di "police" e storie di vita: note sulla storiografia foucaultiana', *Aut aut* 170–1 (1979), p. 64.

13 'Using this new method, theory is not only subordinated to practice but is shown to be one of the essential components through which the organizing practices operate.' Herbert Dreyfus and Paul Rabinow, *Michel Foucault: Beyond Structuralism and Hermeneutics* (Chicago: University of Chicago Press, 1983), p. 103.

14 Roberto Esposito has insisted on this Foucauldian outside in *Bíos: Biopolitica e filosofia* (Turin: Einaudi, 2004), pp. 19–41; *Terza persona: Politica della vita e filosofia dell'impersonale* (Turin: Einaudi, 2007), pp. 163–73; *Da fuori: Una filosofia per l'Europa* (Turin: Einaudi, 2016).

15 Michel Foucault, 'Orders of Discourse', *Social Science Information* 10.2 (1971), p. 10.

16 Ibid., p. 19.

17 'But, once we have distinguished these principles of rarefaction, once we have ceased considering them as a fundamental and creative action, what do we discover behind them?' Ibid., p. 22.

18 Cf. Judith Revel, *Michel Foucault: Un'ontologia dell'attualità* (Soveria Minelli: Rubettino, 2003), p. 98.

19 Foucault, 'Orders of Discourse', p. 21.

20 Ibid.

21 Cf. Angèle Kremer-Marietti, 'De la matérialité du discours dans l'institution', *Revue Internationale de Philosophie* 44 (1990), pp. 241–61; Henry Krips, 'Power and Resistance', *Philosophy and Social Science* 20 (1990), pp. 170–82; Jana Sawicki, *Disciplining Foucault* (London: Routledge, 1991); Jon Simons, *Foucault & the Political* (London: Routledge, 1991).

22 Foucault, 'Order of Discourse', p. 23.

23 Michel Foucault, 'On Popular Justice: A Discussion with Maoists', in Michel Foucault, *Power/Knowledge: Selected Interviews & Other Writings 1972–1977* (New York: Pantheon, 1980), p. 6.

24 Ibid, pp. 8–9.

25 Ibid., p. 10.

26 Ibid., p. 11.

27 Ibid., p. 13.

MACHIAVELLIAN ONTOLOGY

28 Cf. Belden Fields, 'French Maoism', *Social Text* 9–10 (1984), pp. 148–77; Mads Peter Karlson and Kaspar Villadsen, 'Foucault, Maoism, Genealogy: The Influence of Political Militancy in Michel Foucault's Thought', *New Political Science* 1 (2015), pp. 91–117; Richard Wolin, *The Wind From the East: French Intellectuals, the Cultural Revolution and the Legacy of the 1960s* (Princeton, NJ: Princeton University Press, 2010).

29 Michel Foucault, *Society Must Be Defended: Lectures at the Collège de France, 1975–76* (New York: Picador, 2003), pp. 50–1.

30 Ibid., p. 52. Cf. Philippe Chevallier, *Michel Foucault: Le pouvoir et la bataille* (Paris: PUF, 2014).

31 'In the general struggle he is talking about, the person who is speaking [. . .] is necessarily on one side or the other.' Foucault, *Society Must Be Defended*, p. 52. Translation modified.

32 'It is always a perspectival discourse. It is interested in the totality only to the extent that it can see it in one-sided terms, distort it and see it from its own point of view.' Ibid., p. 52.

33 'This discourse established a basic link between relations of force and relations of truth [. . .] In a discourse such as this, being on one side and not the other means that you are in a better position to speak the truth.' Ibid., pp. 52–3.

34 'On the contrary, [this discourse] is interested in defining and discovering, beneath the forms of justice that have been instituted, the order that has been imposed, the forgotten past of real struggles, actual victories, and defeats which may have been disguised but which remain profoundly inscribed.' Ibid., p. 56.

35 Michel Foucault, 'Nietzsche, Marx, Freud', in Gayle Ormiston and Alan Schrift (eds), *Transforming the Hermeneutic Context: From Nietzsche to Nancy* (Albany, NY: SUNY Press, 1989), pp. 59–67. Cf. Édouard Jolly and Philippe Sabot (eds), *Michel Foucault à l'epreuve du pouvoir* (Lille: Presses Universitaires de Septentrion, 2013); Judith Revel, 'Resistance et subjectivation: du "je" au "nous"', in O. Irrera and S. Vaccaro (eds), *La pensée politique de Foucault* (Paris: Éditions Kimé, 2017), pp. 29–40.

36 Michel Foucault, *The Order of Things* (London: Routledge, 2002), pp. 55–6.

37 On these problems, cf. at least Deborah Cook, 'History as Fiction: Foucault's Politics of Truth', *Journal of the British Society for Phenomenology* 22 (1991), pp. 139–47; Arnold Davidson, 'Conceptual Analysis and Conceptual History: Foucault and Philosophy', *Stanford French Review* 8 (1984), pp. 105–22; Michael Mahon, *Foucault's Nietzschean Genealogy:*

FOUCAULT'S GENEALOGY

Truth, Power, and the Subject (Albany, NY: SUNY Press, 1992); Alan Megill, 'The Reception of Foucault by Historians', *Journal of the History of Ideas* 48 (1987), pp. 117–41; Paul Veyne, 'Foucault rivoluziona la storia', in Paul Veyne, *Michel Foucault: La storia, il nichilismo et la morale* (Verona: Ombre corte, 1998), pp. 7–65.

38 Cf. Ferdinand de Saussure, *Corso di linguistica generale* (Bari: Laterza, 1967), p. 174n.

39 Michel Foucault, 'On the Archaeology of the Sciences: Response to the Epistemology Circle', in James D. Faubion (ed.), *Essential Works of Michel Foucault (1954–1984), Volume Two: Aesthetics, Method, and Epistemology* (New York: The New Press, 1998), p. 300.

40 Michel Foucault, 'On the Ways of Writing History', in Faubion (ed.), *Essential Works of Michel Foucault (1954–1984), Volume Two*, pp. 280–1.

41 Michel Foucault, 'Return to History', in Faubion (ed.), *Essential Works of Michel Foucault (1954–1984), Volume Two*, p. 423.

42 This is research, quickly abandoned, in which Althusserianism and thus the Marxist problematic was still quite present: 'Yet this Hegelian dialectics has nothing to do with all these logical relations that the aforementioned sciences are in the process of empirically discovering. What one is trying to find in Marx is something that is neither the deterministic assignation of causality nor logic of the Hegelian type, but rather a logical analysis of the real.' Michel Foucault, 'Linguistics and Social Sciences', *Theory, Culture, & Society* 40.1–2 (2023), p. 263.

43 Foucault, 'Return to History', pp. 427–8.

44 Ibid., p. 428.

45 Ibid., pp. 429–30.

46 Ibid., p. 430.

47 Cf. Judith Revel, *Dictionnaire Foucault* (Paris: Ellipses, 2008), p. 41.

48 See Saussure: 'For in order to set out the history of a language in detail following the chronological sequence, we would have to be in possession of an infinite series of photographs of the language, taken moment by moment. But this condition is never fulfilled [. . .] So the forward-looking method, with its reliance on direct documentation, must be abandoned in favour of going in the opposite direction, proceeding retrospectively against the chronological sequence of events.' Ferdinand de Saussure, *Course in General Linguistics* (London: Bloomsbury, 2013), p. 253.

49 Michel Foucault, 'Nietzsche, Genealogy, History', in Rabinow (ed.), *The Foucault Reader*, p. 76.

50 Ibid., pp. 80–1.

51 Ibid., pp. 85–6.
52 Ibid., p. 87.
53 Ibid., pp. 88–9.
54 Cf. Mahon, *Foucault's Nietzschean Genealogy*, pp. 81–128; Colin Koopman, *Genealogy as Critique: Foucault and the Problems of Modernity* (Bloomington: Indiana University Press, 2013), pp. 58–86; Evangelia Sembou, *Hegel's Phenomenology and Foucault's Genealogy* (Farnham: Ashgate, 2015).
55 Foucault, 'Nietzsche, Genealogy, History', p. 88.
56 Ibid., p. 89.

2

Schmitt: Conflict as Enmity

It has been common practice to describe Carl Schmitt as an ambivalent, if not ambiguous, thinker.[1] This persists despite the role of Schmitt's theses in fulfilling fundamental needs within contemporary political thought: among others, the break with a strong origin, the discovery of an empty structure at the heart of politics, and a rereading of European modernity in light of these philosophical points.

> Schmitt's greatness lies in his genealogy, i.e., in his idea that in order to understand politics, it is necessary to understand the concrete origin of a concrete structure of power and knowledge. And this origin must be not be understood as a stable origin, but rather an energy, an imbalance, a conflict within every order, which relativises it but also keeps it alive; concreteness, in Schmitt, always comes with nihilism. The theoretical discovery of the 'origin of politics' thus has as a counterpart a practice that can be revolutionary (activating a new origin in the conflict: revolutions, constituent power) but also a 'politics of origin,' i.e., the extra-legal, decisionist defense of an existing political order, through reference to its originary legitimacy as a stabilising factor against internal enemies (and therefore, a stabilisation through exclusion).[2]

Here the ambivalence of a mediation emerges in order to grow over time into a rigid alternative and a relation of mutual exclusion. It is the systemic incapacity, so to speak, of Schmitt's thought to articulate form and energy, order and conflict, thereby producing interpretative oscillations between a conflictualist and empty result and a homogenising, excluding, and full anchorage. This can be defined, preliminarily and thus summarily, as a manifestation of Schmitt's Hegelianism,[3] whose substitution by Marx as a reference for a theory of conflict can perhaps illuminate some of the widespread approaches in contemporary thought.[4] We will try to show this by first focusing on the production of this elementary alternative through a process of disarticulating form and energy, in order to then analyse the first conceptual effects of the Schmittian doctrine of political conflict and its consequences for the relation between antagonism and history.

1. Form or Energy

In order to think politics in its specificity (namely, outside of a direct relation with the normativity immanent to the economic and the social), it is necessary to construct conditions marked by the character of undecidability – this assumption seems to be the foundation of a large part of recent political philosophy. As we have already observed, however, undecidability, informality, and disorder are ideas of a primary structure, whose prerogatives are influential for what is found above them. In Schmitt, the awareness of the essential nature of what does not have the usual form of essence and foundation finds one of its primary points of reference. One of his best-known passages deals with the spirit of exception: 'Contrary to the imprecise terminology that is found in popular literature, a borderline concept is not a vague concept, but one pertaining to the outermost sphere. This definition of sovereignty must therefore be associated with a borderline case and not with routine.'[5] The systemic character of the exception as the basis of a politics that is taken here, typically, as decision is not external to the strategic results that are to be obtained. In short, it is not simply one methodological aspect among others. The two-way link between the specificity-limit of the situation of exception and its generality has the following function: 'The assertion that the exception is truly appropriate for the juristic definition of sovereignty has a systematic, legal-logical foundation [. . .] Because a general norm [. . .] can never encompass a total exception, the decision that a real exception exists cannot therefore be entirely derived from this norm.'[6]

In this way, the conceptual knot in this opening passage of Schmitt's discourse links two different moments of the argument: the methodological presupposition of the plural and differentiated nature of the primary elements of politics, which the juridical tradition would to some extent try to relativise and place at the margins, and the epistemological thesis of the central and systemic location of these differently fundamental structures. The blurring of the exception not so much into the rule,[7] but into the normality of its epistemic constitution, concerns precisely these aspects. These aspects preside over the accomplishment of a double theoretical and political result. Offering this image as the origin of politics, at least as a limit-possibility, first allows the relevance of the current system to be bracketed for the purposes of the decision, in this way opening the path to the emptying of the foundations of politics as such. Strictly speaking, however, rather than blurring, we can note in this renewed schema the disarticulation between a personal instance carried out on the level of undecidability and a normative background, or, we will see elsewhere, an energetic and conflictual background which is no longer capable of affecting the former.

> A jurisprudence concerned with ordinary day-to-day questions has practically no interest in the concept of sovereignty [. . .] Such a jurisprudence confronts the extreme case disconcertingly, for not every extraordinary measure, not every police emergency measure or emergency decree, is necessarily an exception. What characterizes an exception is principally unlimited authority, which means the suspension of the entire existing order [. . .] The existence of the state is undoubted proof of its superiority over the validity of the legal norm. The decision frees itself from all normative times and becomes in the true sense absolute.[8]

Separation and distinction, but not without reason or rule. The triangulation between exception, sovereignty, and order is inherent in a peculiar and circumscribed structure of politics, capable of replacing the harmonious or conciliatory convergence between form and energy. In other words, exception is not chaos, or merely disorder, but a presence that lacks real articulation with anything else. From this demarcation, this present draws the possibility of a politics, or for the moment and provisionally, a decision:[9] 'the exception remains, nevertheless, accessible to jurisprudence because both elements, the norm as well as the decision, remain within the framework of the juristic'.[10]

The proper place of sovereignty, its chosen ground, is therefore in this context political creation, whose essential condition is given by the fluidity and uniformity of the background on which it is crafted. If full and empty take on a borderline, indistinct aspect, it is precisely for this reason: both describe a

SCHMITT: CONFLICT AS ENMITY

primarily undifferentiated field, within which the instance of decision can freely move, without faults or points of friction. Thus 'the two elements of the concept legal order are then dissolved into independent notions and thereby testify to their conceptual independence'.[11] In this delimited sense, full and empty come to correspond to one another. In one case form and energy open a distance between them that cannot be bridged by politics and law – and on the contrary, the action of the former is rigorously permitted by such an assumption – while the other option is that of superimposing them up to an identity. This is a theoretical move that now knows its specific nature – and which will be typical of multiple twentieth-century philosophico-political experiences – effectively revoking the possibility of an encounter or clash between politics and what is not political, whether it be economic determinism or whatever form of social production. There is no real divergence between separation and superimposition from this perspective, but instead a common theoretical project, poles of an apparent dialectic that constantly rotates on itself.

> There exists no norm that is applicable to chaos. For a legal order to make sense, a normal situation must exist [. . .] The exception reveals most clearly the essence of the state's authority. The decision parts here from the legal norm, and (to formulate it paradoxically) authority proves that to produce law it need not be based on law.[12]

What emerges clearly in this passage is the schema of juridical filling as essentially subsequent to the action of politics. Order is established in absence, and only the presence that follows it is susceptible to ordering, just as the exception is the condition of order. Law is thus applicable after the state and within it, but

49

not prior to or outside of the normal situation. The juridical context favours the assumption of such a thesis – of a rigorously modern structure, as opposed to a juridical institutionalism in which the autonomisation of the parts from the whole actually recalls a pre-modern, pluralistic framework – and the theoretical weight of this thesis was perhaps most clearly visible when it was, at times in an improvised way, generalised outside the context of an election. Indeed, there is no doubt that such a thesis is endowed with a rigour close to the obviousness within the juridical framework, but if the laws of economics and society replace the laws of right, to what extent is it still possible to hold to the discourse?[13] The flat uniformity of politics can only be the result of a structure for which 'the rule proves nothing; the exception proves everything: It confirms not only the rule but also its existence'.[14]

However, it is not here a question of the correct functioning of the theory as much as the observation of the theoretical effects of an argument. At this point, we can indeed recognise the conceptual crux of starting a theory of political conflict with definite characteristics, to which we will return. For the moment, it is necessary to observe how on this ground we can identify, as we anticipated above, a certain Hegelianism in Schmitt. Rather than a stretched notion of the dialectic – which for Schmitt focuses only on the constant restlessness of the negative,[15] but can be led back to a positivity or overcome – or in the different relation established between mediation, negation, and totality (which is also influential on the strictly political side of both authors),[16] Schmitt's Hegelianism can be seen in the lack of a scanning between levels and stages that ends up assuming the form of a sphere that lacks autonomy, albeit relative autonomy. Whereas the Hegelian conjunction of spheres tends to give rise to a spiritual totality, which therefore removes the difference between the parts, making them uniform to manifestations of a homogeneous principle (*pars totalis*), Schmitt's emptying and superimposition never produces relations between different elements, whose connection must precisely be established, measured, or even contested.[17] That effect of uniformity and pure immanentisation that gives rise to a unified and flat plan, lacking faults and distinctions, thus operates in this way on the level of politics. This is so whether it is empty or full. In this sense – perhaps more than in the directions frequently taken up by interpreters in terms of the affinity and difference between the two – Schmitt's totality appears as a whole, if not exactly thorough in a Hegelian way, finally analogous, although obtained by other means.[18]

In this framework, the clearest and most obvious articulation would seem to concern Schmitt's doctrine of enmity and the conflict connected to it as the nucleus of the political. However, the configuration that this conflict assumes in Schmitt's text, gradually and not without gaps, seems to converge, and to some extent derive, from this primitive schema of understanding the internal politics of the exception.

2. The Symmetry of Conflict

At the origin, there is thus a constitutive instability, a primary energy that is systematically the source and the failure of politics. This is a politics whose autonomy paradoxically emerges in the double crisis of state and society: a state that is no longer the exclusive domain of politics and a society no longer capable of organising its own internal life. This is an autonomy of politics that, again, has the task of managing the void through the most radical form of decision. Such a practice is, then, paradoxical, because it is deeply connected to a lack of foundation and balance, but it is equally 'foundationalist' in its unfolding as a decisionism that transforms the conflict into exclusion. This is a case of Schmittian ambivalence and oscillation, between the lack of foundation and the 'politics of origin' in the autonomy of politics, as well as between politics itself and social determinisms. When super- or, at the limit, extra-legal legitimacy sets for itself the goal of stabilisation and legitimation of both the political and economic spheres, there is a further occurrence of the relation between separation and superposition that we have already identified. Lacking classical mediation in either the rationalist or dialectical manner, but also through distribution, opposition, and articulation, this connection never becomes a true relation between differences. For the *autonomy of politics*, it generates what has been called the 'politics of origin', that is, a paradoxical attempt to resort to the origin itself in a framework that has been characterised as unfounded, absolutely lacking a stable beginning, while in the elaboration of the *autonomy of the political*, it will run into another impasse.

The lack of relation, the oscillation between identity and distinction of elements – this is a philosophical principle which seems to return:

the equation state = politics becomes erroneous and deceptive at exactly the moment when state and society penetrate each other. What had been up to that point affairs of the state become thereby social matters, and, vice versa, what had been purely social matters become affairs of the state [. . .] In such a state, therefore, everything is at least potentially political, and in referring to the state it is no longer possible to assert for it a specifically political characteristic.[19]

SCHMITT: CONFLICT AS ENMITY

In the search for the specificity of the 'political' and the claim of its autonomy from the other, that is, the assumption that the specificity of its domain cannot derive from the outside, one of the most typically Schmittian arguments is given by the opening of politics beyond the state.[20] An immediate consequence of Schmitt's logic is the mutual penetration between society and politics, of which the latter represents the occurrence of a particular intensity in its relations. His reasoning is here focused on polemicising with positions that postulate a rigid continuity between society, economics, and politics, effectively cancelling the domain of politics itself, as well as in the attempt to claim a certain political realism. What stands out less apparently is his superimposition of politics and society which derives from these distinctions, or rather the effective subsumption of society by politics which owes much to his perspective and the historical moment. Once again, however, these theses, as full and empty homogenisation, are made under certain conditions with general philosophical assumptions, and not without the collaboration of Schmitt himself, and they have configured an overall modality of the understanding of politics within a flat and fluid terrain on which it encounters no restraints.[21]

> The specific political distinction to which political actions and motives can be reduced is that between friend [*Freund*] and enemy [*Feind*]. This provides a definition in the sense of a criterion and not as an exhaustive definition or one indicative substantial content [. . .] In any event it is independent [. . .] in that it can neither be based on any one antithesis or any combination of other antitheses, nor can it be traced to these.[22]

Enmity is therefore the definition of the imbalance, at once productive and lacking stable form, that characterises the political if isolated from further instances.[23] From this perspective, the presence of the successive distinctions, both relative to the frame of reference (politics rather than morality or aesthetics), as well as in the elements of the relation, seems aimed at preventing the reactivation of a balance and homogeneity, whether internal or deriving from the outside: 'the distinction of friend and enemy denotes the utmost degree of intensity of a union or separation, of an association or dissociation'.[24] There is no detonation in Schmitt's concept of the political, but only intensity, which is obtained not only by means of the regressive movement of the particular Schmittian phenomenology (or as we have said, genealogy), but above all by the subtraction of the figures of the private enemy, of economic competition, against which the re-proposal of a harmony appears possible on the surface.

Schmitt summarises a constitutive and exhausted imbalance in two fundamental characteristics of the relation: first in the polemical nature of properly political terms, the qualification of which simultaneously denotes their concreteness and thus the materiality and generality of the references. Second, Schmitt emphasises the connection with the possibility of a struggle, according to the model of civil war, to which it will be necessary to return. Struggle is again understood in the service of disharmony, whose battle is 'to the death',[25] with a radical existential significance. In this way, an origin in the proper sense is configured, albeit one with a peculiar structure: 'War is neither the aim nor the purpose nor even the very content of politics [but is] an ever present presupposition as real possibility.'[26] In what direction does this instability lead? What movement does it produce? Among the many criticisms addressed to this definition of the political, from irrationalist activism to the reverse, the

54

ontologisation of conflict, the discussion of the specific structure that Schmitt assigns to politics, the particular form in which the relation presents itself, has assumed less centrality. This is a relation that at first glance is profoundly asymmetrical. Indeed, what greater difference can be given than that between friend and enemy? The connection of enmity, including Schmitt's clarifications against objections, shows itself as a radical interference, which is programmatically aimed at giving an account of the always conjunctural nature of politics and the provisional character of its acquisitions. This is a dichotomy now qualified not by ambivalence, such as that between fullness and the void, but that to which emptying itself seems to give a direction that cannot bend towards asymmetry.

Yet the radicality of Schmitt's assertion of conflict as the original background to politics appears to overturn its own profile as soon as we look to its connection with the specific position in which it is placed, on the one hand, and to the outcomes that it produces, on the other. The process of emptying from, and of the possible superposition to, every circumscribed field implies an anonymity of the factors of discord, an indistinction between the poles of antagonism that renders the presupposition of asymmetry an attribution of right rather than what is done. Friend and enemy, in their respective and reversible positions, then appear as aspects of a relation destined by paradox – this time not sought after – to a stabilisation of instability.[27] By claiming and attempting to account for the conjunctural status of every given political, there is a continuous centre of gravity found below the phenomena to which they can be brought back, which interprets every conflict as always equal to itself. This is an origin whose form presents itself as symmetrical in this way, through the attribution of the same role to every social, economic, or moral actor who from time to time comes to fulfil the role of the pole of enmity.

> The political can derive its energy from the most varied human endeavors, from the religious, economic, moral, and other antitheses. It does not describe its own substance, but only has the intensity of an association or dissociation of human beings whose motives can be religious, national (in the ethnic or cultural sense), economic, or of any other kind and can effect at different times different coalitions and separations.[28]

Outcomes, productive capacities, are thus limited to repetition: a single symmetrical notion of political conflict that structures the origin of every phenomenon that can qualify as such. This repetition is non-differential and therefore precisely of the same, insofar as it is marked by the social, economic, or moral anonymity of its factors, from whose exit, however, what would be obtained is not so much a submission of the political to external conditioning as the encounter and interference with diversified fields with respect to which a relation is defined. This is a conflict that, in the last instance, cannot be resolved due to the formation of a stasis that does not attribute divergent tasks and purposes to the parties involved. It is an abstraction relocated to the empty origin, which is aimed at accounting for a claimed concreteness of politics: lacking mediation, consigned to the splitting and fusing, but never open to articulation.

The identification between politics and (civil) war is consubstantial with this logic, which Schmitt will consolidate and transform in the post-war period.[29] This is a conflict conceived according to a rigid military model:

SCHMITT: CONFLICT AS ENMITY

1. The intrinsic nature of the political assumes a *binary schema* at its origin. Every phenomenology is traced to this schema by starting from the elements that emerge. It is a prototype that displays asymmetry while assuming the guise of perfect symmetry by means of a process of emptying and superposition.

2. This model is configured as *struggle*, investing in itself the paradigm of civil war and in the last instance always reproducing the same figure of struggle, in a way that is consistent with the military matrix. There is no outcome here because of the genealogical framework that is sketched, and its search for concreteness changes into abstraction.

3. Every possible objectivity with regard to politics, understood as a mirroring between energy and order, is therefore subject to final judgement. This is an epistemological background which, in the history of interpretations, has not struggled to translate itself into a vindication of the perspective, reproducing this thesis on the cognitive terrain.

4. If there is thus a truth of politics, it is that of not being susceptible to a knowledge that is not *conjunctural*. But this is a conjuncture that, we will see, finally presents itself as subtracted from history rather than as a factor of radical historicisation. In this way the specific moment is opposed to the eternal, not the sequence or the process.

5. Finally, it is a political that is structured but alien to any form of closure, constitutively open but only to repetition. A rupture with the essence that, even in the search for origins which Schmitt carries out, does not justify the possibility. In short, far from irrationality, it is a choice for *immanence*.

The lack of a landing place for politics through this hollow form now seems to have Schmitt draw close to a number of

Nietzschean positions, particularly regarding the centrality of negation.[30] However, it is worth noting how, in the first place, for Nietzsche the negative is the place of the subsumption of this flat, irreducible contrast – in other words, that there is exactly a negation of this perspective. For Schmitt, instead, negation is always of order, the constitutive impossibility of a protection from its bottomless origin. In the same way, the coincidence of the genealogical perspective was authoritatively emphasised in the figure of *Enstehung*, or emergency, which, however, presents a divergence concerning the end between the two: for Nietzsche, the liberation of contrast and power; for Schmitt, the search for the origin of form, to the point of being configured as *arché*. This distinction cannot be underestimated: to the Nietzschean liberation of form Schmitt opposes contingency, which is, however, rooted in something like an originary form of the particular structure.[31] It is this structure, as we have seen, that probably generates effects of proximity and distance at the same time, for different reasons, between Hegel and Nietzsche: with respect to the sphere as *pars totalis* in the former and the liberation of the will in the latter, Schmitt places, as a halfway point, the specific model of political enmity. This is a flat relation between anonymous parts, such as the identical nuclei of dialectical and expressive totality, and a permanent relation between forces that does not produce development, such as the counterposed will to power. The effect is a stasis on the smooth plane of symmetrical conflict, of the manifestations of totality and the dispersion of forces.[32]

3. History and Passivity

In a text such as *Theory of the Partisan*, theoretical questions concerning the relation between politics and its origin at first seem to fade in favour of a more clearly historical reflection. However, in the background of this text there are some questions that orient Schmitt's thought for almost its entire course: the role and level of the relevance of politics, the crisis of the state, the tension towards form, and again, the advance of technology and the end of the territorial dimension. Analogously, the deep philosophical nucleus of Schmittian thought on politics and the political seems to be re-proposed through a glance that carries out its own questions not only on the constitution, but also the transformation of political form.

Empty and full are in this way theoretical elements that significantly change their sign, proposing new options. In particular, the figure of the revolutionary, as opposed to the partisan, introduces a 'full' modality of politics and the conflictuality underlying it, rooted in a renewed centrality of the economic and social framework. Partisan and revolutionary confront one another as two frontally divergent forms of enmity, both responses to a crisis that also determines the possible outcomes. The proposal of a 'full' figure against an 'empty' one that Schmitt makes here, we can anticipate, will work to recover the centrality of the dynamic between emptying and levelling described in the previous section: a conflict filled with social, historical, and economic content in order to be left empty.

The first connotation of the partisan is the irregularity of its position in the context of war, which is correlated to his particular form of enmity, namely that against the regularity of the soldier in uniform. We observe here a case of that anonymous and structured enmity through the contrast that Schmitt has gradually defined, lacking reference to the context and field of conflict.[33] It is a character that merges with its political commitment, of a specific nature and intensity, a further consequence of that escape from the antagonism of the state that is the primitive nucleus of this reflection: 'the partisan [. . .] fights on a political front, and it is precisely the political character of his action that brings to the fore again the original sense of the word *partisan*. The word is derived from *Partei*.'[34] An assumption we have already encountered is confirmed again in this case, namely the direct, non-mediated, non-dialectical passage between war and politics. This is an osmosis that is not only capable of justifying the reasoning in the light of the transformations of modern war, but also allows for interpreting some civil phenomena through a military gaze.[35]

Mobility is the third aspect that qualifies the partisan, associating him in Schmitt's eyes to the extra-state impulse to mobility, towards a conflict that expands beyond traditional borders.[36] The fourth characteristic of this figure, however, seems to contradict or partially amend this judgement, and this will be one of the main points in the division between partisan and revolutionary. Indeed, for Schmitt the partisan has the land as his place of belonging, and the nature of his action is fundamentally connected to its defence: '[the tellurian character] is significant for the essentially defensive situation of the partisan [. . .] whose nature changes when he identifies with the absolute aggressiveness of a world-revolutionary or technologizing ideology'.[37]

The differences between the figure of the partisan and his revolutionary counterpart begin to emerge clearly at this point. In particular, what is emphasised here is his telluric bond in the perspective of delimiting conflict, both on the level of the covered space and in the solely defensive and non-aggressive character of his action.[38] What belongs to the framework of the real or concrete enmity of the partisan is limitation, whereas the revolutionary tends to bend his logic into a moment of abstract and universal, indistinct justice. The other factors which Schmitt has noted also undergo a twist in the perspective of the revolutionary: irregularity and belonging, joining a party, are in this figure accentuated to the point of becoming all-encompassing, and in the Schmittian interpretation exceed any boundaries and determination. In this way, mobility translates into an aggressiveness that is the daughter of the paradigm of technicisation, eroding the internal limits of war understood in the traditional sense. The passage 'from Clausewitz to Lenin' is what decrees the breaking of such limits:

> What Lenin learned from Clausewitz, and he learned it well, was not just the famous formula of war as the continuation of politics. It involved the larger recognition that in the age of revolution the distinction between friend and enemy is the primary decision [. . .] Only revolutionary war is true war for Lenin, because it derives from absolute enmity. Everything else is a conventional game.[39]

The transition between modern partisan and revolutionary, because of its particular characteristics, gives the story of this figure a turning point that does not lack philosophical consequences. The revolutionary is not now an empty polarity as is the case with the partisan, but neither is there an oscillation between emptying and superposition – that is, the institution of an anonymous duality and its application to every form of politics through the genealogy of origin – rather, politics encounters a separate field in the image of the revolutionary, one which is not political: the sphere of society and its interests. In the economy of Schmitt's discourse, this occurrence presents itself as a reversal, or better, as a complete change of terrain. Filling is thus not a levelling of the empty model of every actual experience, but the encounter between the problem of the origin of politics ('the political') and something that breaks its non-derivability, its constitutive autonomy in the place of origin. This opens up a distance between partisan and revolutionary, concrete enmity and absolute enmity, equal to the distance between play and war:

> the distinction between war [*Woina*] and play [*Igra*] is accentuated by Lenin himself in a marginal note [. . .] Its logic entails the decisive step that tears down the containments which the state war of European international law had managed to establish in the eighteenth century [. . .] Clausewitz had not yet really considered their elimination. In comparison with a war of absolute enmity, the contained war of classical European international law, proceeding by recognized rules, is little more than a duel between cavaliers seeking satisfaction.[40]

Thus, there is a change of the model, starting from the change in the factors involved in it. In Schmitt's eyes, the acceleration created by Lenin's break with the paradigm of *jus publicum europæum* results exactly from the interference with the terrain of the economy, society, and in the last instance, class struggle. The revolutionary, in comparison with the partisan, does not then only struggle for a part, but for a cause and for specific objectives, which are not reducible to the regulated game of international law. Certainly, the associations Schmitt makes between the subversion of the limits of the law and the advancement of phenomena such as technicisation and globalism (which inform us more about Schmitt's specific sensitivity than the constitutive notes of his theory) play a role in his judgement, but the gap between two prototypes of conflict is precisely captured in these pages. In the last instance, the global dimension and excess with respect to established norms are nothing more than the reflections of a deeper transformation, which shifts the perfectly symmetrical axis of the friend–enemy relation through an intervention of the third element, an irreducible level that activates the filling of such hollow figures:

> The war of absolute enmity knows no containment. The consistent realization of absolute enmity provides its meaning and its justice. The only question therefore is this: is there an absolute enemy and who is it *in concreto*? For Lenin, the answer was unequivocal, and his superiority among all other socialists and Marxists consisted in his seriousness about absolute enmity. His concrete absolute enemy was the class enemy, the bourgeois, the western capitalist and his social order in every country in which they ruled [. . .] His comprehension of the partisan rested on the fact that the modern partisan had become the irregular proper and, in his vocation as the executor proper of enmity, thus, the most powerful negation of the existing capitalist order.[41]

Absolute enmity in this way represents a form of conflict whose geometry essentially differs from the political in its original form.[42] It is first of all a complete antagonism, in which the two poles of the relation are socially characterised, not anonymous and not distributable over any relation that reaches a certain level of intensity. Consequently, this kind of enmity gives rise to an asymmetrical conflict in which the actions, because of their socio-economic characterisation, play different roles, have antithetical ends, do not start from identical points, and adopt opposed instruments. Third, this antagonism exceeds the limits imposed by the game that is purely a game 'of position' in international law, which assigns roles and constraints according to a link that is structured by law and military custom. It is not exactly without limits, but it certainly acts outside of the established rules. Because of this excess, the fourth essential trait, it is a matter here of an enmity that concludes with the dissolution of one of the parts, an outcome that, despite its expressed radicalism, Schmittian politics wants to avoid. This dissolution provokes a fifth character, a complete upheaval of the starting ground and the construction of a field of a different sign. This is an upheaval that, again, is not the patrimony and objective of every actor implied in the contest, but instead only concerns one of the agents of the conflict, in the circular relation of cause and effect that this aspect knows with respect to the asymmetry of the subjects themselves, among which the subordinate will have more interest in the transformation of the starting field. Finally, an antagonism that does not present itself as permanent but that can be resolved by going beyond the existing given is therefore very different from 'the political' as the autonomous, originary, and unsurpassable level of politics.

In this regard, Carlo Galli has noted that

> Schmitt thinks war and politics as reciprocally implicated in a non-dialectical but genealogical sense, and that for him, war reveals its true nature (a manifestation of originary hostility, of exceptional origin) both when it is external and, even more so, when it is internal to the political order; and that, finally, conflict always arises between ontologically 'equal' contenders.[43]

But the discovery of the unequal conflict that belongs to absolute enmity introduces a gap and a selection without appeal into the logic of Schmitt's discourse. On the one hand, there is a regulated, symmetrical, and limited antagonism, and on the other, absolute, asymmetrical conflict that is aimed at dissolution. Beyond the numerous reasons that have emerged, which are connected to the revulsion towards the emergence of technology and the opening of the global 'maritime', it is perhaps not completely clear that such as decisive choice is made for the first option. The defence of the prerogatives of the *jus publicum europæum*, at the moment in which its crumbling is decreed, does not fully justify taking the position, just as the stigma towards the destruction of the adversary appears to underestimate the phenomenon of exclusion that is inevitably associated, albeit in another epoch, with the constitution of every political form. Thus, why the choice of such a party?

> None surmised what the unleashing of irregular war meant. None considered how the victory of the civilian over the soldier would play out when one day the citizen put on a uniform, while the partisan took it off in order to fight on without a uniform. Only this failure of concrete reflection has completed the destructive work of the professional revolutionary. This was a great misfortune, for with those containments of war, European man had succeeded in accomplishing a rare feat: the renunciation of criminalizing opponents at war, in other words, relativizing enmity, the negation of absolute enmity.[44]

The absolute enemy of the revolutionary is not really a party, a group – at the limit, it can be a social class – but Schmitt clearly grasps that the authentic adversary of this new kind of partisan is a specific order, a historically determinate political form. The aim of the professional revolutionary is to subvert that form, thus adopting a different model of political conflictuality, overturning the polemological and military paradigm. Indeed, the latter, as we have seen, presents itself as the prototype of a conflict among equals, a conflict that is symmetrical, and which only produces

MACHIAVELLIAN ONTOLOGY

its repetition.[45] And it does so because of its specific structure. The revolutionary – this is perhaps Schmitt's fear of his paradigm – intends to build a different order, in this way reactivating the course of history.

> In a world in which the partners push each other in this way into the abyss of total devaluation before they annihilate one another physically, new kinds of absolute enmity must come into being. Enmity will be so terrifying that one perhaps mustn't even speak any longer of the enemy or of enmity, and both words will have to be outlawed and damned before the work of annihilation can begin. Annihilation thus becomes entirely abstract and entirely absolute. It is no longer directed against an enemy, but serves only another, ostensibly objective attainment of highest values, for which no price is too high to pay. It is the renunciation of real enmity that opens the door for the work of annihilation of an absolute enmity.[46]

What is the meaning of the formula 'absolute enmity'? What is understood by 'annihilation thus becomes entirely abstract and entirely absolute'? In this context, annihilation is not so much physical destruction freed from the bonds of international law, but the overcoming of a world and a social order, the establishment of a different political framework. A process possible only through the conception of a new model of political conflict, the inverse of a prototype of eternal polarisation between friend and enemy. In short, a paradigm that thinks the succession of forms beyond empty decidability, the field of politics that in the last instance lacks prerogatives. What fails in Schmitt's discourse, as well as its uses in democratic and authoritarian guises, which this point invariably keeps firm, is the historicity itself of politics. This is a connotation that refers to the processes of constitution, and to their failure, to their being conjunctural but not punctual,

SCHMITT: CONFLICT AS ENMITY

to their constant testing of duration. Finally, we grasp here the given of a model of conflictuality, and even more of the origin of politics, which first empties and then fills up through the differential encounter with the economic and social level only to be left empty again, through choice and stigma. However, by contrast, the emergence of a form of asymmetrical conflict, which is not socially anonymous and aimed at the prefiguration of a new order, clearly shows the attempt to remove historicity from politics, confining it in a field in which the undecidability of the political is associated with the neutralisation of history.

Notes

1 Cf. Giuseppe Duso, *La logica del potere: Storia concettuale come filosofia politica* (Rome: Laterza, 1999), p. 189. See also Giuseppe Duso, 'Carl Schmitt: teologia politica e logica dei concetti politici moderni', *Daimon: Revista de filosofia* 13 (1996), pp. 77–98.

2 Gerardo Munoz, 'Intervista a Carlo Galli sulla nuova edizione spagnola di "Genealogia della politica"', *Cuarto Poder*, 2 May 2019.

3 Cf. Jean-Francois Kervegan, *Hegel, Carl Schmitt: la politique entre spéculation et positivité* (Paris: PUF, 1992).

4 See Mario Tronti, 'Marx e Schmitt: un problema storico-teorico', in Giuseppe Duso (ed.), *La politica oltre lo Stato* (Venice: Arsenale Cooperative Editrice, 1981), pp. 25–40. For a balance sheet, see Mattia Di Pierro, 'Mario Tronti lettore di Carl Schmitt: Da Marx alla teologia politica', *Storia del Pensiero Politico* 2 (2017), pp. 261–80. There is curiously no reference to the 'Italian' interpretation of Schmitt, even in passing, in Matthew G. Specter, 'What's "Left" in Schmitt? From Aversion to Appropriation in Contemporary Political Theory', in Jens Meierhenrich and Oliver Simons (eds), *The Oxford Handbook of Carl Schmitt* (Oxford: Oxford University Press, 2016), pp. 426–54. This interpretation in many ways anticipates the problems Specter highlights in the readings of Schmitt by Habermas, Mouffe, Kalyvas, Balakrishnan, and Werner Müller.

5 Carl Schmitt, *Political Theology: Four Chapters on the Concept of Sovereignty* (Cambridge, MA: MIT Press, 1985), p. 5.

MACHIAVELLIAN ONTOLOGY

6 Ibid., pp. 5–6.

7 Cf. Giorgio Agamben, *Homo Sacer: Sovereign Power and Bare Life* (Stanford, CA: Stanford University Press, 1998), pp. 11–12.

8 Schmitt, *Political Theology*, p. 12.

9 On this, see at least Pierangelo Schiera, 'Dalla decisione alla politica: la decisione in Carl Schmitt', in Duso (ed.), *La politica oltre lo Stato*, pp. 15–24, and Roberto Racinaro, *Esistenza e decisione in Carl Schmitt* (Naples: Guida, 1986).

10 Schmitt, *Political Theology*, pp. 12–13. Cf. at least George Schwab, *Carl Schmitt, la sfida dell'eccezione* (Rome: Laterza, 1986); G. Gomez Orfanel, *Excepcion y normalidad en el pensamiento de Carl Schmitt* (Madrid: Centro de estudios costitucionales, 1986); G. Motzo, 'Carl Schmitt e lo stato d'eccezione', *Quaderni costituzionali* 3 (1986), pp. 525–33.

11 Schmitt, *Political Theology*, p. 12.

12 Ibid., p. 13.

13 Cf. Tronti, 'Marx e Schmitt', p. 25.

14 Schmitt, *Political Theology*, p. 15.

15 Cf. Carlo Galli, *Genealogia della politica. Carl Schmitt e la crisi del pensiero politico moderno* (Bologna: Il Mulino, 1996), p. 27.

16 Ibid., p. 28. On this see also José Luis Villacañas, *Poder y conflicto. Ensayos sobre Carl Schmitt* (Madrid: Biblioteca nueva, 2008), p. 191.

17 Cf. Kervegan, *Hegel, Carl Schmitt.*

18 Cf. Geminello Preterossi, *Carl Schmitt e la tradizione moderna* (Rome: Laterza, 1996); John P. McCormick, *Carl Schmitt's Critique of Liberalism. Against Politics as Technology* (Cambridge: Cambridge University Press, 1997). Jurgen Habermas has not fully appreciated how, for Schmitt, political homogeneity can be given not only as a 'full' totality in an ethnic or nationalistic sense, but also as an emptying with respect to the materialist distinction between social groups. This anti-Schmittian preoccupation, however it is unilaterally grasped, has contributed to the pluralisation and emptying of sovereignty through which Habermas has proposed a competitive stagnation to which, as we will see, Schmitt's reasoning can also lead. Cf. Jurgen Habermas, *Between Facts and Norms: Contributions to a Discourse Theory of Law and Democracy* (Cambridge, MA: MIT Press, 1998).

19 Carl Schmitt, *The Concept of the Political* (Chicago: University of Chicago Press, 2007), p. 22.

20 Gianfranco Miglio, 'Presentazione', in Carl Schmitt, *Le categorie del "politico"*, ed. G. Miglio and P. Schiera (Bologna: Il Mulino, 1972), pp. 7–14. Cf. Duso *La logica del potere*, p. 214.

SCHMITT: CONFLICT AS ENMITY

21 On several problems which derive from a kind of *philosophia perennis* in Schmittian thought, see Gabriele Pedullà, 'Oltre Carl Schmitt', *Le parole e le cose*, 1 February 2016, http://www.leparoleelecose.it/?p=21894 (accessed 12 January 2024).

22 Schmitt, *Concept of the Political*, p. 26.

23 Galli, *Genealogia della politica*, pp. 739–40.

24 Schmitt, *Concept of the Political*, p. 26.

25 Ibid., p. 71.

26 Ibid., p. 34. Translation modified.

27 Schmitt often refers to stasis in his writings. For example: 'stasis means in the first place quiescence, tranquility, standpoint, status [. . .] But stasis also means, in the second place, (political) unrest, movement, uproar and civil war.' Carl Schmitt, *Political Theology II: The Myth and Closure of Any Political Theology* (London: Polity, 2008), p. 123. Cf. Banu Bargu, 'Stasiology: Political Theology and the Figure of the Sacrificial Enemy', in Winifred Fallers Sullivan, Robert A. Yelle, and Mateo Taussig-Rubbio (eds), *After Secular Law* (Stanford, CA: Stanford University Press, 2011), pp. 140–4.

28 Schmitt, *Concept of the Political*, p. 38. 'Also a class in the Marxian sense ceases to be something purely economic and becomes a political factor when it reaches this decisive point [. . .] The real battle is then of necessity no longer fought according to economic laws but has—next to fighting methods in the narrowest technical sense, its political necessities and orientations, coalitions and compromises, and so on'. Ibid., p. 37.

29 Cf. Ibid., pp. 32–4.

30 Cf. Carlo Galli, 'Nichilismi a confronto: Nietzsche e Schmitt', *Filosofia politica* 1 (2014), pp. 99–120.

31 Cf. Galli, *Genealogia della politica,* pp. 129–30.

32 And thus, an identity between competitive plurality (enmity) and homogeneous totality (empty decision), which remains misunderstood for those who have attempted a progressive appropriation of Schmitt in the name of an abstract agonistic pluralism, as an alternative to conflict. Cf. Chantal Mouffe, 'Carl Schmitt and the Paradox of Liberal Democracy', in Chantal Mouffe (ed.), *The Challenge of Carl Schmitt* (London: Verso, 1999), pp. 38–53; Chantal Mouffe, *The Return of the Political* (London: Verso, 1993); Chantal Mouffe, *On the Political* (New York: Routledge, 2005); Gopal Balakrishnan, *The Enemy: An Intellectual Portrait of Carl Schmitt* (London: Verso, 2000); Andreas Kalyvas, *Democracy and the Politics of the Extraordinary: Max Weber, Carl Schmitt and Hannah Arendt,* (Cambridge:

Cambridge University Press, 2009). Jan-Werner Müller rightly compares these options to the aporias of Tronti's interpretation in Jan-Werner Müller, *A Dangerous Mind: Carl Schmitt in Post-War European Thought* (New Haven, CT: Yale University Press, 2003).

33 Carl Schmitt, *Theory of the Partisan* (East Lansing, MI: Michigan State University Press, 2004), pp. 9–10.

34 Ibid., p. 11.

35 Ibid.

36 Ibid., pp. 11–12.

37 Ibid., p. 13.

38 'Schmitt's partisan, instead, is far from the revolutionary and his discriminatory and absolutely aggressive logic that makes him a particularly intense expression of the senseless uprooting that is typical of the age of technology and its "globalisms".' Galli, *Genealogia della politica*, p. 767.

39 Schmitt, *Theory of the Partisan*, p. 35.

40 Ibid., p. 36.

41 Ibid.

42 'A thought, once again, oriented towards a concrete order capable of "taming" unchained technology, universalism, and absolute conflictualism'. Galli, *Genealogia della politica*, p. 769.

43 Ibid., p. 769.

44 Schmitt, *Theory of the Partisan*, p. 64.

45 Roberto Esposito has written widely on the binary role of negation in Schmitt: 'As soon as the enemy is placed before the friend and war before peace, the inevitable effect is a loss of boundaries and an identification between opposites. Identified with its enemy, the political subject ends up sharing the implosion. When the logic of negative determination transmutes into an ontology of enmity, annihilation is poised to become self-annihilation.' Roberto Esposito, *Politica e negazione: Per una filosofia affermativa* (Turin: Einaudi, 2013), p. 12. Cf. Roberto Esposito, *Due: La macchina della teologia politica e il posto del pensiero* (Turin: Einaudi, 2013), in particular pp. 42–8; Roberto Esposito, *Categorie dell'impolitico* (Bologna: Il Mulino, 1988).

46 Schmitt, *Theory of the Partisan*, p. 67.

3

Arendt: Competition and Distinction

If it is possible to identify a single term that reflects Hannah Arendt's intellectual posture, and more generally the underlying epistemological horizon of her thought, then 'distinction' perhaps accomplishes this task. To distinguish, indeed, is not only one of the prevailing gestures of the author of *The Origins of Totalitarianism*, but perhaps her main exhortation towards the human condition: politics and history, ideology and thought, political revolution and social revolution, labour, work, and action – these are just some of the binary and ternary distinctions found in her texts. These are all cases of association to escape from, to subvert by breaking the constitutive link. In this sense, distinguishing presents itself here as a synonym for disarticulating. From Arendt's perspective this disarticulating takes place with respect to a gap that always generates, a vertical order that tends to subsume one term to the other, in which therefore the filling of one always corresponds to the emptying of the other.

The continual recurrence of such an operation of distinction perhaps shows a recurring need in this philosophical perspective: the levelling only obtainable by way of separation, and therefore the isolation of factors internal to a problematic. In what follows, we will first analyse the main epistemological equipment in order to show the image that politics and conflict in particular take on, with the form and results that derive from it. Finally, we will observe the repercussions of this conceptual structure on the idea of the course of history, on the aspect of its presence and the eventuality of its absence. The disturbing character of distinction will thus be the criterion that guides the attempt to reconstruct the Arendtian nexus between epistemology, politics, and history:

> Arendt also understands the autonomy of the political in the sense of its being a separate sphere with, as it were, contents of its own. This corresponds to her attempt to make a clear-cut *distinction* between political problems or questions and those pertaining to the spheres of morality, social welfare, private life, the economy, or the protection of basic human rights [. . .] This *disturbing* tendency is also apparent in her inclination to take the idea of a council system literally, while stripping it of all the social, administrative, and economic responsibilities which it had always taken upon itself whenever one emerged during a time of revolution.[1]

1. Ideology and Identification

The processes that Arendt describes in *The Origins of Totalitarianism* perhaps have as their object the technical term that is most clearly opposed to the semantics of distinction (which is pervasive throughout the text): identification, its lack, its fulfilment that is poured into assimilation and homogenisation. The historical events of statelessness can only focus on this kind of issue. But it is in the final definition of the nature and lived experience of totalitarianism that the role of these terms is clearly shown:

> Totalitarian policy does not replace one set of laws with another [. . .] It promises to release the fulfillment of law from all action and will of man; and it promises justice on earth because it claims to make mankind itself the embodiment of the law. *This identification of man and law* [. . .] seems to cancel the discrepancy between legality and justice.[2]

Liberating and distinguishing, identifying and obliterating: the peculiarity of the totalitarian phenomenon here appears to overturn even this initial binary scan of Arendtian analysis because, by identifying man and law, it tends to liberate man from the effort to fulfil the law, which will happen through an automatism, so to speak. This automatism abolishes alternatives and separations, establishing links that soon dissipate into indistinct unification: 'instead of saying that totalitarian government is unprecedented, we could also say that it has exploded the very alternative on which all definitions of the essence of governments have been based on political philosophy, that is the alternative between lawful and lawless government, between arbitrary and legitimate power'.[3] Whatever the specific form of this reduction to essence that, by a paradox, proceeds according to successive associations rather than isolation, Arendt is not slow to point it out: it is the assimilation, in a determinate historical structure, of a particular content to politics as such. The gradual emergence within politics of something that is not politics transparently shows the risk attached to a politics that does not distinguish, that is related to its other and, essentially, subordinated to it: '[totalitarianism] is quite prepared to sacrifice everybody's vital immediate interests to the execution of what it assumes to be the law of History or the law of Nature'.[4]

Command, which for Arendt is intimately connected to modern politics, thus does not fail through the path of a liberation but through the appearance of a lack: the loss of that traditional legitimation embodied in the law which reveals, among other things, all shadows of power, which is selective but necessary in it. According to Arendt, totalitarianism obliterates this price paid to the social order that is articulated in the positivity of the law, referring to a politics that is no longer marked by any opacity. On the contrary, in the totalitarian perspective, this would be nothing but a transparent replication of a necessity inscribed elsewhere: in the automatism of fields such as biology or history.[5] In other words, the operation of linking politics, its tasks, and its functions to something that does not pertain to its autonomous sphere makes the legality that is both the burden and guarantee of modern politics evaporate.[6] The 'laws' of nature and history, indeed, do not provide for any artificially obtained positivity, but instead introduce processes of formation and the arrival at immediate and spontaneous types of necessary outcomes into politics. This attraction between divergent polarities also generates flows and orientations that dominate the single individual, depriving them of their specificity and uniqueness, thereby destining humanity to be only an expression of logics which are entirely unpremeditated.

> In the interpretation of totalitarianism, all laws have become laws of movement [. . .] Underlying the Nazis' belief in race laws [. . .] is Darwin's idea of man as the product of a natural development [. . .] just as under the Bolsheviks' belief in class-struggle as the expression of the law of history lies Marx's notion of society as the product of a gigantic historical movement.[7]

Distinction *or* identification, identification *and* development: if politics comes into contact with other levels of the social or natural whole, it not only allows them to contaminate it, but also to integrally direct it.[8] In particular, this happens if these spheres are characterised by the centrality of the notion of development, that is, an internal legality of the object that leads the movement: 'the tremendous intellectual change which took place in the middle of the last century consisted in the refusal to view or accept anything "as it is" and in the consistent interpretation of everything as being only a stage of some further development'.[9] Every development, Arendt here argues as key to the philosophy of history, tends as such to overdetermine politics, whose historicity (to which we will return) instead has a punctual, singular, distinct, and individual character. In this key, the articulation and positive filling of politics demonstrate themselves as factors of its decay, of its introduction within a necessarily asymmetrical relation, which thus creates hierarchy and the subordination of one element to another.

According to Arendt, we thus observe a double movement, both horizontal and vertical, in the totalitarian configuration: the essentialisation of politics through a movement of vertical association with a background of reference (as noted in the biological example of Darwin or the historical prototype of Marx)[10] is followed by a horizontal dynamic of contracting the articulation which ends up transforming into homogeneity. In Arendt's words: 'by pressing men against each other, total terror destroys the space between them [. . .] Totalitarian government [. . .] destroys the one essential prerequisite of all freedom which is simply the capacity of motion which cannot exist without space.'[11]

At the heart of this problematic we find a notion that bridges the distance between thought and politics, individual and society: ideology (in its Arendtian version). The concept of ideology connects a form of thought – we could say an entire categorial apparatus elaborated by the tradition – to a certain number of historical-political consequences, and again to a specific interpretation of the historical events of the twentieth century. In this way, the caesura between politics and a number of its specific historical and social manifestations is restitched.

> All ideology is quite literally what its name indicates: it is the logic of an idea. Its subject matter is history, to which the 'idea' is applied; the result of this application is not a body of statements about something that is, but the unfolding of a process which is in constant change.[12]

Here again we find the argumentative chain that identification, in opposition to distinction, associates with the emergence of a development, whose outcome is a contraction of space. It is now under the charge of a very general set of political phenomena – one of the clearest heuristic limits of Arendt's notion of ideology – but also a modality of thought: from logical deduction to dialectical processuality, an entire season of modern reflection comes to be grasped, certainly *in nuce*, as totalitarian. In other words, it is susceptible to a use, originally external to it, that is capable of abolishing both the synchronic (the space of relation) and diachronic (the event of action) distinctions of politics.[13] Politics emerges transfigured, transformed into nature or history by a reason whose instruments seem in these pages to be the authentic theoretical knot in question.[14] It is a sort of absolute political evil.[15]

However, as we anticipated, the adversary of such a positive conception (which we will examine) in these pages already seems to be indistinct homogeneity rather than articulation and connection: indeed, there are numerous Arendtian notes on isolation as the final result of the totalitarian practice and on isolation as a political problem. For example: 'Isolation is that impasse into which men are driven when the political sphere of their lives, where they act together in the pursuit of a common concern, is destroyed.'[16] Yet, if Arendt rejects homogeneity, which she sees as the ultimate outcome of every connection, the role of relation against isolation is also paramount for the purposes of isolating the ends of possibility of political action.[17] Nevertheless, and here perhaps is the solution of ambivalence, political isolation probably appears as the ultimate effect of homogeneity, of the contraction of space, rather than the explosion of relation. In short, it is the adhesion to a politics of the 'whole' of a development that is always tendentially totalising and compromises both the public and private spheres, whose correlation is where politics itself lives. The flow of totalitarian becoming thus loses both distinction and articulation: 'while isolation concerns only the political realm of life, loneliness concerns human life as a whole. Totalitarian government [. . .] bases itself on loneliness, on the experience of not belonging to the world at all, which is among the most radical and desperate experiences of man.'[18]

2. Action, Distinction, Competition

The contrary of distinction – opposition – does not share Arendt's usual reasoning procedures. This is probably also due to the tendential pluralisation of the objects of this kind of thought, which are extraneous to binary divisions and crossroads.

Multiplicity is a factor within which some parts are more clearly traceable than others. This is the case in the relation between *labour* and *action*, which are components of the human condition whose historical disposition includes and is interpolated by the element of *work*. Thus, although this third space is present, Arendt's reflection seems to grasp something else between the two poles that is a main opposition. In order to identify the main characteristics of the theory of action Arendt carries out in *The Human Condition*, it will therefore be useful to closely observe the qualities and problems of the fundamental trait of late modern societies[19] according to her, namely labour. It is an eminent example, however, of the practice of distinction and separation that is antithetical to connections and fusions:

> The common characteristics of both, the biological process in man and the process of growth and decay in the world, is that they are part of the cyclical movement of nature and therefore endlessly repetitive [. . .] laboring always moves in the same circle, which is prescribed by the biological process of the living organisms and the end of its 'toil and trouble' comes only with the death of this organism.[20]

There is no aspect of Arendt's thought where the tendential fusion between the epistemological approach and the orientation of the contents can be verified more than in her conception of labour.[21] Comparing it first to work, Arendt emphasises how this modality of the human condition produces a sort of paradox of productivity – 'man's metabolism with nature', according to the Marxian definition. This gives rise to products whose permanence always results in the outcome of a rapid consumption, since labour is not oriented from the beginning towards the permanence of its objects, but rather to their disposition in relation to the necessities of life.[22]

In this sense, method and development, form and content, tend to coincide in Arendt due to a structural separation between labour and action that remains functional to the rupture between automatisms in the former and the priority of distinction in the latter. Her critique of Marx similarly unfolds in the key identified above regarding the presupposition of distinction with respect to the double polarity of homogenisation and isolation.[23] The first axis is clearer, and immediately derivable from the main connotation attributed to labour. It is a double axis, however, in the sense of a double form of levelling that Arendt argues can be traced in Marx's philosophy: on the one hand the description of a society, that typical of the capitalist mode of production, which is integrally characterised by the prerogatives of man as *animal laborans*, that is, by the strict link with nature and its processes, which as such is deprived of every possibility of autonomous decision regarding its own destiny. On the other hand, there is the future society, which Marx imagines (in Arendt's interpretation) as a haven beyond the necessity of productive labour, the most important human faculty in her framework. This gives way to a uniform void that is not different from the capitalist fullness of production and consumption, which is a dystopian outcome for Arendt.

> The fact remains that in all stages of his work he defines man as an *animal laborans* and then leads him into a society in which this greatest and most human power is no longer necessary. We are left with the rather distressing alternative between productive slavery and unproductive freedom.[24]

Bringing the economic close to politics, or better put, identifying in the former the place of the subsumption of the latter – as well as the other instances of modern societies – gives rise to a deterministic horizon in which properly political action no longer has any place.[25] It is therefore the logic of articulation that is under accusation here: just as was the case with regard to the conformation of ideology – also structurally destined for a repetition without deviations – here the connection between the sphere of labour and politics simply makes the latter impossible, annulling it in the mesh of biological processes.

> The only activity which corresponds strictly to the experience of worldlessness, or rather to the loss of world that occurs in pain, is laboring, where the human body, its activity notwithstanding, is also thrown back upon itself.[26]

More precisely, what can be observed in these passages is the impossibility of thinking, in Arendt's framework, an effective relation between these fields of labour, work, and action. Every link is here without hierarchical mediation, vertical ordering, subsumption. This can only give rise to the alternative between a homogeneous union of instances (which is synonymous, eventually, with isolation as the loss of context) and a singularisation of the same. Distinction will then be the instrument of the liberation, both conceptual and practical, of the specific modalities of action.

Indeed, when defining the proper nature of action in its chosen place, with Greece and its *poleis*, Arendt seems to construct a model that is symmetrically opposed to labour: doing and acting are in this way taken in a dualism that afflicts and gives value to the human condition. It is a conceptual structure that revolves around a fundamental triangulation, within which the individual factors reciprocally define each other. It is within this structure that distinction is found, as a difference that is united in a couple with equality, and this binomial characterises the instances of plurality.[27] The latter is the trait that most strongly emerges in a space that allows action and, vice versa, that typically human connotation that is the condition of possibility itself of action and its necessary correlate, discourse. Furthermore, it is this primary structure that determines the modality through which Arendt thinks political relations among individuals, and it is perhaps a consequence of what has been observed until now that relations can exist exclusively between individuals.

Arendt argues that equality allows for understanding among people, which is memory as the capacity to understand others in the past, and project understood as an imagination of needs in the future. Difference instead opens the inter-human space that avoids superimposition and fusion, a space that is the proper place of action and discourse: 'in man, otherness, which he shares with everything that is, and distinctness, which he shares with everything alive, become uniqueness, and human plurality is the paradoxical plurality of unique beings'.[28] In this there is a processual qualifying of acting: in discourse and action, individuals are not distinct as much as they 'distinguish themselves' according to a development that leads them to distance themselves from each other without excluding the public sphere, to the point that Arendt attributes to this development of action two main properties capable of characterising its status: the possibility of innovation and the emergence of subjectivity.[29] Acting as insertion into the human world configures an authentic 'second birth' for Arendt,[30] in which the individual stimulus takes the place of biological necessity and utility. In this key, the effect of man is to produce the unexpected that breaks with custom and tradition, and it is only in this acting that the agent reveals himself as subject.[31]

> Because of its inherent tendency to disclose the agent together with the act, action needs for its full appearance the shining brightness we once called glory, and which is possible only in the public realm.[32]

If thinking the intertwining of different spheres solely as super-positioning and levelling leads to an emptying of the concrete meaning of politics, then establishing an economically, historically, and socially anonymous prototype is its necessary reverse. This leads to three main consequences.

First, this configures a notion of mute difference, which is not characterised by the encounter with the other and is therefore integrally political. Observing the rigid relation of consequentiality of such an outcome with respect to its epistemological background, however, can only be followed by the observation of the modelling abstraction of such a proposal.[33] This generates a problematic relation between this prototype and its historical references, to which we will return below, as well as an immediate emptying of any possible content that is capable of specifying the position, the quality of agents and their action. Indeed, we find here an aspect, which we observed differently in the preceding chapters, which interpreters have sometimes assimilated to the so-called 'autonomy of politics'.[34]

For these reasons, as a second important consequence, the Arendtian schema of action describes a form of symmetrical conflict, that is, a relation among different horizontal differences that are never staggered with respect to a plane of reciprocal immanence. In short, a conflict that does not foresee deviations from the terrain of departure, in which novelty is nothing other than the affirmation of the prevailing individuality.

However, it could be argued that Arendtian politics does not foresee a centrality of conflict and therefore cannot be analysed through such a filter. Yet beneath the immediate surface, this kind of philosophical discourse about politics appears to contain an eminently conflictual, agonistic, and competitive nucleus.[35] Arendt's interpretation of the 'Greek solution' with respect to the risks of action, its futility and unpredictability, shows what the historical point of reference of this paradigm is, and how the model is shaped by the author:

> The original, prephilosophic remedy for this frailty has been the foundation of the *polis* [. . .] The *polis* was supposed to multiply the occasions to win 'immortal fame,' that is, to multiply the chances for *everybody to distinguish himself*, to show in deed and word who he was in his unique distinctness.[36]

Such a conception is configured as a paradigm, whose essential function is to judge what does not confirm to it, as in the example of labour we analysed.[37] There is therefore an agonistic direction of Arendtian discourse around politics, whose public space is populated by conflictual relations which generate free individuals in the course of their processual unfolding. We can synthesise its characteristics as follows:

1. Politics assumes, as already noted, the trait of *plurality* as a determining factor for the construction of public space, that is, a terrain that is simultaneously circumscribed, as in the example of the walls of the *polis*, and entirely composed of discrete factors. It is a circumscription, in other words, whose scope allows them to differentiate.
2. A differentiation that shows itself as a *symmetrical conflict*, namely the competition for the same ends with the same tools. The memorable action that remains etched in collective memory, which is also possible only thanks to the circumscribed and to some extent regulated space of the *polis*, is thus the result of a politics of this kind.
3. It is also further a *competitive* terrain because a new inequality, emanating from the same starting points, is the result.

Becoming *aristoi*, the best, is the aim of the collective political construction.

4. The result is an *abstract* field, endowed with a strong modelling tension but one that is cut out of historical experience and ends up losing it. It is a prototype that translates into a paradigmatic instance, which is thus called upon to judge and decide on particular historical experiences.

5. Finally, it is a field, which on the whole is *immanent*, whose distinction with respect to further spheres does not allow any external measure that is capable of shifting its internal symmetry and flatness.

We then observe a paradigm selectively deduced from a historical experience that finally, third among the results we alluded to above, judges the historical experience itself, and on this basis builds a typology (labour, work, action).[38] Reflecting on the antagonism internal to the *poleis*, Hans-Joachim Gehrke has noted how 'what in the modern ideology of the market is exalted as free competition and as competition with positive values dominated unchallenged in the political field'.[39] We could then ask if the historical origin of a certain conception of political conflict, or even of simple antagonism, cannot elucidate some aspect of its abstract figure.[40] Or if it can elucidate some aspect of the abstraction derived from it. In other words, one could ask if the formula of a regulated competition between equals, understood as anonymous in terms of positioning, tools of operation, and objectives, and aimed at immortality, of both fame and distinction from others, a moment in which only something like subjectivity emerges – one can ask if this formula can return to endow itself with historicity. In short, if this conflict allows a change in terrain that produces a deviation from the point of departure and with it, diachronic succession. For the moment this highly codified philosophical and historiographical interpretation appears induced rather by paradigms of the author than archaic experience, however important. This is an outcome that again projects its shadow on to a past that is perhaps transfigured, and certainly oriented and selected. The form that this abstraction can assume in the context of historical judgement properly understood, and the reflection it can provide on a specific idea of historicity, is what must then be investigated.

3. Revolutions Without History

Miguel Vatter has argued that there is a clear tendency in contemporary philosophy to establish a field proper to politics that is separate in various ways from the domains of economy and society which for a long time have been held to determine it.[41] But this methodological approach, so to speak, has often found immediate political versions; among these, the one Arendt carries out in *On Revolution* and some other essays is certainly among the most radical.

The question presents itself as a historico-political transposition of the theses which we have previously developed on the level of reflection and philosophical modelling concerning the proper nature of action, as well as the relation with the other spheres of the human condition. On this ground, Arendt poses a problem regarding the authoritarian turns of modern revolutions and their intrinsic violence, which is destined to have a long-lasting influence:

MACHIAVELLIAN ONTOLOGY

The perplexity consisted in the task of foundation, the setting of a new beginning, which as such seemed to demand violence and violation, the repetition, as it were, of the old legendary crime (Romulus slew Remus, Cain slew Abel) at the beginning of all history.[42]

As we see here, Arendt relocates a key feature of her position regarding the possibility of action in general on to the level of pure political reflection. Even in this case, there is action only if it produces the new, which here means to confer on it an extra-legal meaning. Violence and extraneity to order are now synonymous, however. Reactivating another element of her meditation on action, Arendt points out how arriving at the generalisation of violence does not emerge because of a constitutive quality of political action but, once again, because of its subordination to something else, to economic or social ends. It is indeed the 'social' side of the modern revolutions, both French and Russian, that produces the violent drift, as a consequence of the aspiration to escape from the state of necessity.[43] According to Arendt, freeing man from necessity means rendering him an absolute means for a project of emancipation, unlike in the case of political revolutions (essentially the American), which in thinking of freedom exclusively from political domination, look at man as an end in itself.[44] In her words:

the direction of the American Revolution remained committed to the foundation of freedom and the establishment of lasting institutions [. . .] The direction of the French Revolution was deflected almost from its beginning from this course of foundation [. . .] it was determined by the exigencies of liberation not from tyranny but from necessity, and it was actuated by the limitless immensity of both the people's misery and the pity this misery inspired.[45]

Again, if politics that is subjected to biological and social processes overdetermines individual action into an uncontrollable flux, and if this results in a structurally violent and arbitrary general situation, then it is a matter of separating these spheres, both by defending a closed space of politics and by circumscribing the ends of the revolutionary moment.

How then should the *constitutio libertatis* be thought, the effective presence of a historical framework that is capable of proposing an uncontaminated action, one which is detached from the normativity of the social? This is a question that concerns, on the theoretical level, the crystallisation of the novelty that action imposes, the construction of an order that keeps the spirit of the foundation act alive without betraying it, guaranteeing its permanence and stability. In short, this is the now classic problem of the internal relation between constituent and constituted power, which in Arendt is connected to the triangulation between action, conflict, and history.[46]

> To the extent that the greatest event in every revolution is the act of foundation, the spirit of revolution contains two elements which to us seem irreconcilable and even contradictory. The act of founding the new body politic, of devising the new form of government involves the grave concern with the stability and durability of the new structure.[47]

In other words, according to Arendt, freedom brings with it an inevitably extra-constitutional trait, but at the same time, action requires a moment of formalisation in order to be effectively practicable and mature. In this sense, what is defined as *constitutio libertatis* presents an attempt to solve an aporia that appears constitutive. On the one hand, the very act of the foundation of an at least relatively stable form offers historical consistency to the process of action as plurality that is typical of associated people. On the other, however, this aspect remains rigorously circumscribed to the moment of foundation, and risks being lost in what comes to be constituted. Indeed, it is a moment with a punctual duration which, moreover, in Arendt's conception should not be capable of establishing any function of command, which is effectively external to its specific nature. Thus, if the constitution of freedom here remains something different than the simple constitutional government, the latter reproduces the diachronic impasse: the extra-constitutional act of founding a new order remains external to any authority capable of supporting precisely the novelty which it intended to give rise to.[48]

The structure of freedom that Arendt thinks in action as absolute novelty therefore produces a double impossibility on the historico-political terrain. On the side of constituted power, the side of authority and order, it does not allow freedom to be founded because it is understood as unconditional spontaneity that does not allow for heteronomy. On the other side, constituent power presents itself as a punctual moment that finds the fulfilment of freedom precisely in the internal relation with what will be created, as such being the bearer of authority and legitimacy, always situated on this side of them.[49]

However, it is by reversing the meaning of this double incapacity that Arendt believes she can resolve this question, which is apparently related to every form of relation between the gesture of beginning and political structure. This is a connection that, perhaps now in a clearer way, runs through the articulation of politics itself and history, insofar as the conformation of the former defines the modality of destitution and reconstitution that characterises the latter. Arendt's reversal takes place, in this context, by considering how foundation itself responds to the characteristics of action, which are not immediately superimposable on the indistinct flow of constituent power that precedes political form. In other words, the foundation corresponds to that absolute beginning that characterises action. This is a moment in which freedom and power are organised in an aggregate, beyond the unattainable constituent purity, as an order in itself, in which extra-constitutional propulsion is now lost.[50] In this sense, Arendt seems to bring the two poles together by contracting the space between them, against the tendency to see them as separate. On the level of order as such, this proximity is embodied in the idea that authority always emanates from an act of beginning, but that authority, far from betraying its spirit, is endowed with institutions capable of keeping this beginning alive.[51]

However, analysing the role of authority as an extension and repetition, it is possible to observe how it is now the status of the latter that is in question, once again in a double alternative between the inexhaustible re-proposition of an origin that is binding once and for all, or in the permanent activation of the new, as an unprecedented constitutional configuration. If repetition is rooted in institutions, the second hypothesis immediately appears to account for a mechanism that Arendt conceives precisely in searching for stability and duration, while the former alternative appears ambivalent. Arendt's historical reference is republican Rome, whose order [*ordinamenti*] would at least partially resolve these aporias:

> The very concept of Roman authority suggests that the act of foundation inevitably develops its own stability and permanence [. . .] This notion of a coincidence of foundation and preservation by virtue of augmentation [. . .] was deeply rooted in the Roman spirit and could be read from almost every page of Roman history.[52]

This 'Roman' and 'Atlantic' interpretation connects authority and freedom, foundation and constitution, in a way that now seems unbalanced on a beginning given once and for all. The relation between beginning and repetition here becomes external rather than internal. In short, it is the knot that instead of tightening, as seen in Arendt's claim of the impossibility of separating the two powers, tends to loosen. Repetition and beginning, in a sort of inversion of direction, rather than moving towards a coincidence in which each repetition is none other than a new beginning, are interpreted by Arendt in a 'Roman' way in which the repetition of beginning means the expansion of the influence, spirit, and modalities of command that it has initiated. Finally, the 'coincidence'[53] between origin and its institutionalisation returns to configure something as a homogeneous and indistinct flux, not unlike the perpetual immanence in itself of a constituent power that is thought as autonomous.

What is the image of history that appears now, in the framework of politics thought as action and placed in the context of the events of modernity? In short, how is a certain theory of action and conflict reflected in the figures through which permanence and succession, transformations and durations, are conceived? The political action Arendt historicises and understands as necessarily destined to be inscribed within a design, or better, as the covering of the interval between what is constituent and what is constituted, seems to discount the presence of a notion of origin that projects its shadow over the entire course that follows it. Authority as broadening seems to absolve this origin from the act that it was capable of performing, that is, from erupting as absolute newness. In this direction, the repetition it orders is configured precisely as a new affirmation of those same institutions which, once founded, appear immutable.

This is a thesis that thus seems to situate itself with a decision for the permanence itself of the constituted.

One variant of this Arendtian operation is given by the insistence of some authors on the specificity of the notion of beginning. Its reiteration would thus correlate to its historicity, which is in itself immune to every stability. In other words, the repetition of the origin, the event of innovative action, could be read as the moment of the destitution of the given order without this event coming to activate a further stability, which would be constituted as a substantially aleatory recomposition following the event.[54] The interpretative effort with respect to the internal link between freedom and authority that Arendt tries to circumscribe, in which the foundation unites rather than separates these discrete moments, is clear. However, it is an undoubtable aporetic outcome of such an attempt, that is, the institutionalisation of an origin in a strong sense, that the possibility of a different reading exists, which focuses on the tension and reciprocal resistance between event and form.[55] This tension outlines a new type of relation, in which events punctuate the history of orders without being able to take charge of the process, only deconstructing its stability.[56] If this option is certainly rooted in a primary inheritance from Arendt, the constitutive need for the action of permanence, it is here replaced with practice understood as inert novelty, as destitution rather than creation.[57]

Whether it searches for stability or destitution, it could finally be argued, Arendt's notion of action produces a merely simulated beginning. Or, otherwise, thinking a revolution without history. That is the dehistoricised prototype of the *polis*, cut out from its aristocratic guise and founded on a conflict that stands between the competition among equals for distinction, affirmation, and memorability, or the internal relation between a principle that, starting from the new that represents, becomes an archaic origin, both unavoidable and perpetual, or even an event that displaces any given structure, a destituent insurgency without succession – in each of these cases the problem seems to lie elsewhere. Perhaps it is found in the place of what was excluded in the first place: the possibility of the articulation between different segments of historical and social space, a non-anonymous and therefore internally differentiated space, populated by discrete and characterised agents, and finally the possibility that not all events and all political aggregates can be thought as equal, mute, and undifferentiated. It is thus probably in distinction as the ultimate philosophical principle, which arranges the epistemological field by immunising action from any contact with the outside – and which then thinks the process as internal relation to a flat plurality, immanent to itself, and that systematises the historical terrain by separating rather than connecting order and conflict – that such a link can be traced.

Once again it is within the fundamental operation between distinction and identification, as the positive and negative of a horizon of overall meaning, that it is possible to trace the basic coordinates that lead to such outcomes. Indeed, if every connection is grasped as subordination and fusion among different levels, the destiny can only be thinking the gap as a necessary solution. But this leads without mediation to a closure of politics within a narrow field, in which the binary and dualistic options end up reflecting one another. To these resolutions of politics in the economy and in society, or those in which – as we have frequently seen – the ultimate outcome is separation and distinction, there are perhaps different semantics that have opposed to the differential encounter between motives and actors deeply characterised, but not for this reason incommensurable, strategies of construction against and beyond individuation, notions conceived as measurement and evaluation of the forces that traverse them without necessarily betraying their aims.

To articulate rather than distinguish, to suture rather than pluralise, to make equal and not level, translate and not empty. These could perhaps be the pivots around which to build a different semantics. But for this, we will need to turn to another line of thought.

Notes

1 Albrecht Wellmer, 'Arendt on Revolution', in Dana Villa (ed.), *The Cambridge Companion to Hannah Arendt* (Cambridge: Cambridge University Press, 2001), p. 232. My emphasis.

2 Hannah Arendt, *The Origins of Totalitarianism* (New York: Harcourt Brace, 1973), p. 462. My emphasis.

3 Ibid., p. 461.

4 Ibid., pp. 461–2. Cf. Margaret Canovan, *Hannah Arendt: A Reinterpretation of Her Political Thought* (Cambridge: Cambridge University Press, 1992), pp. 107–15.

5 See Simona Forti, 'Introduzione', in Simona Forti, *Hannah Arendt* (Milan: Bruno Mondadori, 1999), p. xiv. Cf. Simona Forti, *Vita della mente e tempo della polis. Hannah Arendt tra filosofia e politica* (Milan: FrancoAngeli, 1996).

6 For a recognition and problematisation of this thesis, see at least Margaret Canovan, 'Arendt's Theory of Totalitarianism: A Reassessment', in Villa (ed.), *The Cambridge Companion to Hannah Arendt*, pp. 25–43, and Margaret Canovan, *The Political Thought of Hannah Arendt* (New York: Harcourt Brace & Jovanovich, 1974).

7 Arendt, *The Origins of Totalitarianism*, p. 463.

8 Cf. Forti, 'Introduzione', p. xviii.

9 Arendt, *The Origins of Totalitarianism*, p. 464.

10 Cf. Hannah Arendt, *Marx e la tradizione del pensiero politico occidentale*, ed. Simona Forti (Milan: Cortina, 2016).

11 Arendt, *The Origins of Totalitarianism*, p. 466.

MACHIAVELLIAN ONTOLOGY

12 Ibid., p. 469.

13 Ibid., pp. 471–2.

14 Ibid., p. 477.

15 Cf. Simona Forti, *I nuovi demoni:. Ripensare oggi il male e il potere* (Milan: Feltrinelli, 2012), particularly pp. 157–245.

16 Arendt, *The Origins of Totalitarianism*, p. 474.

17 Cf. Forti, 'Introduzione', p. xxi.

18 Arendt, *The Origins of Totalitarianism*, p. 475.

19 Cf. at least Carlo Galli, 'Hannah Arendt e le categorie politiche della modernità', in Carlo Galli, *Modernità. Categorie e profili critici* (Bologna: Il Mulino, 1988), pp. 205–24; Seyla Benhabib, *The Reluctant Modernism of Hannah Arendt* (Thousand Oaks, CA: Sage, 1996); Jean-Michel Chaumont, 'Individualisme et modernité chez Tocqueville et Arendt', *Les Cahiers de Philosophie* 4 (1987), pp. 115–46.

20 Hannah Arendt, *The Human Condition* (Chicago: University of Chicago Press, 1998), p. 98.

21 Cf. Christine Buci-Glucksmann, Barbara Cassin, Françoise Collin, and Myriam Revault d'Allonnes (eds), *Ontologie et politique. Actes du Colloque Hannah Arendt* (Paris: Éditions Tierce, 1989); Laura Boella, 'Hannah Arendt "fenomenologa". Smantellamento della metafisica e critica dell'ontologia', *Aut Aut* 239–40 (1990), pp. 83–110.

22 Arendt, *The Human Condition*, pp. 99–100.

23 See again Arendt, *Marx e la tradizione del pensiero politico occidentale*.

24 Arendt, *The Human Condition*, p. 105.

25 Ibid., pp. 115–16.

26 Ibid., p. 115.

27 Cf. Bonnie Honig, 'Identità e differenza', in Forti (ed.), *Hannah Arendt*, p. 195. Cf. further Bonnie Honig, 'Arendt's Accounts of Action and Authority', in Bonnie Honig, *Political Theory and Displacement of Politics* (Ithaca, NY: Cornell University Press, 1993), pp. 233–42; Bonnie Honig (ed.), *Feminist Interpretations of Hannah Arendt* (Philadelphia: Penn State University Press, 1995). See also Alessandro Dal Lago, 'Il pensiero plurale di Hannah Arendt', *Aut Aut* 239–40 (1990), pp. 1–10.

28 Arendt, *The Origins of Totalitarianism*, p. 176.

29 Cf. Roberto Esposito, 'Polis o communitas?', in Forti (ed.), *Hannah Arendt*, p. 106. See also Roberto Esposito, *L'origine della politica. Hannah Arendt o Simone Weil?* (Rome: Donzelli, 1996).

30 On this oft-discussed aspect of Arendt's philosophy, see at least Ronald Beiner, 'Action, Natality and Citizenship: Hannah Arendt's Concept of

ARENDT: COMPETITION AND DISTINCTION

Freedom', in Zbigniew Pelczynski and John Gray (eds), *Conceptions of Liberty in Political Philosophy* (London: Athlone Press, 1984), pp. 349–75; Miguel Vatter, *The Republic of the Living* (New York: Fordham University Press, 2014).

31 Cf. Miguel Abensour, *Hannah Arendt contro la filosofia politica* (Milan: Jaca Book, 2010). In this regard, see also Étienne Tassin, 'L'azione "contro" il mondo. Il senso dell'acosmismo', in Forti (ed.), *Hannah Arendt*, pp. 136–54; Étienne Tassin (ed.), *Hannah Arendt. L'humaine condition politique* (Paris: L'Harmattan, 2001).

32 Arendt, *The Human Condition*, p. 180.

33 Cf. Forti, *Hannah Arendt tra filosofia e politica*, p. 88..

34 Cf. Ernst Vollrah, *Grundlegung einer philosophischen Theorie des Politischen* (Würzburg: Königshausen, 1987); Teresa Serra, *L'autonomia del politico. Introduzione al pensiero di Hannah Arendt* (Teramo: Facoltà di Scienze Politiche, 1984); Roberto Esposito, 'Irrappresentabile polis', in Esposito, *Categorie dell'impolitico*, pp. 72–124; Roberto Esposito (ed.), *La pluralità irrappresentabile. Il pensiero politico di Hannah Arendt* (Urbino: QuattroVenti, 1987).

35 Bonnie Honig, 'Towards an Agonistic Feminism: Hannah Arendt and the Politics of Identity', in Judith Butler and Joan Wallach Scott (eds), *Feminists Theorize the Political* (London: Routledge, 1992), pp. 215–35.

36 Arendt, *The Origins of Totalitarianism*, p. 197. My emphasis. Cf: 'Arendt returns to the elitism of an aristocratic republicanism in her diagnosis of the fundamental ills of modern society. This is, perhaps, most apparent in her conclusion to *On Revolution*, where she proposes that we distinguish between an active, political minority (with all the rights of political participation, including the right to vote) and the broad, passive majority of consumers/citizens, who have (in effect) abdicated these rights. For Arendt, making this distinction official seems one way out of the "dangerous, destructive" tendency of mass democracy to "widen the gap between rulers and ruled." Yet this solution – a "self-chosen" political aristocracy which wields greater power by dint of its greater political virtue – is as utopian as the sociological background of her view of contemporary society is reactionary.' Hauke Brunkhorst, 'Equality and Elitism in Arendt', in Villa (ed.), *The Cambridge Companion to Hannah Arendt*, p. 196.

37 Cf. Simona Forti, 'Hannah Arendt e la facoltà di giudicare: considerazioni su un'eredità contesa', *Teoria politica* 3 (1992), pp. 123–55; Forti, 'Introduzione', pp. xxvi–xxxiii. Finally, see also Simona Forti, 'Per un ethos della libertà. Note su soggettività e potere', in Mattia Di Pierro and

Francesco Marchesi (eds), *Crisi dell'immanenza* (Macerata: Quodlibet, 2018), pp. 49–74.

38 Cf. Alessandro Del Lago, 'La Città perduta: Introduzione', in Hannah Arendt, *Vita activa. La condizione umana* (Milan: Bompiani, 2008), pp. vii–xxxiii.

39 Hans-Joakim Gehrke, *Stasis: Untersuchungen zu den inneren Kriegen in den griechischen Staaten des. 5 und 4. Jahrunderts v.Chr.* (Munich: C.H. Beck, 1985), p. 453. Cf. 'in this way, a process of social differentiation took place in which, starting in the eighth century, a class of nobles was formed which became increasingly distinct from the lower classes. These nobles in particular became the bearers of the mentality described above.' Ibid., p. 455.

40 Cf. Claude Lefort, 'La questione della politica', in Forti (ed.), *Hannah Arendt*, pp. 12–13.

41 Cf. Miguel Vatter, 'Legality and Resistance. Arendt and Negri on Constituent Power', *Kairos* 20 (2002), pp. 192–3: 'A new radical democratic theory, having as some of its most important referents thinkers as diverse as Arendt, Lefort, the late Althusser, and Negri, takes much of its impetus from the reappropriation of Machiavelli, both with and against Marx. This return to Machiavelli betrays, first, a need to salvage the "autonomy" or "separateness" of the political from its reduction at the hands of Marxist economism and Weberian sociologism.'

42 Hannah Arendt, *On Revolution* (London: Penguin, 1990), p. 38.

43 Cf., for example, Ferenc Fehér, 'Freedom and the "Social Question". Hannah Arendt's Theory of the French Revolution', *Philosophy and Social Criticism* 1 (1987), pp. 1–30.

44 Cf. Robert Nisbet, 'Hannah Arendt e la rivoluzione americana', *Comunità* 183 (1965), pp. 81–95.

45 Arendt, *On Revolution*, p. 92.

46 Cf. Bonnie Honig, 'Declarations of Indipendence: Arendt and Derrida on the Problem of Founding a Republic', *American Political Science Review* 1 (1991), pp. 97–113; Miguel Vatter, 'La fondazione della libertà', in Forti (ed.), *Hannah Arendt*, pp. 107–35; Miguel Vatter, *Between Form and Event: Machiavelli's Theory of Political Freedom* (New York: Fordham University Press, 2014).

47 Arendt, *On Revolution*, pp. 222–3.

48 Cf. Patchen Markell, 'The Rule of the People: Arendt, Archè, and Democracy', in Seyla Benhabib (ed.), *Politics in Dark Times: Encounters with Hannah Arendt* (Cambridge: Cambridge University Press, 2010),

p. 82. See also Marco Goldoni and Christopher McCorkindale (eds), *Hannah Arendt and Law* (Oxford: Hart, 2012).

49 Hannah Arendt, *Sulla violenza* (Parma: Guanda, 1996), pp. 38–9. Cf. Françoise Collin, 'Les deux visages de la violence', *B@bel* 3 (2007), pp. 37–47.

50 Cf. Hannah Arendt, 'What Freedom and Revolution Really Mean', *Literary Hub*, https://lithub.com/never-before-published-hannah-arendt-on-what-freedom-and-revolution-really-mean/ (accessed 12 January 2024).

51 Arendt, *On Revolution*, p. 194. Cf. Kei Haruta (ed.), *Arendt on Freedom, Liberation and Revolution* (London: Palgrave Macmillan, 2019).

52 Arendt, *On Revolution*, p. 202.

53 'The coincidence itself is perhaps best illustrated in the Latin word for founding, which is *condere* and which was derived from an early Latin field god, called Conditor, whose main function was to preside over growth and harvest; he obviously was a founder and a preserver at the same time.' Ibid., pp. 202–3.

54 Cf. Reiner Schürmann, *Le principe d'anarchie: Heidegger et la question de l'agir* (Chicago: University of Chicago Press, 2022); Reiner Schürmann, *Des hégémonies brisées* (Mauvezin: Trans-Europ-Repress, 1996).

55 Cf. Anne Amiel, *Hannah Arendt: Politique et événement* (Paris: PUF, 1996).

56 Arendt, *On Revolution*, pp. 264–5.

57 Cf. ibid., pp. 212–13: 'What saves the act of the beginning from its own arbitrariness is that it carries its own principle within itself, or, to be more precise, that beginning and principle, *principium* and principle, are not only related to each other, but coeval [. . .] The Greek language, in striking agreement, tells the same story. For the Greek word for beginning is *arché* and *arché* means both beginning and principle.'

Part 2

Asymmetrical Conflict – The Psychic Model

4

Lacanian Suture

Turning the conceptual axis of political conflict does not appear to be a simple task in light of the recent tradition. This tradition is centred on the contestation of order and an essential orientation of politics from distinction to destitution, up to the pure fragmentation of political aggregates. However, there is more that can be distilled from contemporary approaches which identify a different tendency, particularly around antagonism and politics in general. This is the case concerning the set of philosophico-political positions that generally refer to Jacques Lacan and the renewal of psychoanalytical practice.[1]

If it is necessary to trace a starting point, if not exactly the origin, we could certainly turn to the experience of the *Cahiers pour l'analyse*, a journal from the late 1960s which was animated by a group of École Normale Supérieure students who had a Lacanian-Althusserian orientation in philosophy and a Maoist orientation in politics.[2] Starting from this main segment made up of the *Cercle d'épistémologie*, there have been a number of expressions of this approach, from the Ljubljana school of Žižek, Dolar, and Zupančič to that of Ernesto Laclau and Chantal Mouffe at the University of Essex. However, here we are not particularly interested in the historical articulation of this tradition, but rather the philosophical structure which lies at the base of a first and partial rotation of the conceptual axis for understanding conflict and politics. We will show how this line, together with others we will indicate throughout this second part of the book, might appear on the one hand as a significant advance in the research direction compared to what we examined in Part 1, while on the other hand, we will note how these approaches seem to reproduce the same traps from the opposite side, thus inviting a more decisive change in terrain.

As Alain Badiou has argued, the most original outcome of this set of reflections lies in the union between a highly speculative analysis of ideological, discursive, and philosophical discourses and an interest in the theory of the subject, usually at some distance from this first axis of research.[3] The idea of an alternative, so to speak, between the 'efficacy' of structures and the presence of a subject, conceived in a particular impersonal and anti-humanistic form, thus assumes the characteristic trait of this philosophical horizon. The way this contributes to the analysis of conflict and politics is soon clear, as it is the first factor of the destitution of existing structures, but at the same time it is an element of the reconstitution of the new, a further system that can take the place of the previous one.[4]

It is thus a question of reconstituting the coordinates of what has also been called the 'Lacanian left',[5] starting from some original trajectories and proceeding through at least two fundamental options of the triangulation between conflict, politics, and history that persist today. One is concentrated on an ethics of the real or its lack, thus focusing on the enhancement of the lacuna that this tradition grasps at the heart of every system. The other aims to develop a politics understood as the continuous construction of structures and orders. Lack and suture will be

LACANIAN SUTURE

the poles that characterise a terrain always open to testing this constitutively unstable relation, suspended between complementarity, articulation, and opposition.

1. The Politics of Lack

Not too long ago, one could read in a British journal that 'an approach to politics drawn from Lacanian psychoanalysis is becoming increasingly popular of late among theorists who consider themselves "critical" and/or "radical" [. . .] Indeed, this approach to theorising politics is today perhaps second in influence only to analytical liberalism.'[6] In this way, Andrew Robinson identifies the link capable of tying together a number of lines of research in the *politics of lack*. He describes these in this way:

> The guiding theme in the work of Žižek, Badiou, Laclau, Mouffe, and Stavrakakis is the idea of 'constitutive lack'. This basic idea refers to a first principle or zero-point of 'the human condition' or (in the case of the Essex School) of social life which is asserted at a high level of generality, as ontology or 'social ontology' [. . .] all [of them] take approaches traceable to Lacan's thesis that existence is grounded around the repression of a fundamental, unrepresentable and impossible negativity.[7]

At the centre of this field would be an impossibility attributed at times to the lack of an essence in its most general and philosophical sense, or to the constitutive openness and irrepresentability of the social, or again to that irreducible residue of negativity typical of psychic life. A certain number of options are as such concentrated around the Lacanian matrix which pose the problem of lack as the structural given of politics, identifying different

MACHIAVELLIAN ONTOLOGY

possibilities for valorising, managing, or governing a given that in some measure is primal. According to Yannis Stavrakakis:

> it is true that the relation of knowledge to experience is only one of the modalities assumed by the relation between the symbolic (and the imaginary), on the one hand, and the real, on the other. The fact, however, that the symbolic can never master the real, that theory can never totally capture experience, does not mean that one should abstain from symbolising: Lacan is clearly against any such tabooing of the real.[8]

It is therefore a matter of a problematic that starts from the idea that every set of objects, whether given by psychic events or parts and groups of society, does not establish a positivity as such. This set of objects, parts, differences must be *sutured*, since no arrangement is perfectly integral or systematised. And it is precisely by filling this lack, by marking it, that a psychic signifier or collective representation sutures the system.[9]

The frame of reference for this approach starts from the Lacanian problematisation of identity. Indeed, for Lacan, Freud's main achievement is precisely to have traced a complex of intimately plural and multiple agents and forces in the identification underneath personal unity understood as a synthesis. In this direction, identity is poised to become impossible, never coinciding with this unrepresentable set of instances, always destined towards structurally fragile processes of identification.[10] In this regard, there has been talk that this is a new essentialism. However, Lacan's reference to the *spaltung*, while generalising Freud's thesis, does not present itself as a new productive essence:[11] on the contrary, it appears as a division and difficulty internal to every essence, which in order to constitute itself must repress this element of openness, which finally re-presents itself to threaten its solidity.[12]

In this sense, the real, the negative, lack are always 'second' rather than 'first': they emerge in the background of the system, as a constant anomaly, and punctuate the scanning of the structures themselves, thus ending up as a blind spot and passage. It is a constitutive deficiency, then, which qualifies only as the reversal of systems that are apparently closed. However, in homage to another typically psychoanalytic principle, such approaches believe that in every system the lack that underlies or is excluded from it tends to reappear in disguised and dissimulated forms, like an authentic return of the repressed. Dreams, missed acts, neuroses also present themselves in the social field and in discursive ensembles in general for this reason.[13]

To summarise, we here see a schema of political reflection whose structural and psychoanalytical derivation allows institutional systems to be grasped as immediately inadequate for the representation of their object: here the Lacanian symbolic mediates the comprehension of always failed totalities, which work through the exclusion and repression of what is placed outside of them. In this way, there is no primary identity. Rather, what appears is a multiplicity of processes of identification, and with them, the remainders that they leave behind.[14] Thus again from these remainders, it is possible to derive strategies of valorisation for them, for their irreducibility to the system — and conflict will be one of these — or to formulate hypotheses for the use of such lacks in order to construct new political structures. In this regard, Stavrakakis has noted how 'in the face of the irreducibility of the real of experience, we seem to have no other option but to symbolise, to keep on symbolising, trying to enact the positive encircling of negativity [. . .] to "institutionalise" real lack, the (negative) trace of experience'.[15]

Thus, the epistemic knot that binds politics and lack to a different theory of conflict and, implicitly, its historicity, is clear. This epistemological field constitutively holds together two parts of a single discourse: not only structures and the subject but the deficiency, the void, the missing link, and the system with its relative closure. The fact that no representation can ever coincide with its matter, and that the constitution of the object always results from an act which is somewhat violent, does not lead, as we saw in other theoretical experiences, to an abandonment of totality. On the contrary, this invites the identification of institutionalising strategies which are capable of circumscribing and taking on lack in order to give it a form. On the other side of the multiple oppositions that this field tends to structure, we observe the idea of the valorisation of lack and the void, of the event that destitutes the structure, of the real that suddenly breaks the normality of psychic and social life. A politics of symbolisation can thus be countered with a politics of the event.[16]

These divergences are, however, only the latest results of a problematic that, in its moments of formation, attempted an operation that was at once more cautious and more radical: connecting the emergence of the real as an internal conflict to an order with its immediately subsequent reconstitution.

2. The Action of the Structure

The politics of lack analysed here, we could say, was established with a single gesture in Jacques-Alain Miller's essays 'La suture (Elements de la logique du signifiant)' and 'Action de la structure'. Written and circulated between 1964 and 1965, and only published in the *Cahiers* between 1966 and 1968, these essays focus on several decisive notions in the formation of this line of thought.

It is perhaps not by chance that these essays move from, or arrive at, a definition of a field of objectivity. And this is so not only for the positivism that was still active starting from the structuralist matrix of the human sciences in France shortly before 1968 – which represents a decisive turning point on this terrain – but also for the intimate correlation between epistemological discourse and political affirmation that is captured in this context. In 'Action de la structure', for example, Miller begins with a definition of Georges Canguilhem's theoretical work: 'to work a concept [*travailler un concept*] means to make its extension vary and generalise its comprehension [. . .] in short, to progressively confer on it, with regulated transformations, the function of a form'.[17] If 'working' a concept thus means varying its extension and what it comprehends, Miller traces the start of his elaboration in a transformation, correction, and widening of the notion of structure. Indeed, Miller intends to extend the possibilities of formalisation to what usually appeared precluded from it, namely immediate experience:[18] 'the distance from experience over which models prevail [. . .] this distance must now disappear, and an exact integration of the lived into the structural must now be made to operate'.[19] Against the structures described by anthropology and linguistics – constituted through the exclusion of subjectivity, of historicity, or the alteration between the immanence of the causal level – the structure of psychoanalysis allows these factors to be integrated into the topology of the system, since this is 'indiscernible from the progress of their constitution'.[20]

It is a structure with two dimensions. On the one hand, there is its structuring quality, the action that the system exerts on its own elements, while on the other hand, there is its structured side, a subjectivity that is subject to laws that have come to be defined. The second meaning is what is offered for observation, the present modality of its status, while the former has a virtual character from which it is possible to deduce all its future states: in short, the laws of its internal dynamic.

Up to this point, however, such an idea of structure appears limited to the positivity of its movement: according to Miller, the specificity of psychoanalytic structure instead emerges when the movement of its reflexive duplication is observed.

> But if we now assume the presence of an element that turns back on reality and perceives it, reflects it, and signifies it, an element capable of redoubling itself on its own account, then a general distortion ensues [. . .] From the moment that the structure involves the element we have mentioned,
>
> – its actuality becomes an experience or experiment,
> – the virtuality of the structuring [*le structurant*] is converted into an absence,
> – this absence is produced in the real order of the structure: the action of the structure comes to be supported by a lack.
>
> The structuring [*le structurant*], *by not being there*, governs the real. It is here that we find the driving discordance: for the introduction of this reflexive element, which suffices to institute the dimension of the structured-insofar-as-it-lives-it, as taking its effects only from itself, arranges an *imaginary* organization, contemporaneous with and distinct from the real order yet nevertheless coordinated with it, and henceforth an intrinsic part of reality.[21]

Miller maintains that the system, in its structured character, produces effects on the elements that compose it. These effects are given by its reflexive reduplication, that is, by the modality in which the parts of the whole, such as the individuals or a social system or the conscious part of a psyche, for example, perceive the system itself. And they perceive it in the form of an immediate, undisputed experience, whose laws of motion they do not grasp. For this reason, Miller claims, the virtuality of the structured part is converted into an absence, into a lack. This is because the reflexive reduplication tends to fix the present state, to close it by placing its virtualities outside of the visible spectrum. This imaginary order, in Lacanian language, is not secondary: on the contrary, it is the main means of the crystallisation of the structure itself, and the efficacy of its action on the elements.

Lack is, then, the support that allows the system to hold, the void opened by the absence of historicity. There is therefore a circular relation here between the whole and the absent. If the former generates the latter as an effect of its efficacity, that is, as an outcome of a reflexive reduplication that establishes the elements to the system, obscuring its historicity and contingency, the latter is the support of this stability, the primary void that returns to the imaginary order in disguised forms as a counter-effect of the constitution of the whole. For these reasons, Miller emphasises that at the level of structuring, there is neither reflexivity or lack, while at the level of the structured, of the subjected subject, there is both reflexivity and lack. At the basis of reality as perceived in immediate experience, there is in this way an essential *miscognition* (of the real):

> the relation of the subject to the structure [. . .] *dissymmetrical* since it is an insertion, proves to be inconceivable without the mediation of an imaginary function of miscognition, re-establishing reality in its continuity by means of the production of representations that respond to the absence in the structuring, and compensate for the production of lack.[22]

MACHIAVELLIAN ONTOLOGY

Miscognition is here not the secondary function that hides what might be able to appear in full light, but on the contrary is a necessary outcome for the organisation of the system. It is a product of the structuring moment which is its cause, and yet it only exists in order to dissimulate the reason for its existence.[23] The imaginary, the domain of representation, therefore presents itself as an intermediary level between the real of structuring causality and the symbolic of the structured system.

The role of theory in this framework will, then, be to measure the effects of this 'lateral causality' by reconnecting its origin to a principle that is lacking.[24] Analysis, the name that this group gave to philosophical work in homage to psychoanalytic discipline, is central because lack, a sign of the obscuring of the structuring moment, never appears in full light, but is always closed, sutured: 'lack is never apparent, since what is structured [*structuré*] mis-cognizes the action which forms it [. . .] in this place where the lack of the cause is produced in the space of its effects, an element that interposes itself that accomplishes its suturation'.[25] Every system miscognises the action that structures it, and it is precisely in this aspect that it is possible to identify 'the action of the structure': not only in the movement of structuring, but also in what, in doing this, cancels its sign. The void left by the structuring function is thus occupied by a substitute [*leurre*], by a specific covering, which sutures the symbolic chain of signi-fiers, which re-marks what is lacking: that point, that link, Miller argues, is always the weak link of the structured chain, the place where the whole shows itself to be attackable. 'We can further distinguish the function of this element that never tallies and that always misleads the eye, and by virtue of which all perception becomes miscognition, by naming as its place *the utopian point* of the structure, its improper point, or its point *at infinity*.'[26]

The conception of structure proper to psychoanalysis thus presents itself as duplicated, divided between the emerged moment of the structured and its transcendental given by the structuring dynamics. Or more: the moment of the subjected subject is constituted through a third intermediary level, the imaginary, which adapts representation to its chosen terrain, in this way closing the systematised space to the change that it brings with itself.[27] A diagonal reading, as Miller defines it, is thus one that practises this intermediary space between different levels, noting how the asymmetry between them offers a terrain for political action, in order to pass from the *action of the structure* to *action on the structure*.[28] In this sense, the main opposition shifts from the duality between structuring and structured, between system and subject, to that between subject and lack.[29] Every space for politics and conflict is configured here as the open terrain between these two levels, between the void of a stabilisation and the sign that absorbs and hides it.[30]

The kind of politics and conflict that is configured by starting from this elementary schema is perhaps now clearer. If action is situated in the space that passes between the base of structuration and its closed state, albeit through the imaginary, the role of conflict will present itself as a moment of vertical interference between these non-symmetrical levels. Knowledge is now mobilised in search of the suture point of the system that represents the place of its fragility, in a sort of reinterpretation of the theory of the weak link of the chain.[31] It is a model, we can here anticipate, that we will find elsewhere in the course of the second part of this book. Passing from the action of the structure thus first means practising a space of conflict and specific articulation between two levels, in order to break open the closure by learning a new field that allows for the system to be affected.[32]

And it is precisely by starting from that specific difference, from that link in the chain, that a new totality can be re-established, thereby recombining the disrupted parts of the earlier symbolic formation in a different form. This is a matrix that characterises conflict as follows:

1. In the first place it is conflict between different, strictly *asymmetric* forces. It is certainly oppositional but not binary: it is indeed the relation between elements and places of a topic posed on different levels, the action on the lack and the action of the structure, laying the foundations for an explicit characterisation of the forces on the ground.
2. It is a conflict, for these reasons, in which the parties move towards *different ends*, with different means. It is entirely irreducible on the formal level to the military paradigm that we observed earlier, because this relation is not between comparable forces within a relationship that is always the same, but is constructive, articulating moments of destitution and constitution.
3. What is essential for it is the assumption of a *viewpoint on the whole*, on the structure, which is not dislocated or partial. Partiality is on the contrary assumed as the maximum place of ideological blindness, which can only be circumvented through knowledge understood as science.
4. The attempt is therefore to assume the role of *experience* within *formalisation*, avoiding the contrast between event and totality, between a third element and a binary clash. Experience is here nothing more than the effect of a system, the outcome of its reflexive duplication that closes the signifying chain and inhabits conflict. In other words, it is what politics must primarily deconstruct.

5. This is a politics that, finally, knows its proper place in the *relative transcendence* between the levels of the whole: not the binary opposition of a symmetrical antagonism but the distance of an unequal relation, the space between two successive orders.

It has been said that the effect of the closure of the symbolic space starting from the imaginary terrain produces the loss of the historicity of structure: the action of politics, the action on the structure, must then primarily reopen the diachronic ground of the system. In this way, the domains of politics, conflict, and history are strictly connected in this schema. If the emergence of the latter is connected to the work of the former, they will have an intimately historical dimension.[33] We will see that two options open up from this perspective: one in which the form of an ethical valorisation accentuates destitution, and the other which, in the guise of a political construction, emphasises the importance of the affirmative act of a new, and different, closure.

3. Ethics and Politics of the Suture

Alain Badiou writes the following in a strategic passage of *Being and Event*:

> It is not antagonism which lies at the origin of the State, because one cannot think the dialectic of the void and excess as antagonism. No doubt politics itself must originate in the very same place as the state: in that dialectic. But this is certainly not in order to seize the State nor to double the State's effect. On the contrary, politics stakes its existence on the capacity to establish a relation to both the void and excess which is essentially

different from that of the State: it is this difference alone that subtracts politics from the one of statist re-insurance.[34]

In this passage, one of the main lines of research that originates from the framework we are discussing here emerges (perhaps the most popular), namely that which captures the gap between order and conflict, being and event, state and antagonism, a value that the Lacanian philosophical prototype allows us to emphasise.[35] Although it is not the only direction generated by this approach, this side of the problematic clearly seems to resonate with the theses encountered in the first part of this book. Indeed, if antagonism is understood as a primary given with respect to order, as an event that breaks the continuity of being, then it is certainly possible to bring the paradigm of neo-Lacanian politics back to the posture that reads conflict as irreducible to any institutionalisation, however partial. Of course, in these interpretations the moment of antagonism is always connected to structure as its own field of visibility and, inevitably, intervention, and yet the emphasis here falls not on the general reflections of this necessary exclusion, or on the modalities of integrating it, but on its presenting itself on the scene as a punctual subversion of the system, an immanent production of something that cannot be constituted, or that, in being so, loses its inmost nature. It is therefore a matter of emphasising what is found outside the structure as such: 'the real is "an impasse of formalisation", which means that it must be grasped in the element of formalisation [. . .] This exception is the unconscious, the pure subject, rupture, revolution [. . .]'.[36] It is thus a question of grasping the reasons and articulations of a discourse open to different purposes, among which some tend to connect conflict, order, and historicity, while others instead loosen the knot.

The central notions that perhaps allow us to grasp this divergence of intentions and effects are the real and the subject. It has been said that in order to constitute itself, every set of objects must act as an exclusion which gives rise to a system with an empty point or missing link. This constitutive lack must be re-marked, closed, sutured in order to allow for the overall whole to hold, and this role is assumed by a signifier, an element of the whole, a specific difference, which thus places itself in a particular symbolic position, that of the subject. In other words, the subject here is that part that becomes universal, incarnating the possibility itself of symbolisation. It follows, as we have seen, that it represents, so to speak, the weak link of the chain, that is, that which by lacking produces the opening of the signifying chain, thereby destituting the symbolic whole. In this way, it is clear that the subject is what articulates the successive structures, through its presence or its lack. It is the substitute for a primary lack and is therefore the element that unites and divides a before and after. On this ground it communicates with the real.

> An ethics of the Real is not an ethics orientated towards the Real, but an attempt to rethink ethics by recognizing and acknowledging the dimension of the real [. . .] The term ethics is often taken to refer to a set of norms which restrict or 'bridle' desire – which aim to keep our conduct [. . .] free of all excess. Yet this understanding of ethics fails to acknowledge that ethics is by nature excessive, that excess is a component of ethics which cannot simply be eliminated without ethics itself losing all meaning.[37]

Alenka Zupančič's theoretical project has involved the idea of translating the order of Lacanian discourse into the field of ethics, reading the Kantian lesson through this filter, while also starting from Lacan's own treatment of Kant.[38] It is an introduction, therefore, of the Lacanian Real into the ethical context. However, it is also an ethical view on the Real. As already partially noted, the 'Real' is one of the names, perhaps the most faithfully Lacanian, of the constitutive lack of every symbolic form. It is a trait that potentially generates conflict within the structure and between it and its outside. On this ground, Zupančič notes that the ethical domain is not free from this void, even in the rigorous Kantian approach which at first glance would seem to be its antithesis. However, the eventual success of such an experiment would imply the admission of the possibility of an 'ethical' treatment of the Real, and not only the introduction of the Real into ethics. Excess and deficiency, which in this key are synonyms, can thus undergo a treatment that is aimed at their inclusion and the governing of their valorisation and affirmation, always in light of the double implication between them and the system, through the act of the remark on the part of the subject, the substitution of the void.

However, an ethics of the Real does not correspond to a politics of the Real. Zupančič clarifies the former as possible:

> The ethics of the real is not an ethics of the finite, of finitude [. . .] The basis of ethics cannot be an imperative which commands us to endorse our finitude and renounce all 'higher', 'impossible' aspirations [. . .] the infinite is not impossible to attain; rather, it is impossible for us to escape it entirely [. . .] The absence of the beyond, the lack of any exception to the finite, 'infinitizes' the finite [. . .] The problem of the infinite is not how to attain it but, rather, how to get rid of its stain, a stain that ceaselessly pursues us.[39]

An ethics of the Real assumes the finite structures and problematises them through the infinite Real. A politics of the Real assumes this intrinsic problematicity and tries to govern it, to trace strategies of symbolisation. The former grasps the future and historicity in the lack that underlies even the most apparently solid systems, while the latter poses the theme of succession through the thought of a new order, of the alternation between structures. For these reasons, some ethics of the Real represent a transition to politics, to history, while others remain in a pre-political stage. Indeed, if the forms of being are contrasted with events that break up the signifying chain within them, the passage to the next order will be accomplished with difficulty. If instead the role of deficiency is emphasised as a matrix not aimed at freeing its autonomous power, but as an invitation to persevere in symbolisation, to order the chain again, to measure again and always the articulation of differences through the closure of a subject, then it will be possible to grasp the space and terrain for a politics.[40]

Halfway between an ethics of the unlimited productive plan and the moralism of the finite and the present, an ethics of the Real grasps the necessary relation between the polarities of the symbolic and the Real in order to build the former by starting from the latter, to build a system knowing what is absent and partially empty in it, and finally by emphasising the work of this continuous constitutive apparition without deluding oneself as to its autonomy as an entirely deconstructed event, incapable as such of an institutive act. Starting from this outcome, we can grasp the point of a possible politics of the Real to which Miller had already alluded in his essay on the concept of suture.

> Suture names the relation of the subject to the chain of its discourse; we shall see that it figures there as the element which is lacking, in the form of a stand-in [*tenant-lieu*]. For, while there lacking, it is not purely and simply absent. Suture, by extension – the general relation of lack to the structure – of

MACHIAVELLIAN ONTOLOGY

which it is an element, inasmuch as it implies the position of a taking-the-place-of [*tenant-lieu*].[41]

This is a definition whose central elements have already been observed, but whose orientation leads exactly to evaluating the relation that is established here between lack, conflict, and diachrony: in other words, subject and structure in their relation as inseparable and asymmetrical. This leads without mediation towards the clarification of what is understood by a politics of constitutive lack. Thus, let's see the definition. Miller here reprises a term that was used only in passing by Lacan, also tracing a clarifying question of this political proposal within it. The suture is thus the name of a relation, that between the subject and its discursive chain, or the knot that tightens the structure to itself by way of closing (precisely the suture) its lack, its opening. The *tenant-lieu*, moreover, is the element of the structure, the lack that is a part of it, but in the 'sutured' version of the system it is nothing more than a substitute, which re-marks an absence that presents itself precisely through its supplement.[42] As already emphasised, this substitute pertains to the reflexive folding of the system on itself, allowing its closure and thus its hold in time. In this way, we rediscover the infinite and the void which constitute the finite and the full from the inside rather than threatening it from the outside: the emphasis in Miller's definition, however, was from the beginning on a notion of suture as relation between subject and system, contrary to later interpretations which aimed to decide in favour of one part or the other. In this sense, it is already possible to note how the elementary definition of the relation, from which numerous and different traces then departed, brought with itself a fundamental constructive orientation.

118

In the last instance, the analytical approach of the *Cahiers* leads to an attempt to articulate the moments of deconstruction and restructuring, and to the elaboration of a politics of lack and suture. The central role of the subject emerges here. It is not

> an autonomous sphere of self-consciousness, and not for a redu-
> plicated and therefore lacunary subject, the imaginary subject-
> agent of the structured, the subject-support, element, of the
> structuring [. . .] But an alienation is essential to the subject
> since it can only be effectuated as an agent in the imaginary, by
> taking account of the effects of structuring, in which he or she
> is already accounted for.[43]

Understood in this way, a subject presents itself as the first systemic element to eradicate in order to open, through conflict, the dimension of structuring and with it historicity. If in the imaginary the suture of the whole is given precisely in the subjective function, the destitution of the same presents itself as a necessary condition also of the reconstructive function.[44] From the viewpoint of analysis, the meaning of this Millerian passage is precisely this: to generate a notion of the subject lacking any link to the level of the imaginary. It is a strategy of deposition, and, subsequently, reconstruction, mediated by the role of knowledge, science, theory, and analysis. In this way, the close connection between knowledge and politics returns in this philosophical frame, which highlights the immediately active role of theory itself.[45]

The result is a sort of destituent conflict: the role of politics in the face of structures is thus understood, that is, endowed with solidity because of a reflexive folding back into the form of a supplement called subject that is essentially found in the identification and deconstruction of the weak link of the chain.[46]

> We must break the reciprocal determination whereby the elements of an object are orchestrated into a structured network [*réseau*] [. . .] We will therefore consider the whole of a text as the circling of a lack, principle of the action of the structure, which thus bears the marks of the action that it accomplishes: *the suture* [. . .] We will thus explore the space of the determination's displacement. At once univocal, repressed and interior, withdrawn and declared, only *metonymic causality* might qualify it. The case is metaphorized in a discourse, and in general in any structure – for the necessary condition of the functioning of structural causality is that the subject takes the effect *for the cause*. Fundamental law of the action of the structure.[47]

So the process goes from the action of the structure that subjects a passive and overdetermined subjectivity, to the action on the structure, opened by the rupture of the reciprocal determination between the system and a subject as support for the constitutive opening of the whole. A strategy of decomposition and knowledge aimed at the identification of the node on which to act: these are the focal points of Miller's discourse. Once the structuring dimension of the system, that is, the internal activity of its laws of development, is reopened to visibility, it remains the case in this context that this movement is understood as automatically tending to the new. The modalities of the fixation of the whole prevent the movement from giving itself beyond mere reproduction: when they were unblocked, there would be no need for anything else to produce unprecedented historical forms. In short, the strategy of restructuring is entirely contained in its negative version of deconstruction. In this sense, the politics of lack seems to stop at a step before history. It alludes to it, offers an explanation of its eventual *stasis* – since indeed, systems present themselves as always-already sutured and must be desutured in order to activate the diachronic level – and it gives an account of the modalities in which history can occur, but it does not offer solutions regarding the positive gesture of the re-suturing. Its specific lack is in this way given by its affirmative reversal.

Notes

1 Cf. Elisabeth Roudinesco, *Jacques Lacan. Profilo di una vita, storia di un sistema di pensiero* (Milan: Cortina, 2019). Further, see Elisabeth Roudinesco, *Histoire de la psychanalyse en France*, 2 vols (Paris: Fayard, 1994); Davide Tarizzo, *Introduzione a Lacan* (Rome: Laterza, 2003).

2 Cf. Peter Hallward, 'Introduction: Theoretical Training', in Peter Hallward and Knox Peden (eds), *Concept and Form Volume 1* (London: Verso, 2012), p. 24.

3 Alain Badiou, 'Theory from Structure to Subject: An Interview with Alain Badiou', in *Theory from Structure to Subject: An Interview with Alain Badiou*, in Hallward and Peden (eds), *Concept and Form Volume 2* (London: Verso, 2012), p. 1392. Cf. ibid., pp. 1395–6

4 Cfr. Jason Barker, *Alain Badiou: A Critical Introduction* (London: Pluto Press, 2001); Gabriel Riera (ed.), *Alain Badiou: Philosophy and its Conditions* (Albany, NY: SUNY Press, 2005); Peter Hallward, *Badiou* (Minneapolis: University of Minnesota Press, 2003).

5 See, in particular, Yannis Stavrakakis, *Lacan and the Political* (London: Routledge, 1999), who has attempted to systematise the relation between Lacan and politics. See also Stavrakakis, *The Lacanian Left*.

6 Andrew Robinson, 'The Politics of Lack', *British Journal of Politics and International Relations* 6 (2004), p. 259. Cf. Andrew Robinson, 'The Political Theory of Constitutive Lack: A Critique', *Theory & Event* 1 (2005).

7 Robinson, 'The Politics of Lack', p. 259.

8 Stavrakakis, *The Lacanian Left*, p. 9.

9 Cf. Oliver Marchart, 'The Absence at the Heart of Presence: Radical Democracy and the "Ontology of Lack"', in Lars Tonder and Lasse Thomassen (eds), *Radical Democracy: Politics Between Abundance and Lack* (Manchester: Manchester University Press, 2005), pp. 17–31.

10 Cfr. Richard Boothby, *Freud as Philosopher* (London: Routledge, 2001).

MACHIAVELLIAN ONTOLOGY

11 Stavrakakis, *The Lacanian Left*, p. 11.

12 'The roots of this conception of subjectivity can be traced back to the Freudian idea of a *Spaltung* (splitting) characteristic of the human condition [. . .] Lacan, for his part, sees this split as something constitutive of subjectivity in general [. . .] While Freud does not refer to the concept of the subject which has mainly philosophical relevance, Lacan, from the very start of his teaching, focuses his theoretical edifice on the idea of subjectivity, which he understands as fundamentally split, thus generalising Freud's idea of the *Ich-spaltung*.' Ibid., p. 16.

13 Cf. Jacques-Alain Miller, 'The Experience of the Real in Psychoanalysis', *Lacanian Ink* 16 (2000), pp. 7–27; Diana Coole, *Negativity and Politics* (London: Routledge, 2000); Philippe Julien, *Jacques Lacan's Return to Freud: The Real, the Symbolic and the Imaginary* (New York: New York University Press, 1994).

14 Cf. Jason Glynos, 'From Identity to Identification. Discourse Theory and Psychoanalysis in Context', *Essex Papers in Politics and Government: Subseries in Ideology and Discourse Analysis* 11 (1999).

15 Stavrakakis, *The Lacanian Left*, pp. 9–10.

16 Cf. Robinson, 'The Politics of Lack', p. 268.

17 Georges Canguilhem, 'La dialettica e filosofia del «non» in Gaston Bachelard', in Georges Canguilhem and Dominique Lecourt, *L'epistemologia di Gaston Bachelard* (Milan: Jaca Book, 1969), p. 116.

18 Cf. Yannis Stavrakakis, 'Theory and Experience. The Lacanian Negotiation of a Constitutive Tension', *Journal of Psychoanalysis and Culture* 1 (1999), pp. 146–50.

19 Jacques-Alain Miller, 'Action de la structure', *Cahiers pour l'analyse* 9 (1968), p. 94.

20 Ibid., p. 95.

21 Ibid., pp. 95–6. Miller's emphasis.

22 Ibid., p. 96. Miller's emphasis.

23 'Structuration functions covertly, and in this sense the imaginary is its means. But it is at the same time its effect: the representations are put into play by what they conceal [. . .] *they exist only in order to hide the reason for their existence.*' Ibid.,

24 Cf. Shuli Barzilai, *Lacan and the Matter of Origin* (Stanford, CA: Stanford University Press, 1999).

25 Miller, 'Action de la structure', p. 96.

26 Ibid., p. 97. Miller's emphasis.

27 Cf. ibid: 'But it is at this point, precisely there where the spread-out space

LACANIAN SUTURE

of structure and the "transcendental" space of the structuring interconnect and are articulated, that we must regulate our gaze, and adopt as our principle of organization the placeholder itself.'

28 Cf. Yves Duroux, 'Strong Structuralism, Weak Subject. Interview with Yves Duroux', in Hallward and Peden (eds), *Concept and Form Volume 2*, p. 1148: 'There is the action of the structure itself, which shapes ordinary reality, but action on the structure presumes that the action of the structure has been located and understood.'

29 Cf. Bruce Fink, *The Lacanian Subject: Between Language and Jouissance* (Princeton, NJ: Princeton University Press, 1995); Kareen Ror Malone and Stephen Friendlander (eds), *The Subject of Lacan* (Albany, NY: SUNY Press, 2000).

30 Miller, 'Action de la structure', p. 97.

31 Cf. Hallward, 'Theoretical Training', p. 102: 'At each level, what structure misses or lacks is concealed by ideology but can be exposed by science.'

32 Cf. Miller, 'Action de la structure', p. 98.

33 Cf. Badiou, 'Theory from Structure to Subject', pp. 1393–4.

34 Alain Badiou, *Being and Event* (London: Continuum, 2005), p. 110.

35 On this, see at least Bruno Bosteels, *Badiou and Politics* (Durham, NC: Duke University Press, 2011), especially pp. 250–88; Peter Hallward, 'Consequences of Abstraction', in Peter Hallward (ed.), *Think Again: Alain Badiou and the Future of Philosophy* (London: Continuum, 2004), pp. 1–20; Slavoj Žižek, 'From Purification to Subtraction. Badiou and the Real', in Hallward (ed.), *Think Again*, pp. 165–81; Ernesto Laclau, 'An Ethics of Militant Engagement', in Hallward (ed.), *Think Again*, pp. 120–37.

36 Badiou, 'Theory from Structure to Subject', p. 1378. Cf. Bruno Bosteels, 'Alain Badiou's Theory of Subject: The Recommencement of Dialectical Materialism (Part I)', *Pli: The Warwick Journal of Philosophy* 12 (2001), pp. 200–29; Bruno Bosteels, 'Alain Badiou's Theory of Subject: The Recommencement of Dialectical Materialism (Part II)', *Pli: The Warwick Journal of Philosophy* 13 (2002), pp. 173–208.

37 Alenka Zupančič, *Ethics of the Real* (London: Verso, 1995), pp. 4–5.

38 Jason Glynos also reflects on these problems in 'Thinking the Ethics of the Political in the Context of a Postfoundational World. From an Ethics of Desire to an Ethics of the Drive', *Theory and Event* 4 (2000).

39 Zupančič, *Ethics of the Real*, p. 249.

40 On this level a distance opens between Badiou and Zupančič, among others. On this, see ibid., pp. 253–4: 'In order for the realization of desire to be possible, however, a temporal dimension must also be introduced into

death [. . .] This attitude implies a preference for the eternal metonymy which shows its real face here: it proves to be not an infinite pursuit of some ideal that transcends us, but a flight from the infinite that pursues us in this world.'

41 Jacques-Alain Miller, 'La suture. Elements de la logique du signifiant', *Cahiers pour l'analyse* 1 (1966), p. 39.

42 Cf. Slavoj Žižek, 'Suture: Forty Years Later', in Hallward and Peden (eds), *Concept and Form Volume 2*, pp. 1050–1.

43 Miller, 'Action de la structure', pp. 99–100.

44 See Žižek, 'Suture: Forty Years Later', pp. 1053–4.

45 Ibid., pp. 1056–7.

46 Cfr. Yannis Stavrakakis, 'Lacan and History', *Journal for the Psychoanalysis of Culture and Society* 1 (1999), pp. 99–118; Teresa Brennan, 'History After Lacan', *Economy and Society* 3 (1990), pp. 277–313.

47 Miller, 'Action de la structure', p. 102. Miller's emphasis.

5

Althusser's Overdetermination

Interpreters have never ceased to raise the question of whether or not Althusser can be spoken of as a philosopher of politics. While for some, the author of *For Marx* was essentially an epistemologist oriented towards a more precise definition of the philosophical contribution of Marxism, for others, the role of Althusserian thought was eminently political, both in its immediate reception and in its dissemination beyond the French and European context, up to the more recent emergence of these parallel anxieties which animated the theory of the *matérialisme de la recontre*.[1] Similarly, Althusser can be considered a thinker of political conflict.

Certainly, however, such a set of problems has always found a form of articulation in Althusser which emphasises their diachronic development: the impossibility, in other words, of considering their role and value outside of a historical, and strictly diachronic, horizon, in the temporal interstice that separates and connects historical and political forms that alternate through time. It is, then, the Machiavellian problematic[2] (to which we will return in the conclusion) that connects beginning and duration, or as has been noted, the different translations composed by contingency and ideology, event and process, in which it is

125

MACHIAVELLIAN ONTOLOGY

possible to trace the modalities and position of a conflict immediately thought as an instrument of variation.

For these reasons, the definition of the epistemological
framework, which also underlies the understanding of political
phenomena, will always be found here immersed in historicity,
inserted exactly in the problematic connection between punctual event and processual determination. This aspect, which
has only recently come to the attention of critics with clarity
regarding Althusser's classic works, will be treated in the first
part of this chapter. Following this, I will then turn to the variations of the role and position of politics that lead to the partial
arrangement of ideological apparatuses, in order to finally arrive
at the particular Althusserian construction of the void in the
problematic of so-called aleatory materialism, which, if it comes
to its fulfilment in the 1980s, represents an underground route
along most of his conceptual itinerary.

1. Event and Determination

One consolidated judgement about Althusserian thought in the
1960s, although now considered obsolete by those who special-
ise in his work, concerns the rigidity of structural determination in three directions: investigating the dynamics of structural
or metonymic causality,[3] assuming the heuristic instrument of
the last instance, and, by means of Saussure's linguistics and
Bachelard's epistemology, reclaiming the differential articulation
of synchronic logic and the constitutive opacity of a diachrony
that is not derived from the laws of development of the structure.[4]

The letter of the text perhaps shows a more ambivalent reality: a position that seems to corroborate the theses we have just

mentioned, accompanied by the possibility that there may be a particular rationality regarding the field of successions, one that is irreducible to the linear determinism of the process within a closed system.[5]

The manifesto of the first tendency, which is clearly visible and in a certain way programmatically declared in Althusser's early reflection, is not found in a text by Althusser himself, but in one that is evidently animated by a logic that is in solidarity with it, if not identical to it. This is Balibar's intervention on 'The Fundamental Concepts of Historical Materialism', published in *Reading Capital*:

> Thus the movement from one form to the other can be completely analysed: *not as the mere dissolution of a structure* (the separation of the worker from the means of labour), *but as the transformation of one structure into another.* Nor as the constitution *ex nihilo* of a structure although original [. . .] or as the accidental formation of that structure by the convergence of two abstractions [. . .].[6]

The semantics of transition do not designate a creation *ex nihilo*, and consequently a dissolution, but instead a real transformation, 'a passage from one structure into another'.[7] Such a description thus seems to suggest the existence of a moment of transition, which is not an ontological void, a moment, but a tangible interval. If it is true that 'in Marx as well the subject of historical development is nothing other than the succession of forms of the organisation of labour. Something that does not exist in the mode of other natural or social beings, but rather assumes the form of a relation',[8] then the actual object of analysis must be the forms whose development is grasped. With Balibar, this leads to holding that the transition from one mode of production to another cannot be understood as a theoretical, material, or epistemological void, a caesura that implies a deconstruction of what was there before, without having already given rise to the instance destined to take its place. The passage that we are trying to grasp here is instead something full. In this sense, the processes of transition are nothing more than, again, modes of production: intermediate structures between one system and the other.

In order to grasp the theoretical nucleus of the idea of transition, it is therefore necessary to delimit what has been historically given between the feudal mode of production and the capitalist mode of production. The study of manufacturing, according to Balibar, is the key to accessing this intermediary mode of production, capable of informing us about the conditions of possibility of a transition beyond capitalism itself, and in general about how transition stages function. In short, 'the forms of transition are in fact necessarily modes of production in themselves'.[9] The concept of transition is therefore undoubtedly related to the diachronic level. Its production is precisely connected to resolving the problem of the obscure movement between one mode of production and another, but with equal certainty it has all the characteristics of the static structure of a synchronic order.[10]

Although rigorously derived from premises that are given by a certain vision of complex structure, such an analysis leads without hesitation to a resolution of diachrony into synchrony. If the synchronic is the only framework in which it is possible to highlight a logic, a set of causal relations, for which an already-formed model is at hand, then the solution is to superimpose diachrony on to it. There is no trace of a different design. We are thus in the presence of an authentic interference between distinct levels.[11]

There is a thus a different, if not openly conflictual picture to this framework on a number of Althusser's pages in this period. If these pages do not completely contradict this framework, they certainly disturb it and deviate from it. We can thus turn to these passages, which we cannot analyse exhaustively here, but from which we will try to extract some hypotheses which are perhaps capable of indicating another axis of research.

First, it should be noted that in Althusser's text, the notion of the event is often a polemic target and an example of a misleading concept,[12] but also that in several important places there is a sort of question addressed to this notion. It is not a complete refusal, but the necessity of corresponding to some theoretical needs. A first example can be found in the pages of *Reading Capital* dedicated to the polemic against the Hegelian 'essential section'. Here the transformations of the whole are read solely as the result of contingent processes or events, of which it is not possible to given an account, as they are extraneous not only to the structure, but to any possibility of examination. In other words, the linear cut of diachrony, precisely the essential section, only allows a comparison between different states, and never follows the transformations in their occurring. At times, however, Althusser observes how synchrony may not necessarily be an essential section, and how it is possible to elaborate a different concept, for which it is

> the *conception* of the specific relations that exist between the different elements and the different structures of the structure of the whole, it is *the knowledge* of the relations of dependence and articulation which make it an organic whole, a system [. . .] the adequate knowledge of a complex object by the adequate knowledge of its complexity.[13]

MACHIAVELLIAN ONTOLOGY

What is synchronic is therefore not the simultaneous presence of different levels of the structured blocked into one common stage, but the structuring of the complexities of such plural instances in a way that is adequate to their heterogeneity. A new model of diachrony must necessarily follow this conception of synchrony: the problem is that of a diachrony, Althusser writes, the reduction of what pertains to single events, in which the historical fact is nothing but unexpected, a haphazardness that affects the structure from the outside and causes its change.

> Indeed, by what miracle could an empty time and momentary events induce de- and re-structurations of the synchronic? Once synchrony has been correctly located, diachrony loses its 'concrete' sense and nothing is left of it either but its epistemological use, on condition that it undergoes a theoretical conversion and is considered in its true sense as a category not of the concrete but of knowing.[14]

Here it is a matter of overcoming the model of Saussurean linguistics, according to which the punctual, singular, and isolated event is opaque to knowledge because it is external to any systematic articulation. We cannot directly see the event *de parole* because it lies 'before the system'. Consequently, in Saussure's view we cannot describe its point of impact and its effects on the structure. It is thus what is always external to the theoretical sphere, *la langue*, and what is framed in the context of a pre-conceptual reality, *la parole*. In other words, without differential inclusion in the system, there is no thinkability. Althusser here attempts to free himself from this prototype, in order to think the diachronic fact as an element of knowledge, and not as a real object, as a category and not as a concrete-real: diachrony then becomes the 'development of forms [*développement des formes*]', according to the Marxian expression.

Similarly, in the context of a particular text such as the *Annexe* to 'Contradiction and Overdetermination', there are openings around the nature and use of the concept of event: 'What makes such and such an event historical is not the fact that it is an event, but precisely its insertion into forms which are themselves historical.'[15] An event can therefore pass from the real object to the object of knowledge only if it is articulated within a set of forms of historicity that define its identity through collocation, differentiation, comparison, and relations with other entities on the same level. It must therefore be inserted, in order to allow for its intelligibility, into an ordered structure. This does not necessarily seem to mean that the event, here understood as a fact of diachrony, must be articulated in a synchronic sphere. The main point, in other words, appears to be articulation, not synchrony.

Finally, in the third case, after the moment of negation and the formulation of theoretical conditions, we have a determinate absence. The place where this is most clearly shown is probably when Althusser analyses Engels' introduction to *Capital* Volume 2 in an original and innovative way. These are the pages of a comparison between Lavoisier and Marx on the problem of scientific discovery and the passage from one theoretical structure to the next. The interest here is obviously related to the emergence of a *disturbance* within a theory.[16]

Althusser emphasises that a single inconsistency in a theory with respect to its conceptual apparatus – the empirical observation of a disturbance, an interference between the given categories – is not enough to give rise to a change in paradigm or radical break: it is a matter of questioning the entire universe

MACHIAVELLIAN ONTOLOGY

constituted by the established theory. The event happens, but it needs a new synchronic framework capable of reading its importance and defining its contours, a problematic that tries to accept its prerogatives and that includes it in a context. 'This *correct formulation* of the problem is not a chance effect: on the contrary, it is *the effect of a new theory*.'[17] Correctly posing the question implies reference to a new set of problems, a different framework than the one where the notion originates. But how to introduce a concept that comes from outside into a specific system? In the case of Lavoisier, Althusser, with Engels, emphasises that it is on the basis of a *new* concept that the new problematic has been constructed, while in the case of Marx, it seems that the internal inconsistency of classical political economy has found a new theory waiting that is more adequate. And finally, from what does the new fact emerge, if it is the theory itself that defines the field in which its own problems can emerge? Nothing more is said here than the old 'particular symptomatic conditions'[18] that Althusser examines in presenting, in the opening intervention of *Reading Capital*, the methodology of symptomatic reading, from which the same duplicity emerges: the manifestation of the 'punctual new' and the inclusion in the 'systematic new', which is not followed by an examination of the possibility and the modalities of commensurability between the two moments, as well as the modalities of formation of the new system capable of grasping incongruity and disturbance.[19]

A sort of epistemological void thus emerges: what pertains to the event, to be precise, does not seem to exist in Althusser's theory of historical movement; it is constantly excluded for essentially epistemic reasons.

However, there is perhaps something else: in Althusser's texts, albeit in an underground and not always explicit way, it is possible to identify a certain number of divergent suggestions. They can be formulated starting from the beginning, from the characteristics of what pertains to the event. First, it is always a local event, which affects a point of the system, but whose consequences affect the entire structure. The model, as noted, is that of the event of *parole*: this is a change in the use of a certain term that modifies a peripheral part of the language, but, the latter being a complex and supportive system of differences, is potentially capable of upsetting a large part of the relations and functions by propagating its consequences along the uninterrupted chain of the language. Secondly, it presents itself as an isolated event, lacking any connection with the structure it affects. Third, the movements that follow the emergence of a single event are not predictable in their extent, and it is thus not possible to circumscribe the zone of the system to which their influence will be limited.[20] Finally, we observe the tendency to give an account for the change only *a posteriori*, that is, by starting from a conceptual framework which follows that in which the anomaly that leads to the change is recorded. In this sense, only an indirect reconstruction of the event in its consequences through a comparison between a certain state before and after the event seems possible. In other words, the modality by which to grasp the history of the singular event directly is not given an authentically diachronic model.

If, in this context, knowledge can be given only through the articulation of a concept in a static framework of defined notions, can a horizon of articulation of concepts in motion or relative to motion be thought?[21] The overdetermined distribution of contradictions and deviations as the beginning of a new necessity will be, in this sense, moments of the Althusserian attempt to

MACHIAVELLIAN ONTOLOGY

think conflict and order, events and structures, together in their differential encounter.

2. Conflict in Dominance

Commentators traditionally date the period of Althusser's increased attention to the role of politics, not without reason, to the decade following the Parisian May, within a narrative that is placed, to use Althusser's own formulas, between his 'self-criticism' and his declaration of a 'crisis of Marxism'.[22] Nonetheless, it is clear that the interest in this level of the constitution of social formations is also present in the classical texts of the 1960s. In particular, there are the annotations, in 'On the Materialist Dialectic', about the logical impossibility of a 'Hegelian politics'. The context is well known: in this theoretically central essay of the collection, together with 'Contradiction and Overdetermination', Althusser is engaged, among other things, in the separation of a properly Marxian epistemology (in Marx's mature works) from the primarily lexical residues of Hegelian influence. This task mainly involves a discussion of the adage about 'overturning' the dialectic, finally leading to a rigid division between the nature of the Marxian and Hegelian totalities. On the one hand, the Marxian totality, the mode of production, articulates singular contradictions in a 'complex-structured in dominance whole' – that is, along the chance of relations between instances that are not defined by a common essence or substratum but because of the differential position they assume according to conjunctural distributions. On the other, the Hegelian totality instead lacks this structuring that simultaneously guarantees the rigour of the singularities and the definition of specific links of identity and difference that move from a unity Althusser defines as 'spiritual', and therefore from a separation of the always provisional moment of the history of a unity, indeed destined towards a necessary recomposition. It is a partition that is, then, the momentary alienation of the idea, of which the elements are only the manifestation (*pars totalis*), the superficial presence of a historically determinate principle, which is not actually differentiated but is instead internally homogeneous.

> My claim is that the Hegelian totality: (1) is not really, but only apparently, articulated in 'spheres'; (2) that its unity is not its complexity itself, that is, the structure of this complexity; (3) that it is therefore deprived of the structure in dominance which is the absolute precondition for a real complexity to be a unity and really the object of a practice that proposes to transform this structure: political practice. It is no accident that the Hegelian theory of the social totality has never been the basis for a policy, that there is not and cannot be a Hegelian politics.[23]

For the Althusser of *For Marx*, there is a double implication between differential articulation and dominance:[24] only a hierarchical arrangement, that is, 'determination in the last instance', a principle of regulation and distribution, by the main contradiction (economic: base, structure) allows for the identities and positions relative to further instances to be thought. In other words, it offers a theoretical anchor, a level of the real, a space within totality, on which to act in view of a change in the given distribution: again, put otherwise, it designates the place of social change.[25]

With respect to these Althusserian theses, we can find some important observations in Cesare Luporini's copy of *For Marx*. There are two in particular that are worth highlighting.

MACHIAVELLIAN ONTOLOGY

First, in the margins of the passages we have examined from 'On the Materialist Dialectic', there is a note that denounces the 'mystical' form of Althusserian emancipation,[26] because of the double implication, as we noted, between structural unity and dominance. But already in an annotation to 'Contradiction and Determination', commenting on Althusser's reading of the relation between exception and rule in revolutionary Russia according to Lenin – which he interprets as a lack of articulation (overdetermination) of the different poles and a leading back of individual exceptions to the abstract, purified norm of the dialectical contradiction between capital and labour[27] – Luporini advances the idea that precisely in such a case, the 'political nature' of the Hegelian contradiction is visible. In Althusser's words, which Luporini underlines, the 'virtue resolved by the abstract contradiction as such'. Here Luporini seems to move in the right direction when he grasps, against Althusser's end, the presupposition of the 'dominance' from the beginning of change, the 'lever' of transformation, in the inheritance of variations and hypostatisations of the present. However, at the same time, he does not appear to be entirely correct when he inscribes such an assumption into a framework of differential structuration (while mentioning its presence). If the axiom of 'dominance' on the one hand appears to crystallise an already-given hierarchy, on the other it appears to validate the attribute of a 'political nature' to the reunification in the abstract Hegelian contradiction of dispersed superficial exceptions. But Luporini does not notice the Althusserian reconfiguration of the principle: determination of the last instance in a complex system is in fact a conjunctural redistribution of hierarchal relations (of domination) between the instances, not the linear command over them, in the same way that it is not the lack of an order, but internal homogeneity (and temporary and derived non-homogeneity) to obstruct the domination of the political by Hegelian totality.[28] In other words, production and reproduction appear too close here.

The need for a displacement of this latter in the sphere of politics will be evident in 'Ideology and Ideological State Apparatuses',[29] a text which is intimately traversed by an undeclared but far from marginal division: in a first half governed by the notion of 'dominant ideology', the focus is particularly on reproduction as a moment situated outside of capitalist enterprise, in the superstructure and particularly in the state and its institutional articulations (the 'ideological state apparatuses'), placing the moment of reproduction in the superstructure. The second part instead introduces three Althusserian definitions of 'ideology' in general.[30] First, 'ideology has no history'; it has an eternal existence, it is a fundamental given in any social formation. Second, 'ideology is a representation of the imaginary relation that individuals have with their own real conditions of existence', and thus according to Althusser it is not an imaginary representation of the real conditions of existence of individuals, but rather a representation of the 'imaginary relation' that individuals entertain with their 'real' conditions of existence. In other words, the relation is imaginary, while the representation is real, or better, efficacious: ideology unfolds its effects in the order of the symbolic, in the sense that it has a 'material existence', because it has the capacity to convert representations into customs, rituals, practices, which are also incorporated into institutions. Finally, ideology 'interpellates individuals as subjects'. It tends to conceal the system of dependencies within which social agents are caught, interpellating them as subjects in the sense of theoretical humanism, as free, conscious, and in the last instance autonomous beings. Ideology obscures, in other words, the mode of production, the position of the individual in the system.[31]

Two perspectives conflict regarding the general logic. On the one hand, the theory of ideological apparatuses linearly determined by the dominant ideology which, we can suppose, similarly defines individual behaviour and every element of the system. On the other, an intense 'overdetermination', that is, the construction of identity through the position in the whole, by ideology, which appears to be the vehicle of this differential inscription, which at the same time induces the behaviours and practices and hides their origin external to the individual, interpreting it as an autonomous agent. This approach, which postulates the political evaporation of overdetermination, is cognitively homogeneous with the guiding criterion of the complex-structured whole and determination in the last instance in *For Marx*, which tends to displace the centrality of the 'dominance' present in that text. The image of the last instance that is implicitly formed here is that of an instrument with a regulatory function, of the articulation of the distribution of elements, which does not necessarily require a linear hierarchy within the mode of production, but a 'horizontal location (certainly governed by the economic) of spheres that become a specific relative autonomy'.[32]

Starting from the separation of the state and the political in the second half of the text, and from a substantial convergence around the need for a clarification of the status of politics that would define its relative autonomy with respect to the economic, Althusser moves from a linear determination in order to arrive at a quasi-equivalence of the two spheres in ideological overdetermination.[33] For Althusser, the Marxian architectonic is not sufficient if it is not converted, at least in principle, into a *topique*, that is, into the tendentially horizontal description

ALTHUSSER'S OVERDETERMINATION

of the relations of overdetermination between single instances, whether governed or not by a point of rotation and distribution.

The difference thus passes from muteness to positivity only through the articulation and isolation of meaning through a particular game between differential negation and the affirmation of value. It is what Althusser calls overdetermination, the effect of the structure on its own elements.

How is politics thought in this framework? And what is the relation between difference, conflict, and order, and institution? From the essay on 'Contradiction and Overdetermination', we observe Althusser's sometimes explicit dialogue with the theory of the weak link of the chain. Understanding the relative determination among the elements of the system, whether it is linguistic, historical, or social, is here not so much considered the key for grasping the weak link of that organisation, but rather the specific relation of the parts among each other. Understanding the determination of the mode of production on one's own levels is decisive for Althusser in order to interpret the role of the supra-structural elements with respect to the sphere of production. This is in a way, finally, to be able to determine on which point of the structure to act in order to change it. Thinking the institution given in the articulation of its internal differences is, then, the necessary step, in this horizon, for outlining the possibilities of change. From this, there derives a doctrine of conflict that can be thought in the following terms:

1. The contradictions in conflict give rise to an *asymmetrical* antagonism, operated by forces placed on non-coinciding levels and thought in the specificity of their place in the whole.
2. Conflict here is acted on a *vertical* plane: by means of

comprehending the relations within a system, it is indeed possible to grasp the conjunctural role assigned to the parts of the last instance, in order to understand the role and strength (as well as weakness) of the parts in the whole.

3. It is therefore an antagonism that cannot be experienced without a viewpoint on the system. Without understanding the role of overdetermination in organising the parts of the structure in a historically determinate way, it is not possible to act on any conflict, nor to understand its function.

4. It is a conflict that is thought, however, 'one step back' from the structurality of the whole: the event as interference and crisis of the system, the overdetermination of the contradiction, and, we will see, the aleatory beginning are modalities of understanding the initiation as deeply conflictual and never guaranteed of social determinisms and their necessity which, once established, becomes stringent.

5. Finally, Althusser thinks a sequence of orders and conflicts, a necessity punctuated by the contingency of the new beginning, in which the constituted systematicity is relatively transcended by the succession – a transformation that is always the recombination of dispersed elements, and never creation out of nothing. Althusser's void is indeed different from what we have examined in earlier sections.[34]

3. Deviation and Genesis

The story of the *matérialisme de la rencontre* is by now well known: the aggregating centre of the late Althusser, a sort of parallel current that runs through a large part of his intellectual biography,[35] a conceptual core to a series of heterogeneous texts in terms of measure, spirit, and setting, it is perhaps not a complete theory but probably neither the set of heterogeneous considerations that it can often appear as. Rereading the pages dedicated to this singular ontology of the void and the encounter, a sketch of a general and unfinished research programme, it will perhaps be possible to define the slippage that has taken place with respect to the previous positions we have examined.[36]

> Epicurus tells us that, before the formation of the world, an infinity of atoms were falling parallel to each other in the void. They still are. This implies both that, before the formation of the world, there was nothing, and also that all the elements of the world existed from all eternity, before any world ever was. It also implies that, before the formation of the world, there was no Meaning, neither Cause nor End nor Reason nor Unreason. The non-anteriority of Meaning is one of Epicurus' basic theses.[37]

In this passage on Epicurean ontology, we see the essence of the discontinuity that the materialism of the encounter imposes on the course of Althusser's reflection in condensed form. First, it is undoubtedly necessary to emphasise the blank space in which the primordial *void* is located, a point of departure for the entire doctrine. Essentially, it is not a beginning in a chronological sense, but rather in a logical sense: beneath the apparent solidity of a world (in an ontological key), a consolidated theory (in an epistemological key), and a social and political conjuncture (in a historical key), there is a real and conceptual abyss, a radical temporal becoming. Thus, what is often presented, through examples drawn from the history of thought, as an effective process must be read as a figurative narrative full of theory. However, this is a void that, at first glance, presents itself as singularly filled: in the Epicurean nothing, indeed, atoms whose material consistency can with difficulty be questioned travel without stopping. Althusser, however, focuses on the way these primitive entities move: they move in parallel, and Althusser often emphasises how in Epicurus, such a parallelism is equivalent to Nothing, because nothing is constituted, everything remains in an inexpressed state. There is no internal evolution, or necessary destination. The fall is, then, an effective description of an empty ontological landscape, not always occupied, for example, by those structures which the Althusser of *Reading Capital* maintained could not be ignored, even in the context of the reflection on processes: something must always occupy centre stage.[38] In other words, it is an attempt to subtract the centrality of systems:

> this can be put differently: the whole that results from the 'taking-hold' of the 'encounter' does not precede the 'taking-hold' of its elements, but follows it; for this reason, it might not have 'taken hold', and, *a fortiori*, 'the encounter might not have taken place.' All this is said, – in veiled terms, to be sure, but it is said – in the formula that Marx uses in his frequent discussions of the 'encounter' [*das Vorgefundene*] between raw labour-power and the owners of money.[39]

The second concept on which aleatory materialism is based is deviation, or clinamen, according to the Epicurean and Lucretian prototype. As is well known, in this ontological model the parallel fall of singular entities is disturbed, at a given moment, by a deviation that has the specific role of producing chance: not only because it is impossible to localise the point of incidence and the moment of manifestation, but since, moreover, there is no certainty regarding the extent of its effects, the duration, the result that will be produced.[40] Here once again the Saussurean inspiration that marks the notion of deviation is clear: just like the event of *parole*, it is local, indefinite in its consequences, and it produces and modifies systems with a logic, but does not itself have a stable regulation that renders it intelligible.[41]

Here we observe a discontinuity with respect to what we observed earlier. Indeed, particularly in *Reading Capital*, a horizon of this kind was excluded without hesitation, and moreover, it tended to continually emerge as an interference within the theoretical system, and was always rejected in a space unattainable by theory. The *symptomatic* disturbance that emerges in the texts of classical economics, the articulation of the event in its 'historical' becoming, the construction of a model of transition, and of the structures it rests on – all of these occurrences showed how much the classic Althusserian doctrine does not accommodate the event, deviation, the aleatory. The event, deviation, was a source of haphazardness, and it was in itself unintelligible, but above all it was an isolated, punctual theoretical object, which was not articulated within a system, and which produced the impossibility of its essential determination (i.e., its essence), through relations and differences with other objects. In the context of Althusserian philosophy in the 1960s, then, the event was rejected as such, or better, there was imposed on it, in order to acquire conceptual legitimacy, the need to translate itself into an 'event', that is, to articulate itself within a system, and therefore, in that model, to lose its diachronic character. In other words, to respond to the demands of the law of synchrony and not to its own specific horizon, characterised by the surprises that it can produce, but the unexpectedness of the event, its aleatory laws.[42]

The final notion that characterises this theoretical hypothesis is the conjuncture. It is the result of the aleatory combination of different elements, united by a deviation that, however accidental, does not prevent, on condition of a 'hold' of sufficient duration, the possibility of giving rise to a complex structure with defined and intelligible norms and models of regulation. From this point of view, there does not seem to be significant difference between such a concept and the notion of a *complex structured whole* that dates back to *For Marx* and *Reading Capital*, except for a different reconstruction of the genesis of the one with respect to the other: the conjuncture indeed descends from a destructured horizon of chance, and its epistemological solidity, so to speak, is not guaranteed by any real object of which it would be the 'restructuring' [*remaniement*], but is founded on a continuous reference to the other, to a system of deviations in the ontological void, through which it entirely confesses its nature as an integrally artificial construction, and never natural, objective, factual. The complex whole, on the contrary, always derives from a structure that preceded it in time, with which, moreover, it shares the character of an entity derived from a process that goes back to the foundation, precisely, of a real concrete. Upon closer examination, however, the distances expand: the former indeed appears differently open to the outside than the latter, which is characterised by a radical autonomy. If the complex whole is impermeable towards the outside, immutable inside, and in the last analysis grounds the set of problems that can be posed, the conjuncture, while not losing its structural character, is measured by local changes, overall effects, a process of objectification of greater complexity as it is continuously modified by punctual events.[43] A construction that is integrally artificial, as mentioned, fragile because it continuously refers to the other, always the result of a conjuncture, but solid because it is given, arbitrary, unmotivated. As with the lack of motivation in Saussure's language, it is not possible to criticise what has no reasons, causes, or logic.

The entire meaning of the conjunctural construction is summarised in an Althusserian note from 1966, which is now well known:

> 1. Theory of the encounter or conjunction (= genesis . . .) (cf. Epicurus, clinamen, Cournot), chance, etc., fall, coagulation. 2. Theory of the conjuncture (= structure) . . . philosophy as a general theory of the conjuncture (= conjunction).[44]

Aleatory materialism constitutes a rupture, significant albeit internal, that is, different but relative to the same questions, within Althusser's thought, because it produces a different answer to the question about what pertains to the event. This theory proceeds from the need to give an account of the emergence of the punctual, local, unmotivated event within a complex structure, whether it is a set of concepts, a mode of production, a historical conjuncture: the solution is to hypothesise the possibility of an articulation relative to the diachronic level, of which the examples drawn from the history of thought in this essay, particularly the Epicurean model (and perhaps, the Machiavellian one),[45] are only descriptive representations, not yet corroborated by an adequate terminological and conceptual apparatus. In other words, the attempt appears to be to produce an articulation of diachronic conceptions, void, deviation, conjuncture, in a systematic theory capable of adequately defining them by difference: in this way, it is possible to respect the assumptions of the basic synchronic problematic and support them with a relatively diachronic level.[46] In this sense, there is no self-criticism, but an attempt to resolve issues that remained suspended, which, clearly, also partly modify the original problem. This is not an isolated and incommensurable reflection with respect to that contained in *For Marx* and *Reading Capital*. On the contrary, a doctrine thus constituted does nothing but fulfil the conditions posed in the classic works. In particular, it proposes a model through which the local event is included in an overall arrangement composed of categories of historicity, in order to give rise to a 'historical event' [*evento storico*] or 'event' [*avvenimento*] – categories of historicity, and here is the difference, which are no longer, however, subordinate to a static logic, but endowed with particular modalities of regulation. From this point of view, aleatory materialism is nothing other than the *linguistics of the parole* of Louis Althusser, in which, however, event and structure are in a position of mutual exclusion: if focused on the systemic articulation, the event is cognitively unattainable, but if centred on the singular event, structurality becomes inconsistent.

This is a conclusion that, in this context, seems to relativise both the role of the structural presence and its rare interruption, elements typical of the approach in the texts of the well-known phase of Althusser's thought. The aleatory void, while relative, of his aleatory materialism thus appears to assume a temporality centred on the repetition of encounters that can take hold or not, rather than on the need for the contingency of fully historical processes.

Notes

1 Cf. Étienne Balibar, *Per Althusser* (Rome: Manifestolibri, 1991), p. 47; Fabio Raimondi, *Il custode del vuoto. Contingenza e ideologia nel materialismo radicale di Louis Althusser* (Verona: Ombre Corte, 2011); Emilio De Ípola, *Althusser. L'adieu infini* (Paris: PUF, 2012); Sylvain Lazarus (ed.), *Politique et philosophie dans l'oeuvre de Louis Althusser* (Paris: PUF, 1993); Saül Karsz, *Théorie et politique: Louis Althusser* (Paris: Fayard, 1974).

2 Cf. Louis Althusser, *Solitude de Machiavel et autres textes* (Paris: PUF, 1998); Louis Althusser, *Machiavelli e noi* (Rome: Manifestolibri, 1999); Louis

ALTHUSSER'S OVERDETERMINATION

Althusser, *Sul materialismo aleatorio* (Milan: Unicopli, 2000); Miguel Vatter, 'Machiavelli After Marx: The Self-Overcoming of Marxism in the Late Althusser', *Theory & Event* 4 (2013). Cf. further the entire 'Machiavelli and Marxism' section in Filippo Del Lucchese, Fabio Frosini, and Vittorio Morfino (eds), *The Radical Machiavelli* (Leiden: Brill, 2015), pp. 393–456; Mikko Lahtinen, 'Althusser, Machiavelli and Us: Between Philosophy and Politics', in Katja Diefenbach, Sara R. Farris, Gal Kirn, and Peter Thomas (eds), *Encountering Althusser: Politics and Materialism in Contemporary Radical Thought* (London: Bloomsbury, 2013), pp. 115–26; Mikko Lahtinen, *Politics and Philosophy: Niccolò Machiavelli and Louis Althusser's Aleatory Materialism* (Leiden: Brill, 2009).

3 See at least Vittorio Morfino, 'The Concept of Structural Causality in Althusser', *Crisis & Critique* 2 (2015), pp. 86–107; Étienne Balibar, 'Structural Causality, Overdetermination and Antagonism', in Antonio Callari and David F. Ruccio (eds), *Postmodern Materialism and the Future of Marxist Theory: Essays in the Althusserian Tradition* (Hanover, MA: Wesleyan University Press, 1995), pp. 109–19.

4 Cf. Étienne Balibar, 'Le structuralisme: une destitution du sujet?', *Revue de metaphysique et de morale* 1 (2005), pp. 5–22; Alison Assiter, 'Althusser and Structuralism', *The British Journal of Sociology* 2 (1984), pp. 272–96.

5 Cf. Stephen A. Resnick and Richard D. Wolff, 'Marxist Epistemology. The Critique of Economic Determinism', *Social Text* 6 (1982), pp. 31–72.

6 Étienne Balibar, 'On the Basic Concepts of Historical Materialism', in Louis Althusser, Étienne Balibar, Roger Establet, Jacques Rancière, and Pierre Macherey, *Reading Capital* (London: Verso, 2015), p. 407. Balibar's emphasis.

7 Ibid.

8 Étienne Balibar, 'Les concepts fondamentaux du matérialisme historique', in Louis Althusser, Étienne Balibar, and Roger Establet, *Lire le Capital*, vol. II (Paris: Maspero, 1966), pp. 142–3.

9 Balibar, 'On the Basic Concepts of Historical Materialism', p. 473.

10 Ibid., pp. 423–4.

11 Cf. Étienne Balibar, *Sur Althusser: Passages* (Paris: L'Harmattan, 1993); Gregory Elliot (ed.), *Althusser: A Critical Reader* (Oxford: Blackwell, 1994); Pierre Raymond, *Althusser philosophe* (Paris: PUF, 1997); Jean-Claude Bourdin (ed.), *Althusser: Une lecture de Marx* (Paris: PUF, 2008); Alex Calinicos, *Althusser's Marxism* (London: Pluto Press, 1976); E. Ann Kaplan and Michael Sprinker (eds), *The Althusserian Legacy* (London: Verso, 1993).

MACHIAVELLIAN ONTOLOGY

12 Cf. François Matheron, 'Louis Althusser ou l'impure pureté du concept', in Jacques Bidet and Stathis Kouvélakis (eds), *Dictionnaire Marx contemporain* (Paris: PUF, 2001), pp. 137–59.

13 Louis Althusser, 'The Object of *Capital*', in Althusser et al., *Reading Capital*, p. 255. Althusser's emphasis.

14 Ibid., p. 256.

15 Louis Althusser, *For Marx* (London: Verso, 2005), p. 126.

16 Cf. Althusser, 'The Object of *Capital*', p. 305.

17 Ibid., p. 307. Althusser's emphasis.

18 Cf. Louis Althusser, 'From *Capital* to Marx's Philosophy', in Althusser et al., *Reading Capital*, p. 24: 'They are invisible because they are rejected in principle, repressed from the field of the visible: and that is why their fleeting presence in the field when it does occur (in very peculiar and symptomatic circumstances) *goes unperceived*, and becomes literally an undivulgeable absence.'

19 Cf. Colin Davis, 'Althusser on Reading and Self-Reading', *Textual Practice* 2 (2001), pp. 299–316; Francesco Marchesi, 'Althusser e Derrida. Lettura, sistema, evento', *Décalages* 2 (2016).

20 Cf. Warren Montag, *Louis Althusser* (London: Palgrave Macmillan, 2002); Vittorio Morfino, 'Escatologia à la cantonade. Althusser oltre Derrida', *Décalages* 1 (2012).

21 Cf. Louis Althusser, *Philosophy and the Spontaneous Philosophy of the Scientists* (London: Verso, 1990), p. 75: 'Theoretically, this effect might be expressed by saying that philosophy "divides" (Plato), "traces lines of demarcation" (Lenin) and produces (in the sense of making manifest or visible) distinctions and differences.'

22 On this, see Various Authors, *La cognizione della crisi. Saggi sul marxismo di Louis Althusser* (Milan: FrancoAngeli, 1986).

23 Althusser, *For Marx*, p. 204.

24 Cf. ibid., p. 201: 'That one contradiction dominates the others presupposes that the complexity in which it features is a structured unity, and that this structure implies the indicated domination–subordination relations between the contradictions [. . .] Domination is not just an indifferent fact, it is a fact essential to the complexity itself.'

25 Cf. ibid., p. 206: '*This reflection of the conditions of existence of the contradiction within itself, this reflection of the structure articulated in dominance that constitutes the unity of the complex whole within each contradiction*, this is the most profound characteristic of the Marxist dialectic, the one I have tried recently to encapsulate in the concept of "*overdetermination*".' Althusser's

ALTHUSSER'S OVERDETERMINATION

emphasis. 'Displacement and condensation, with their basis in its over-determination, explain by their dominance the phases (non-antagonistic, antagonistic and explosive) which constitute the existence of the complex process, that is, "of the development of things".' Ibid., p. 217.

26 Louis Althusser, *Pour Marx* (Paris: Maspero, 1965), p. 210. Luporini's copy is held in the Biblioteca della Scuola Normale Superiore di Pisa, Fondo Luporini-Gallinaro, BLG A467.

27 Cfr Althusser, *For Marx*, pp. 115–16.

28 On this, cf. Alfonso Maurizio Iacono, *The History and Theory of Fetishism* (London: Palgrave Macmillan, 2016).

29 As is well known, around May 1968 Althusser was admitted for one of many hospitalizations for psychological issues which never left him. He thus experienced the events that he reflected on in 'Ideology and Ideological State Apparatuses' only indirectly.

30 Cf. Terry Eagleton, *Che cos'è l'ideologia* (Milan: Il Saggiatore, 1991); Isolde Charim, *Der Althusser-Effekt. Entwurf einer Ideologietheorie* (Vienna: Passagen, 2002); Stuart Hall, 'Signification, Representation, Ideology. Althusser and the Post-structuralist Debate', *Critical Studies in Mass Communication* 2 (1985), pp. 91–114; Paul Q. Hirst, 'Althusser and the Theory of Ideology', *Economy and Society* 4 (1976), pp. 385–412; Martin Jay, 'Lacan, Althusser and the Spectacular Subject of Ideology', in Martin Jay, *Downcast Eyes: The Denigration of Vision in Twentieth-century French Thought* (Berkeley: University of California Press, 1993), pp. 329–80; Slavoj Žižek, *The Sublime Object of Ideology* (London: Verso, 1989).

31 Cf. Judith Butler, *The Psychic Life of Power: Theories in Subjection* (Stanford, CA: Stanford University Press, 1997), pp. 106–15.

32 Cf. Steven B. Smith, 'Althusser and the Overdetermined Self', *Review of Politics* 4 (1984), pp. 516–38; Steven B. Smith, *Reading Althusser: An Essay on Structural Marxism* (Ithaca, NY: Cornell University Press, 1984).

33 On this semantic, see further Jean-Marc Lemellin, 'Idéologies, idéologie et idéologique', in Josiane Boulad-Ayoub et al., *Les Épiphanies idéologiques: Théorie, idéologie, société* (Montreal: Université du Québec à Montréal, Département de philosophie, 1981), pp. 63–111; Jorge Larrain, *The Concept of Ideology* (London: Hutchinson, 1979).

34 Cf. Gregory Elliot, *Althusser: The Detour of Theory* (Leiden: Brill, 2006), especially pp. 317–71.

35 Cf. Maria Turchetto (ed.), *Rileggere il Capitale: La lezione di Louis Althusser I-II* (Milan: Mimesis, 2007–2009); Andrea Cavazzini (ed), *Scienza,*

epistemologia, società: La lezione di Louis Althusser (Milan: Mimesis, 2009); Diefenbach et al. (eds), *Encountering Althusser.*

36 On this project, see Djuna Larise, 'Der aleatorischer Materialismus. Ein theoretisches Projekt des späten L. Althusser', *Synthesis Philosophica* 1 (2006), pp. 115–37; Djuna Larise, *Würfelspiel des Zufalls. Aleatorischer Materialismus – ein politisch-philosophisches Projekt von Louis Althusser* (Marbug: Tectum, 2007); Wal Suchting, 'Althusser's Late Thinking About Materialism', *Historical Materialism* 1 (2004), pp. 3–70.

37 Louis Althusser, *Philosophy of the Encounter (Later Writings, 1978–87)* (London: Verso, 2006), pp. 168–9.

38 Cf. Maria Turchetto, 'Scienza, ideologia, società: per una critica a due dimensioni', in Various Authors, *Scienze, epistemologia, società: la lezione di Louis Althusser* (Milan: Mimesis, 2009), pp. 23–40.

39 Althusser, *Philosophy of the Encounter*, pp. 197–8.

40 Cf. ibid., p. 169: 'But the encounter can also not last; then there is no world. What is more, it is clear that the encounter creates nothing of the reality of the world, which is nothing but agglomerated atoms, but *that it confers their reality upon the atoms themselves*, which, without swerve and encounter, would be nothing but abstract elements, lacking all consistency and existence. So much so that we can say that the *atoms' very existence is due to nothing but the swerve and the encounter* prior to which they led only a phantom existence.' Althusser's emphasis.

41 On the status of deviation, see Fabio Raimondi, 'Althusser: l'eccezione senza diritto. Per una "philosophie de la déviation"', in Vittorio Dini (ed.), *Eccezione* (Naples: Dante & Descartes, 2006), pp. 189–218.

42 Althusser, *Philosophy of the Encounter*, pp. 194–5.

43 On the theoretical transformations in which these turning points mature, see at least Warren Montag, *Louis Althusser and His Contemporaries: Philosophy's Perpetual War* (Durham, NC: Duke University Press, 2013).

44 Cited in François Matheron, 'Présentation', in Louis Althusser, *Écrits philosophiques et politiques*, vol. I (Paris: Stock/Imec, 1994), p. 21. As reported by Matheron, this note is dated 1966, but it is among material that up through 1984 Althusser decided not to publish, in order to use it for a book of overall reflection. This note is then indeed internal to the problem of aleatory materialism.

45 Cf. Althusser, *Philosophy of the Encounter*, pp. 173–4: 'A curious *philosophy which is a "materialism of the encounter" thought by way of politics*, and which, as such, does not take anything for granted. It is in the political *void* that the encounter must come about, and that national unity must "take hold". But

this political void is first a philosophical void. No Cause that precedes its effects is to be found in it, no Principle of morality or theology [. . .] One reasons here not in terms of the accomplished fact, but in terms of the contingency of the fact to be accomplished.' Althusser's emphasis.

46 Cf. Vittorio Morfino, *Plural Temporality: Transindividuality and the Aleatory Materialism Between Spinoza and Althusser* (Leiden: Brill, 2014); Francesco Marchesi, 'Attendere Althusser: Continuità e rottura tra testi classici e materialismo aleatorio', *Quaderni Materialisti* 11/12 (2012/2013), pp. 163–82.

6

Laclau and Mouffe:
Antagonism and Equivalence

In the context of a relatively recent comparison with Giorgio Agamben's thought, Ernesto Laclau claimed that a distinguishing feature of his own philosophical activity is flexibility. This is a trait which, evidently in opposition to the rigidity of the author of the *Homo Sacer* series, Laclau uses as a weapon and theoretical expedient in that context. At the centre of this discussion we find the category of sovereignty, in whose original gesture of banishment Agamben identifies its fundamental performance, one that is still present in its contemporary versions. Laclau's investigations concentrate on exactly this ambivalence: the Argentine philosopher asks whether Agamben does not arbitrarily choose the meaning he attributes to sovereignty, considering it the only possible meaning within a spectrum that is actually more extensive. His recourse to the origin, from this perspective, would therefore have the function of rigidifying the multiplicity (which is also historical) of the notion, placing one in the privileged position of the beginning. And this is a beginning whose duration extends to our present.[1] Laclau's comments perhaps emphasise more of an aspect in his own construction of philosophical concepts than a side of Agamben's project. To the original sedimentation of meaning, Laclau prefers the construction of notions that are capable of occupying multiple places and functions, or better, presenting a gradient of options and scales of intensity. This is why they have a specific flexibility that is not synonymous with ambiguity or eclecticism.[2]

We will see how it is on this terrain that Laclau has attempted a synthesis and transformation of some concepts that we have already observed with respect to the triangulation between conflict, order, and historicity, particularly those of the void, suture, and overdetermination. For this reason, the first part of this chapter will be dedicated to the specific Laclauian modality of constructing the void, a recurring theme in the positions we are observing. Laclau constructs the void in its specific relation to the positivity of the social. Once this space for politics has been circumscribed, it will be necessary to observe how Laclau thinks about this construction through the notion of equivalence, which is at the same time a synthesis and representation of conflicts. Finally, we will notice the characteristics assumed by the historicity of a relation between orders and conflicts which are constructed in this way, between, again, hegemonic forms and an antagonism that punctuates their internal life, constituting the basis of their making and unmaking.

1. The Construction of the Void

In the preface to the second edition of *Hegemony and Socialist Strategy*, Laclau and Chantal Mouffe identify the philosophical horizon which inscribes their work on Marxism and political theory in the historical transition of twentieth-century philosophy towards the absence of a referent,[3] the privilege of the signifier over the signified and the banning of so-called essentialisms:

MACHIAVELLIAN ONTOLOGY

> In other works, we have shown that the category of 'discourse' has a pedigree in contemporary thought going back to the three main currents of the twentieth century: analytical philosophy, phenomenology, and structuralism. In these three the century started with an illusion of immediacy, of a non-discursively mediated access to the things themselves – the referent, the phenomenon and the sign, respectively. In all three, however, this illusion of immediacy dissolved at some point, and had to be replaced with one form or another of discursive mediation. This is what happened [. . .] in Marxism with the work of Gramsci, where the fullness of class identities has to be replaced by the hegemonic identities constituted through non-dialectical mediations.[4]

In this context, the work of both authors is presented as an extension of this tendency, mediated above all by deconstruction and Lacanian theory in this case, towards domains which had not yet been attracted to it.[5] However, there are specific reasons that justify such a transition and insert it within a more general freeing, which has already been seen, of contemporary political philosophy from the reference to what is not political, that is, the determinisms and normativity proper to the economy and society. This is a parallel movement to what Laclau and Mouffe claim with respect to the theory of discourse and the sign, which, however, brings its own motivations with it.[6] Finally, alongside it we observe an attempt at renewal and freeing of and from Marxism[7] – a use of some elements in this tradition, considered and combined among others, which thus deprives it of some of its distinguishing elements.

A sort of construction of the void is thus the starting point of this theoretical position, understood as a necessary space for political action and its movement, as well as, correlatively, a terrain that requires a recomposition that in itself is absent. It is in this way that the main gesture of politics itself is identified. Laclau and Mouffe's analysis starts with a discussion of the aporias of Marxism which developed in the context of the Second International – apparently disqualifying, but in fact, particularly in 1985, claiming its discursive richness – in order to then measure their own response to the solutions elaborated in the subsequent tradition, from Lenin to Gramsci, passing through Luxemburg and Sorel, among others.

The difficulty Laclau and Mouffe find in the perspective of the Second International is threefold. It condenses a first attempt to relativise the linear determination of the economic structure of the mode of production on the level of the superstructure, and thus politics and ideology in general. This is initially given in the form of the dualism between a rigidly determined field, the productive sphere, and a completely indeterminate sphere, the superstructure. In fact, if the relative influence of structural determination is assumed, because of the specificity of levels of consciousness or factual and historical concreteness, it is done by grasping an overall indetermination in these sectors, one without norm and its own rule.[8] In this way, the indeterminate becomes a pure supplement of determination, the negative reverse of a necessity without interference.[9]

According to Laclau and Mouffe, the crisis of the Second International thus leads to a third fundamental philosophical consequence: if the paradigm through which politics is conceived is still that of the mirroring between base and superstructure, its crisis connected to the conjunctural fragmentation of class opens in principle the empty space for political action.[10]

The political practice of Leninism significantly changes the terms of the problematic. First, with Lenin the space of economic determination is transformed into a field that is also marked by its political nature,[11] that is, by the chains of unequal development and imperialism, whose weak links must be identified and acted on. Further, politics is given the role of representing the historical interests of the social subject through a pedagogy that, although reflecting the specific nature of the identity in question in a mirror, attributes the burden of constituting its consciousness to the reflexive double of representation. In short, with Leninism, the Marxist tradition identifies a specific role for politics, namely the constitution of alliances around the nucleus of the working class, which is capable, however, of attracting and articulating different parts of social nature, the result of the pluralisation that is connected to the struggle in the economic periphery and the fragmentation of class in the capitalist restructuring of the early decades of the twentieth century.

This is a transformation that, according to Laclau and Mouffe, can give rise to two different and opposite outcomes. They define one as democratic and the other as authoritarian, and it is the latter that will prevail in the doctrine of Leninism.[12] The role that the authors of *Hegemony and Socialist Strategy* seek for politics cannot be superimposed on to that announced by Lenin: in what they call the democratic case, the political act influences the nature of the social agents, when it does not entirely constitute them. In other words, it is the construction of the alliance as a whole that exceeds and precedes the configuration of the parts. Consequently, representation will no longer reflect historical interests which are given once and for all, but will constitute those interests and the identities beneath them. In the second form, which they call authoritarian, political representation has the function of transparently grasping the specific identities of social groups, organising a relation that is proposed as external to the elements that compose it.

It is only with Gramsci, in Laclau and Mouffe's reconstruction, that we observe a transformation of the modality through which such an articulation is thought: no longer alliance between classes, and therefore between elements whose identity remains stable before and after political construction, but hegemony, the construction of a historical bloc in which the individual groups transform their respective points of departure in light of the new overall configuration. This is a change that rests on a different conception of the relation between the economic structure and the superstructure of the mode of production: in particular, in this reading of Gramsci's position, there is a rethinking of the notion of ideology, understood here as an organic totality that is not reduced to false consciousness or a system of ideas, which in short does not only pertain to the sphere of discourse, but instead has a specific materiality. In fact, ideology is found embodied in institutions, social relations, and political apparatuses, and in this way tends to become a vehicle for political action thought as an arrangement between relatively mobile and permeable entities. Elements are no longer or not only represented by the materialistic rigidity of classes, but by the more complex and stratified collective will, which is evidently shapeable by the work of politics and discourse.[13] However, the articulation between different instances, in fact, although internal and logically preceding them, must in any case revolve around a single principle of unification given by the common reference to a fundamental class.[14]

The theoretical need that Laclau and Mouffe try to respond to is already observable here in the reconstruction of the process of the progressive relativisation of economic determination in Marxism. It clearly comes to light through a passage from Derrida that they cite: 'perhaps something has occurred in the history of the concept of structure that could be called an "event", if this loaded word did not entail a meaning which it is precisely the function of structural—or structuralist—thought to reduce or to suspect'.[15] In this passage, Derrida does not refer so much to a hidden function of the structured whole, and thus to its implicit essentialism, but rather looks to the presence, and the absence, of a pivot point, a stable hinge that would limit the circulation of signifiers within the differential chain. This is the Derrida of the criticism of Lévi-Strauss, who looks at the perspective (for some, already poststructuralist, for others still indebted to that inheritance) of a horizontal and non-dialectical totality, one lacking foundation but internally closed, precisely to allow the infinite circulation of its signifiers. It is on this ridge, between Lenin and Gramsci, that Laclau's search for the void can be situated. This is a void that, while radicalising itself in the versions that followed the synthesis in *Hegemony and Socialist Strategy*, will be configured as an open space between the logic of difference and the logic of equivalence, between the infinite dissemination of the most recent Derrida – which Laclau views as a problem and as the schematism of the neoliberal social – and the horizontal construction of the equivalence between differences, in which the limit, the closure, is exactly what allows circulation. In other words, Laclau and Mouffe will constantly re-propose the need for closure, against the proliferation of differences that instead constitute the necessary, undecidable point of departure for political decision. Without void and undecidability (and crisis), there is no politics – a void, again, which is here fluctuation and unrelated difference rather than anonymity and a mute origin, as we observed in the first part of this book.

However, with the need for closure, albeit contingent and unstable, what will gradually re-emerge is the question of the relative transcendence of politics, of its gesture that continually founds and refounds what in its immanent void, in the constant presence to itself of dispersion, cannot be and cannot be instituted – a space for the transformation of articulation and the overdetermination from descriptive hypotheses and heuristic instruments into historical and political tasks.[16]

2. Equivalence and Antagonism

However, in Laclau and Mouffe's work, the construction of the void does not only proceed from a long detour through the history of Marxism, but has also an intimately philosophical side. Oliver Marchart has argued there is a post-foundational thought in Laclau, which is heir to a certain progressive Heideggerianism, whose hinge lies in how difference is grasped, or perhaps better, a specific form of the political translation of Heideggerian ontological difference:

> We tend nowadays to accept the infinitude of the social, that is, the fact that any structural system is limited, that it is always surrounded by an 'excess of meaning' which it is unable to master and that, consequently, 'society' as a unitary and unintelligible object which grounds its own partial processes is an impossibility.[17]

This is a frame of reference that, according to Laclau, implies a double movement of recognition and action.

> This first movement thus implies the impossibility of fixed meaning. But this cannot be the end of the matter. A discourse in which meaning cannot possibly be fixed is nothing else but discourse of the psychotic [. . .] The second movement

therefore consists in the attempt to effect this ultimately impossible fixation.[18]

The Heideggerian difference between the ontological and ontic levels is translated here into the difference between the social and the political, or in Mouffe's Schmittian version, between the political and politics. On the one hand, we have the impossible origin of social relations, which are constitutively disseminated and open. On the other hand, we have the act of their articulation, the always partial and incomplete attempt to fix the meaning of collective representations and confer an order on to the social that is capable of lasting.

In this way, we understand an ambivalence that is non-secondary in Laclau's thought, in the sense that, so to speak, it is originary twice. On the one hand, it is strongly present from the beginning of his thought, while on the other, it actually concerns what he understands as the origin of politics. Indeed, it pertains to the modality in which this void is understood, starting from the identification of a primary difference, in the social, at the beginning of politics. We have noted Marchart's genealogy, which places Laclau (together with authors who are quite different from him such as Badiou, Nancy, and Lefort) into a post-Heideggerian horizon.[19] Moreover, this is an explicit declaration of Laclau himself.[20] However, it is still possible to trace a second important presence here, that of the post-Lacanian context we have already examined, from which the same conceptual tools derive, such as the notion of suture.[21]

What appears problematic and ambivalent is precisely the movement of oscillation between two conceptions of origin, and its relation with the ontic level (in Heideggerian terms) of representation, whether theoretical or political, which radically do not coincide. The deconstructionist position holds not only that every signifier, representation, or supplement results as such from the movement of difference and betrays an inevitable impurity, but also that precisely for this reason, every form of stable order, whether political or symbolic, must be rejected and deconstructed. At the limit, theories of democracy have emerged which respect such a prescription through the regulated alteration of parties in power, insofar as a democratic institution would never offer the conditions for an effective conquest of power by one historico-social agent.[22]

As we have already seen, the neo-Lacanian emphasis is instead on the symbolic order, and on the gesture of its institution, albeit always agitated and founded on a real whose full assumption is impossible. The fact that there is always an excess of the real basis over order does not lead to thinking the impossibility of institution itself, in this case, nor to theorising an order that represents and mimics originary difference, but to accepting this constitutive gap and, with it, the fragility and contingency of every symbolic form.[23]

These are widely divergent hypotheses, albeit on the common bases given by the insufficiency representative of every order, between which Laclau and Mouffe move with divergent results. Although here the theoretical apparatus of the former is in question above all, we could say that Laclau always tends towards the neo-Lacanian option up through his most recent works, while Mouffe more strongly takes on the deconstructionist posture.[24] It is not by chance that Mouffe derives a more explicit theory of democracy from their common reflection. And yet, even in Laclau's case, the latter premise takes on an undeniable centrality.[25] This is a necessary premise about the void and the origin of politics, in their relation with the forms of representation and

MACHIAVELLIAN ONTOLOGY

order, as these authors identify this primitive political horizon precisely with conflict, sometimes in that completed form of what must be represented by politics (Mouffe), and at other times as a gesture that bridges this gap between the dissemination of the social and its political articulation (Laclau).[26]

These are two paths that stem from the same set of theoretical needs and the same argumentative basis.[27] In the first, the possibility of constructing an order is rendered problematic by the background of politics, an intimately divided and antagonistic 'political': 'by "the political", I refer to the dimension of antagonism that is inherent in human relations [. . .] "Politics", on the other side, indicates the ensemble of practices, discourses and institutions which seek to establish a certain order and organize human coexistence.'[28] This basis displaces the possibility of a resolution (albeit relative) of conflict within a defined and structured order, instead looking at the possibility of reflecting the antagonism by introducing it into a controlled framework. What differentiates social antagonism and political agonism is exactly the field of reference, where the latter, while not being able to replicate the indefinite opening of the former, reproduces its divided structure: 'in an agonistic politics, however, the antagonistic dimension is always present [. . .] it is a real confrontation, but one that is played out under conditions regulated by a set of democratic procedures accepted by the adversaries'.[29] In this way, the democratic procedure constructs a frame of reference in which social antagonism can be defined, represented, and made productive, while maintaining its constitutive divergence. It is, finally, a new form of symmetrical conflict. Indeed, it is precisely the turning of antagonism into agonism that makes the status of this position commensurable to the proceduralisms of the most abstract theories of democracy.

The central notion for the purpose of grasping the peculiarly Laclauian conception of conflict is instead equivalence. This notion in part subsumes those of suture and overdetermination which we have already examined. But if the first framed a subject, and the second described positivity, equivalence has its genesis in a political matrix. Indeed, equivalence is first of all a product of politics, the result of its action and a possible description of its effects. Differences, for Laclau, are ultimately equivalent, thought as partial social identities and disseminated social questions. In the theories of disseminated difference, Laclau instead grasps useful instruments to take account of what in his eyes is the main contemporary political problem, the diffusion of partial and unrelated identities (individual and group) which are unable to articulate themselves in an organic form.

And yet the state of dispersion, or better tendential dissemination, which follows a crisis of legitimacy is precisely that in which equivalence, a different form of equivalence, can be built. It is a need for order originally connected to conflict. If in fact conflict was still thought as a disintegrating element with respect to order in theories of suture and overdetermination, here antagonism has an eminently instituting role.[30] In the fragmentation following a hegemonic crisis, for Laclau the role of politics is to trace a line of demarcation with respect to a nucleus of specific differences: in this way, the differences that are located beyond the line of demarcation will tend to become equivalent, because they are antagonistic with respect to an adversary.

> The other, however, can only be another difference, and since we are dealing with a totality that embraces *all* differences, this *other* difference – which provides the outside that allows us to constitute the totality [. . .] The only possibility of having a true outside would be that the outside is not simply one

163

MACHIAVELLIAN ONTOLOGY

> more, neutral element but an *excluded* one [. . .] vis-à-vis the excluded element, all other differences are equivalent to each other – equivalent as is their common rejection of the excluded identity.[31]

In short, conflict establishes equivalence, which through the use of the two notions described above requires a specific difference that acts, in Laclauian language, as an empty signifier that sutures the new hegemonic whole, within which the differences will take on positivity because of an overdetermined causal connection. In this way, on the one hand, the role of overdetermination and articulation are overturned, from a descriptive instrument into a historical task of political action. On the other hand, an order is affirmed that is not a pure reflection of the social division, but an authentic institutional act of a political sign, albeit in the form of a failed totality because it is provisional and, so to speak, artificially sutured. Hence the effectively instituting and ordering torsion of Laclau's proposal: the result is a vertical, asymmetrical antagonism between the differentiated instances of the equivalential chain that is formed through the opposition and excluded identity in the form of the enemy. It is now possible to notice the difference from Mouffe's agonism that always maintains symmetrical and open poles, in a framework of rules that do not allow the act of ordering and the creation of the new by any part of the parties involved.[32]

Equivalence, however, seems capable of constituting a form, albeit a 'failed' one, only through the combination of two factors that have until this moment appeared in opposition: on the one hand, the asymmetry of instances, on the other, the anonymity of actors and the originary void. In Laclau's words: 'this relation, by which a certain particular conflict overflows its own particularity and becomes the incarnation of the absent fullness of society is exactly what I call a hegemonic relation'.[33] Equivalence can only be given in light of this empty space of relative dissemination, which tends to organise and, in this way, fill: bridging and representing absence, however, is at the same time possible only in the asymmetrical form of an equivalence that is accomplished through the conflict with a specific difference, and through taking charge of the suture of the social by a further partial identity, which is in this way made universal. If up to this moment, therefore, the search for and construction of the void had appeared as theoretical claims aimed at the rejection of symbolisation, in Laclau we find asymmetry as the condition of formation of the equivalential chain. Laclauian antagonism thus presents, overall, the following characteristics:

1. It is an *asymmetrical* conflict, in which the game of equivalence and difference can only be given in their relative irreducibility. The one is present as the reversal of the other, not as a binary competition, but in the relation of inequality according to which the one gives rise to a totality, albeit contingent, while the other is the excluded element starting from what further differences are aggregated.

2. It is an antagonism therefore between *high and low*, between instances placed on discrete levels, which is not established in the manner of the horizontal relation between forces. In other words, there is no polemological schema that is assumed. Moreover, the hinge of equivalence, as well as the conflict with the excluded, is itself thought as necessarily empty, in this way able to aggregate even disparate identities under itself.

3. It is a conflict which therefore tends to create a *totality*, breaking with the systematic division of antagonism, while feeding

itself on it. Laclau breaks the dualism between order and conflict in order to reformulate its intimate reciprocity.

4. In this context, knowledge is again asked to *look at the set*, and at a whole which, although incomplete, can be the outcome of political creation. It must therefore act as a third element, capable of assuming the overall fracture of political structures, without, however, renouncing the continuous gesture of ordering and symbolisation.

5. Finally, Laclauian conflict is eminently instituting, in this way situating itself in the horizon of a *relative transcendence* with respect to an indeterminate and undecidable base. It is an assumption of the task of institution that depends on the specific social order, but which does not reproduce its dispersed form.

This configuration, while bypassing the traps of the politics of immanence and origin, identifies a place of reflection in which order, however, seems to assume a duration that is no longer punctual.

3. History and Contingency

If Laclau's conception of conflict immediately presents a certain number of anomalies with respect to many contemporary positions, his analyses of diachrony that result from the link between hegemony and antagonism appear to be connected to clearly established views. The construction of the void on the synchronic level, whose maturation follows the path of an entire intellectual biography accentuating itself over time, is in fact immediately accompanied by the criticism of perspectives which have their own figure in a fullness traced on the temporal level. Fullness and homogeneity are in this way the theoretical opponents of Laclau's conception of time and history, in a relation with the political elaboration that is evolving over the course of his entire mediation.[34]

Already starting from the debate around theories of underdevelopment, the world system and unequal development – among Laclau's earliest theoretical texts – there emerges a sensitivity towards the pluralisation of a unity and homogeneity that necessarily generates, according to him, teleology and continuism on the diachronic ground. In this sense, the comparison with authors such as André Gunder-Frank and Immanuel Wallerstein is important, as Laclau claims they offer a linear and stageist approach:

> Wallerstein started from the correct observation that it is not possible to link the dominant mode of production in a country or a region with a determinate stage of development, since the intelligibility of any process of change depends on an analysis of the world economy as a whole and not of its isolated parts, but instead of concluding that by mode of production we should therefore understand an analytical category devoid of 'stageist' connotations, he has transferred the staged to the economic system and has eliminated—by a distortion—the concept of mode of production.[35]

It is not possible to reconstruct the entire debate here. What is of interest is only to emphasise some important moments in a framework of the theory of history. According to Laclau, the way that above all an author such as Frank, but secondly the entire apparatus of the theory of the world-system, thinks the relations between a world economic centre and its periphery represents a stageist reflection of synchronic homogeneity, and therefore the absence of internal differences from the object under consideration. At issue here is the modality through which the conformation of Argentine society at the time is grasped: on the one hand, there are those who see it rigidly polarised into an advanced, fully capitalist part and a backward, still feudal part. On the other, there are those such as Frank who already read a fully capitalist situation. According to Laclau, this judgement depends on the conceptual apparatus through which Frank interprets the economico-social structure of reference: the notion of an 'economy system', centred on the sphere of exchange and circulation, tends according to Laclau to homogenise internal plurality.[36] In short, if the economic system is judged as capitalist, the entire space within it will fall under this label. On the contrary, through the notion of the mode of production, it is possible to articulate this apparent unity, arguing that within the same economic system, different modes of production (both capitalist and non-capitalist) can exist. In this way, moreover, the relations of dependence between capitalist centre and non-capitalist periphery can be shown, an authentic stake in the overall debate.

We now observe a perhaps originary tension in Laclau's thought, namely that between a homogeneity that seems only to produce teleology and linear development, and an alternative that can change over time. At this level, indeed, his intellectual posture seems to place the Althusserian notion of articulation on the terrain of relations between capitalist centre and periphery, in this way attempting to establish relations of difference within a closed system and relative autonomy among its parts.[37] If the object of analysis presents itself as internally compact and unitary, in short responding to a single developmental principle, then its history will necessarily be that of a linear evolution immediately oriented towards an end.

Laclau here draws a schema in which the internal articulation of systems does not yet have a break from the frame of references: the differences are such because they are connected in the context of a closed and tendentially horizontal network of significations, because it is endowed with a foundation that is weakened over the course of time. A matrix that, if applied to the social, would give rise to an analysis of society understood not as a pure dispersion of unrelated identities, whose unity is achievable only from the outside and in a fragile and contingent form. In this phase, Laclau grasps the relation between politics and historicity within a well-defined structural framework, whose internal reform is precisely outlined in order to remove its teleological and linear temptations. In this sense, it could be asked where the need of breaking with this relational unity stems from, which is central in the mature Laclau.

This passage from the synchrony of the whole to the diachrony of its evolution or transformation, a problematic knot of any structural theory, finds a hypothesis for resolution in Laclau through the notion of contingency. First, the profound concatenation between the moment of the static of structures and the question of their movement is shown:

> now, everything depends on how we conceive this organization which we are now able to give to ourselves [. . .] either that organization is contingent and, therefore, external to the fragments themselves; or else, both the fragments and the organization are necessary moments of a totality which transcends them. It is clear that only the first type of 'organization' can be conceived as an *articulation*; the second is, strictly speaking, a *mediation*.[38]

The internal relation between elements, which for Laclau is attributable to a traditional form of dialectic, indirectly leads

to that compactness which opens the way to an indeterminate
necessity, whose term cannot be other than, in turn, something
internal to its initial logic and development. Contingency is
instead the result of external relations between elements of a
system, in which their combination occurs through a different
logic that is imprinted outside of their sphere of influence.[39]
The union of parts, in this way, is not predetermined by laws
of development and thus is open to external intervention.
According to Laclau, the field of discontinuity opens on to this
terrain, in a framework that seems to substitute pure necessity
with pure contingency:

> The irresoluble interiority/exteriority tension is the condition
> of any social practice: necessity only exists as a partial limitation
> of the field of contingency [. . .] For the same reason that the
> social cannot be reduced to the interiority of a fixed system
> of differences, pure exteriority is also impossible. In order to
> be *totally* external to each other, the entities would have to
> be totally internal with regard to themselves: that is, to have a
> fully constituted identity which is not subverted by any exterior
> [. . .] *This field of identities which never manage to be fully fixed, is
> the field of overdetermination.*[40]

A residual need therefore, a relative and provisional remnant
of a contingency elevated to a central dimension of the temporality of political forms. This has a retroactive effect on the
synchronic dimension in which the overdetermination of the
elements is interpreted in its most radical sense: because there
is pure contingency, it must be read as the infinite circulation
of differential parts, tendentially detached from any systematic
closure. Indeed, this is a basic ambiguity in Laclau's thought, in
which the declared hold on the theme of articulation, and the
equally declared rejection of any structural determination (albeit

of the last instance), gives rise to a passage without mediation from the system to dispersion.

Laclau intends to relativise and moderate this transition through the idea that politics is the place of interconnection and the fixation, contingent and fractured, of an unfounded form which for this reason lacks an ultimate outcome. However, it is clear that the direction of his theses does not foresee intermediate points between closure and foundation on the one side and rupture with the foundation and unrelated dispersion on the other, and thus the complete substitution of contingency for necessity. The hegemonic act of suturing the disseminated social will not strictly encounter any other cohesive sphere, but only the void of an atomistic dissemination. More precisely, and particularly in Laclau's most recent work, the action of articulation is thinkable only at the moment of the crisis of a hegemonic formula, when the knot that allows the whole to hold, the specific difference that becomes empty, loses its aggregating power. In this sense, we can grasp the fact of constitutive fragility and contingency in Laclauian hegemonic articulation, delivered to an almost precise duration:

> here we have a *demand* which initially is perhaps only a *request*. If the demand is satisfied, that is the end of the matter, but if it is not, people can start to perceive that their neighbors have other, equally unsatisfied demands [. . .] If the situation remains unchanged for some time, there is an accumulation of unfulfilled demands and an increasing inability of the institutional system to absorb them in a *differential* way (each in isolation from the others), and an *equivalential* relation is established between them.[41]

This way of thinking history, however, probably does not depend on either the social production of the void, the

MACHIAVELLIAN ONTOLOGY

philosophical side of Laclau's philosophy, or on the dismissal of theories of history that are variously continuist or linearist, which is the historico-critical context of his reconstructions. Rather, what seems decisive again is the doctrine of political conflict, or better, the placement of antagonism in its general reflection. As we have seen, it is thought in part as the necessary reverse of every representative whole, as the real that underlies every symbolic by continually reproducing the act of ordering.[42]

Antagonism is thus the transcendental of Laclau's thought, more so than the renewal of the figure of hegemony or the key words of its lexicon as empty signifier and equivalence: all of these, in fact, depend on and confront conflict, an unavoidable given that decides on the aspect of these key concepts. If at times hegemony results in a contingent and partial form, which manages and in part resolves a vertical conflict between the possible equivalential chain and excluded difference, if equivalence itself is a provisional outcome of the unification of variegated and potentially reciprocally disagreeing instances, if then the empty signifier performs exactly the function of temporarily concealing the dispersion of the social and outlining the thinkability of symbolisation and order – all of this is given by reason of the fracture constituted by antagonism. Indeed, according to Laclau, 'the chasm – the antagonistic moment as such – eludes conceptual apprehension' because 'a notion of constitutive antagonism, of a radical frontier, requires, on the contrary, a broken space'.[43] Every 'conceptual apprehension', that is, every comprehension of conflict, is excluded because it is thought as an impossibility, as the indeterminate reversal of every determination. Breaking with the proliferation of pure difference is certainly what clearly separates this thought from the risk of the postmodern 'anything goes', and yet this limitation does not fully circumscribe the scope of the conflict.[44]

Antagonism owes its status in Laclau's thought, ultimately, much more to its topological position than its inner, completely indeterminate nature: within the triangulation between conflict, articulation/hegemony/order, and the emptiness of the social, it is perhaps in the confrontation with the last instance that antagonism is grasped with greater clarity. Indeed, strictly speaking, it never encounters anything on its own path, being able to give itself only in the deconstruction of a preceding hegemonic order, which always fails due to internal problems. Again, the antagonism between an exclusion and a renewed equivalential chain marks the passage from one articulation to the other in the void of a dispersion that follows a crisis.[45] Only in crisis, therefore, is a politics possible. If all of this perhaps shows some strategic limits of this system, the theoretical question is of interest here: antagonism is mute, unattainable as such, perhaps precisely because it is never measurable, never compared with anything else, with further and irreducible logics. It generates order, it is therefore asymmetrical and instituting, but not fully historical, because it does not conceptually allow for the measuring of its adequacy to – or its predisposition to force – a conjuncture, an economic and social process. In other words, acting in the void and on the void, antagonism always remains homologous to itself and does not allow for the differentiation of hegemonic forms, which are relatively anonymous.

Finally, it is a matter of an antagonism that is not fully historical, because in the encounter with the pure void it tends to produce purely contingent totalities, in a new polarity 'between extremes': just as Laclau thinks, on synchronic terrain, homogeneous structures that are rooted in an origin, or unlimited

MACHIAVELLIAN ONTOLOGY

and proliferating openings (circumscribable only by means of politics), on the diachronic level he describes on the one hand the impossibility of political action overdetermined by a historical necessity, opposing it on the other to its practicability through the simple encounter with the void. In this way, the form produced will have a completely contingent, and at the limit, punctual temporality, conceptually unattainable because it is undifferentiated with respect to the other hegemonic formations. Conversely, the encounter with the other, with a logic that is of different nature than pure political articulation, can perhaps allow the modalities of action to measure their own adequacy, their eventual subordination to a determinism, their relative agreement with the times, or again the conformity to the task of breaking with a defined, structured, but undesirable development. It is the uncertain and occasional, but effective, power that forces the process and the conjuncture.

Notes

1 Cf. Ernesto Laclau, *Le fondamenta retoriche della società* (Milan: Mimesis, 2017), p. 238.
2 On this formal aspect of Laclau's thought (but not only this), see above all two important works: Simon Critchley and Oliver Marchart (eds), *Laclau: A Critical Reader* (London: Routledge, 2004); David Howarth, 'Discourse, Hegemony and Populism. Ernesto Laclau's Political Theory', in David Horwarth (ed.), *Ernesto Laclau: Post-Marxism, Populism and Critique* (Abingdon: Routledge, 2015), pp. 1–20. See also Jules Townshend, 'Discourse Theory and Political Analysis. A New Paradigm From the Essex School?', *The British Journal of Politics and International Relations* 1 (2003), pp. 129–42.
3 Cf. Rodolphe Gasché, 'How Empty Can Empty Be? On the Place of the Universal', in Critchley and Marchart (eds), *Laclau: A Critical Reader*, pp. 17–34.

4 Ernesto Laclau and Chantal Mouffe, *Hegemony and Socialist Strategy: Towards a Radical Democratic Politics* (London: Verso, 2001), pp. x–xi.

5 'The presumed "poststructuralist" motive for the incompleteness or uncertainty that is constitutive of the system is, itself, from the outset, inherent in the description of the effects of the structure.' Étienne Balibar, 'Un feu d'artifice du structuralisme en politique', in Ernesto Laclau and Chantal Mouffe, *Hégémonie et stratégie socialiste: Vers une politique démocratique radicale* (Besançon: Les Solitaires Intempestifs, 2009), p. 11.

6 Cf. David Howarth, Aletta Norval, and Yannis Stavrakakis (eds), *Discourse Theory and Political Analysis: Identities, Hegemonies and Social Change* (Manchester: Manchester University Press, 2000).

7 This is the post-Marxism that Laclau and Mouffe claim for themselves. Cf. Paul Bowman, *Post-Marxism Versus Cultural Studies: Theory, Politics and Intervention* (Edinburgh: Edinburgh University Press, 2007).

8 Laclau and Mouffe, *Hegemony and Socialist Strategy*, pp. 47–8.

9 Cf. Allan Dreyer Hansen, 'Laclau and Mouffe and the Ontology of Radical Negativity', *Distinktion: Scandinavian Journal of Social Theory* 3 (2014), pp. 283–95.

10 Laclau and Mouffe, *Hegemony and Socialist Strategy*, p. ix.

11 Ibid., p. 59.

12 In this context, it is interesting to note the observation of the authors with respect to the innovation of Leninism rooted only on the political terrain and beginning from a military language, which only with Gramsci becomes an innovation in understanding social relations in the strict sense. This observation seems to corroborate the thesis developed here which claims that the military paradigm remains extraneous to the modalities of an effective and historical social and political conflict: 'The terrain of hegemonic relations was, therefore, one of essentially pragmatic discourses. All the terminological innovations which Leninism and the Comintern introduce to Marxism belong to military vocabulary (tactical alliance, strategic line, so many steps forward and so many back); none refers to the very structuring of social relations, which Gramsci would later address with his concepts of historical bloc, integral State, and so forth.' Ibid., p. 57.

13 Cf. Georg Glasze and Annika Mattissek, 'Die Hegemonie und Diskurstheorie von Laclau und Mouffe', in Georg Glasze and Annika Mattissek (eds), *Handbuch Diskurs und Raum* (Bielefeld: Transcript, 2015), pp. 153–81; Jacob Torfing, *New Theories of Discourse: Laclau, Mouffe and Žižek* (Oxford: Blackwell, 1999). See also the criticism in Slavoj Žižek,

'Beyond Discourse-Analysis', in Ernesto Laclau, *New Reflections on the Revolution of Our Time* (London: Verso, 1990), pp. 249–60.

14 Once again, it is interesting how Laclau and Mouffe, returning to the military paradigm of conflict, here criticise its relative persistence due to the relative permanence of political identities within it. We have observed that, generally, the military paradigm more often operates in the sense of the anonymity of the agents involved in the conflict, even more so than in the fluctuations of meaning sought by Laclau and Mouffe. As far as we are concerned, the opposite is true: only socially determined identities, albeit those relatively autonomous to their political positioning, can give rise to conflicts that look to the new order, as Gramsci anticipated through other means.

15 Derrida, *Writing and Difference*, p. 351. Cf. Laclau and Mouffe, *Hegemony and Socialist Strategy*, pp. 70–1.

16 Cf. Jason Glynos and David Howarth, *Logics of Critical Explanation in Social and Political Theory* (Abingdon: Routledge, 2007), pp. 165–208.

17 Cf. Laclau, *New Reflections on the Revolution of Our Time*, p. 90.

18 Ibid., pp. 90–1.

19 Cf. Oliver Marchart, *Post-Foundational Political Thought* (Edinburgh: Edinburgh University Press, 2007), p. 1.

20 'If, as shown in the work of Derrida, undecidables permeate the field which had previously been seen as governed by structural determination, one can see hegemony as a theory of the decision taken in an undecideable terrain.' Laclau and Mouffe, *Hegemony and Socialist Strategy*, p. xi.

21 Ibid.

22 For example, cf. Philippe Lacoue-Labarthe and Jean-Luc Nancy (eds), *Les fins de l'homme. À partir du travail de Jacques Derrida (Colloque de Cerisy, 23 juillet–2 août 1980)* (Paris: Galilée, 1981); Philippe Lacoue-Labarthe and Jean-Luc Nancy (eds), *Rejouer le politique* (Paris: Galilée, 1981); Nancy Fraser, 'The French Derrideans: Politicizing Deconstruction or Deconstructing the Political?', *New German Critique* 33 (1984), pp. 127–54; Simon Critchley, *The Ethics of Deconstruction* (Edinburgh: Edinburgh University Press, 2014).

23 Torben Bech Dyrberg, 'The Political and Politics in Discourse Analysis', in Critchley and Marchart (eds), *Laclau: A Critical Reader*, pp. 241–55.

24 Cf. Chantal Mouffe (ed.), *The Challenge of Carl Schmitt* (London: Verso, 1999); Chantal Mouffe (ed.), *Deconstruction and Pragmatism* (London: Routledge, 1996).

25 'Post-foundationalism [. . .] must not be confused with anti-foundationalism

or a vulgar and today somewhat outdated "anything goes" postmodernism, since a post-foundational approach does not attempt to erase completely such figures of the ground, but to weaken their ontological status.' Marchart, *Post-Foundational Political Thought*, p. 2.

26 Cf. Fred R. Dallmayr, 'Hegemony and Democracy. On Laclau and Mouffe', *Strategies* 30 (1988), pp. 29–49.

27 Cf. Jason Glynos and Yannis Stavrakakis, 'Encounters of the Real Kind. Sussing Out the Limits of Laclau's Embrace of Lacan', in Critchley and Marchart (eds), *Laclau: A Critical Reader*, pp. 201–16; Norval, 'Hegemony After Deconstruction'; Aletta Norval, 'The Impurity of Politics', *Essex Papers in Government and Politics / Sub-series in Ideology and Discourse Analysis* 18 (2002).

28 Chantal Mouffe, *The Democratic Paradox* (London: Verso, 2000), p. 101.

29 Chantal Mouffe, *Agonistics. Thinking the World Politically* (London: Verso, 2013), p. 39.

30 On these problems, see Oliver Marchart, 'The Other Side of Order. Towards a Political Theory of Terror and Dislocation', *Parallax* 1 (2003), pp. 97–113; Oliver Marchart, 'Institution and Dislocation. Philosophical Roots of Laclau's Discourse Theory of Space and Antagonism', *Distinktion. Scandinavian Journal of Social Theory* 3 (2014), pp. 271–83.

31 Ernesto Laclau, *On Populist Reason* (London: Verso, 2005), pp. 69–70.

32 Cf. Ernesto Laclau, 'Glimpsing the Future', in Critchley and Marchart (eds), *Laclau: A Critical Reader*, pp. 279–328. Cf. also Urs Stäheli, 'Competing Figures of the Limit: Dispersion, Transgression, Antagonism and Indifference', in Critchley and Marchart (eds), *Laclau: A Critical Reader*, pp. 226–40.

33 Ernesto Laclau, *Emancipation(s)* (London: Verso, 2007), p. 43. Cf. 'In a situation of radical disorder, "order" is present as that which is absent; it becomes an empty signifier, as the signifier of that absence [. . .] To hegemonize something is exactly to carry out this filling function.' Ibid., p. 44.

34 Cf. Samuele Mazzolini, 'Laclau lo stratega: populismo ed egemonia tra spazio e tempo', in Fortunato Cacciatore (ed.), *Il momento populista. Ernesto Laclau in discussione* (Milan: Mimesis, 2019), pp. 33–74.

35 Ernesto Laclau, *Politics and Ideology in Marxist Theory: Capitalism, Fascism, Populism* (London: New Left Books, 1977), p. 44.

36 Ibid., p. 33.

37 'The symbolic – i.e., overdetermined – character of social relations therefore implies that they lack an ultimate literality which would reduce them

MACHIAVELLIAN ONTOLOGY

to necessary moments of an immanent law.' Laclau and Mouffe, *Hegemony and Socialist Strategy*, p. 98.

38 Ibid., p. 94.

39 Ibid., p. 99.

40 Ibid., p. 111.

41 Laclau, *On Populist Reason*, p. 73.

42 Cf. Oliver Marchart, 'Politics and the Ontological Difference: On the "Strictly Philosophical" in Ernesto Laclau's Work', in Crichley and Marchart (eds), *Laclau: A Critical Reader*, pp. 54–72; Marchant, *Post-foundational Political Thought*, pp. 146–9.

43 Laclau, *On Populist Reason*, pp. 84–5.

44 Cf. Mazzolini, 'Laclau lo stratega', p. 70; Fabio Frosini, '"Spazio-tempo" e potere alla luce della teoria dell'egemonia', in Vittorio Morfino (ed.), *Tempora multa: Il governo del tempo* (Milan: Mimesis, 2013), pp. 225–54; Doreen Massey, 'Politics and Space/Time', *New Left Review* 196 (1992), pp. 65–84; Esteve Morera, *Gramsci's Historicism: A Realist Interpretation* (London: Routledge, 1990), pp. 90–102; Anna Marie Smith, *Laclau and Mouffe: The Radical Democracy Imaginary* (London: Routledge, 1998), pp. 76–90.

45 Cf. Oliver Marchart, 'On Drawing a Line. Politics and the Significatory Logic of Inclusion/Exclusion', *Soziale Systeme* 1 (2002), pp. 69–87, special issue 'Inclusion/Exclusion and Socio-Cultural Identities', ed. Urs Stäheli.

Part 3
Machiavellian Ontology

7

Three 'Ontologically Oriented' Concepts: *Inimicizie, Ordini, Riscontro*

Machiavelli never constructed anything like an ontology, at least in the sense that we understand this term.[1] In other words, he never carried out a reflection on being, even as political or social being. Moreover, the time that divides us from his work makes any re-proposal of it a risk, including on the level of pure theory. And yet the commentators who have identified ontological potentialities in his discourse on politics and history have neither been few nor marginal.[2]

Those who have traced this possibility have often done so on the basis of the break that Machiavelli's discourse imposed with regard to several themes in the earlier tradition. This is a discontinuity that does not only concern political concepts, but the entire representation of historical, social reality, including its ontological background. It is therefore first in the light of the historical and theoretical situation of his time, as well as that rooted in some of the habits of ancient and Renaissance thought, that we will observe the specific difference of Machiavellian notions of conflict (expressed in his lexicon as *tumulti, disunioni, inimicizie,* and *romori*),[3] institutions (*gli ordini*, from the plebeian tribunate to the senate), and history (illustrated in the images of the *riscontro* and return to principles).

1. Conflict Against Competition and War

In the eyes of the tradition which precedes Machiavelli, conflict represents a problem for political life, an adversary to every community, and even a taboo whose appearance must be avoided at all costs. However, this is not the case in the same way for every form of antagonism, but only its specific modality, which will be that favoured by Machiavelli.

At the beginning of the Western philosophical tradition, Plato and Aristotle had radically opposed conflict within the city, but they did not oppose it to forms of regulated competition. As Neal Wood has written:

> Competition presupposes wide acceptance of ends, and disagreement over means as to the person or the policy that will best achieve the ends. Competition is a game situation; competitors may be athletes on the playing field, candidates for public office, members of a deliberative assembly, business and processional rivals. Though in practice the precise line between competition and conflict is often difficult to draw, conflict is generally characterized by tension, hostility, and defiance that may erupt into violence and warfare. Typically, extensive and intensive disagreement over ends and, frequently, an unwillingness to abide by the rules of the game lead to conflict.[4]

Classical Greek thought, from this point of view, carries out a decisive choice in favour of competition and against conflict. In the political orders that Plato and Aristotle theorise, while it is differently articulated in each, political life always assumes the sign of harmony, that is, concord between parties. In Plato, this harmony tends to be transformed into the compactness and rigidity of roles, while the most mobile Aristotelian social sectors are always brought back to a harmony by the middle class who embody a sort of just means of political nature.[5] The plurality of parts is in this way either channelled into an order that assigns each group its specific end, or an order that subordinates the interaction between classes to the collective telos of the common good.[6] If competition anticipates unity in the ends and distinction in the means to reach them, whereas in conflict there is the presence of different goals which are reachable through instruments that are also different, then here we are certainly in the presence of a form of competition.

These judgements are part of a wider tendency, rooted in the Greek world in particular, that imposes silence, if not denial, towards conflict. Nicole Loraux's work has in this sense shown how in antiquity the memory of the city of Athens is pervaded by a narrative in which conflict is constantly excluded or sublimated: rather than admitting the division of citizen unity that one prefers, as Aristotle does, it is sublimated into the transformation of orders (*metá-stasis*, constitutional change, rather than *diá-stasis*, division), or it is explicitly prohibited.[7] This is the case of the law promoted by Thrasybulus after the government of the Thirty Tyrants and the return to democracy (403 BCE), which puts amnesty for political adversaries next to imposing silence about past conflicts.[8] At the root of this tendency is the line of demarcation that is traced between *stásis*, domestic conflict, and *pòlemos*, war towards the outside. While the latter is admitted and sometimes encouraged, the former is associated with a disease of the body politic that interrupts its internal harmony, nullifying its overall health.

This tradition extends up through the Renaissance period, passing through the Roman world. Indeed, it is to Cicero, perhaps more than any other author, that we owe the spread of the formula of *concordia ordinum*: in the aristocratic republic that

Cicero imagines, the government of the people by the aristocracy should take place without conflicts, in the name of the concord between orders which in this case is also conceived as harmony. Instead, the citizen-soldier should channel his antagonistic tendency towards the outside, that is, into war.[9] In humanistic literature, and not only in politics, this trace returns and is reinforced: in the face of the endemic partisanship of public life in Italian Renaissance cities, mainly arising from conflicts between rich noble or magnate families and their respective clienteles, the judgement of authors from this period (which immediately precedes Machiavelli) is oriented among other things towards a maxim taken from Sallust's *Bellum Iugurtinum*: *concordia parvæ res crescunt, discordia maxime dilabuntur* ('small states grow in harmony, while the large ones are destroyed by discord').[10] Decontextualised and elevated to an oracular image (as often happened in the medieval and early modern reception of classical texts), this argument used by the character of Micipsa had a very wide circulation starting from the fourteenth century, not only in publications but also on all types of medals, coins, and inscriptions, to the point of being considered a sort of divine revolution by the fourteenth-century humanist Francesco Patrizi.[11]

Machiavelli opposes this consolidated opinion regarding political conflict both by re-evaluating its overall role and by clarifying its difference with respect to competition and war. First, he traces a different ancient tradition, rooted in the concreteness of political action, especially Roman political action, rather than in the words of its writers. In this retelling, of which the work of Livy gives the detailed account, conflict is a usual practice in republican Rome, which contributed decisively to its growth in power and geographical spread. Alongside Livy, authors such

INIMICIZIE, ORDINI, RISCONTRO

as Polybius and Dionysius of Halicarnassus, to whom we will return, provide Machiavelli with a point of reference endowed with that authority that only the ancients possessed in the period during which he was writing. Secondly, already in *The Prince* (1513), Machiavelli insists on the immediately conflictual nature of political relations, both between the people and the great and between the great and the prince, but also in that sort of alliance he proposes between the people and the prince.

From the beginning, according to Machiavelli, a divergence can be seen regarding the political aims of the people and the great: 'for in every city these two diverse humors are found, which arises from this: that the people desire neither to be commanded nor oppressed by the great, and the great desire to command and oppress the people'.[12] Reformulating the medical theory of humours, originally fourfold and oriented towards equilibrium in the version of Hippocrates and Galen, Machiavelli identifies two prevailing orientations in every political community, which naturally tend to clash due to their difference. The great, which is both the Roman patriciate and an allusion to the Florentine magnates of the time, are the constant adversary and polemical target of Machiavelli's work. He describes them as being animated by a desire to oppress the people, in order to acquire major political offices of the city, but also with respect to the protection and accumulation of enormous wealth.

On the other hand, the people are presented as apparently passive and concerned only with their own security and defence from oppression. In reality, this is not the case in Machiavelli's work: the people (from the Roman plebs to the multiplicity of classes and groups that compose the Florentine people) are able to direct their conflictual actual in a positive way, that is, not only in terms of defence, but also in order to acquire greater freedom and equality, if organised through a leader (the prince, the captain of the people) or through institutions (the tribunate of the plebs, the *proposti*).[13] In this way, the people provide an indispensable contribution to the construction and duration of every political form, whether princely or republican, ancient or modern. Through this connotation, which is so to speak originary of politics, Machiavelli intends to oppose the tradition of the oblivion of conflict and the *concordia ordinum*, showing first that the political life of every city or state depends on a constitutive asymmetry, that between the great and the people.

Particularly in *The Prince*, Machiavelli describes a sort of strange convergence between the people and the prince, in common opposition to the great. What is more interesting, however, is that this same alliance is productive and potentially successful against the Florentine oligarchy only insofar as it is internally conflictual. Machiavelli tries to show how it works from the opening dedication to the prince (addressed to a political leader of this kind, Lorenzo de' Medici):

> Nor do I want it to be reputed presumption if a man from a low and mean state dares to discuss and give rules for the governments of princes. For just as those who sketch landscapes place themselves down in the plain to consider the nature of mountains and high places and to consider the nature of low places place themselves high atop mountains, similarly to know well the nature of peoples one needs to be prince, and to know well the nature of princes one needs to be of the people.[14]

Generalising his own condition as a popular writer who takes the liberty of advising a prince, Machiavelli describes the broader relation between prince and people. This is a necessarily asymmetrical relation, between unequal parts, but precisely for this reason also a productive relation: only a man of the people – far

INIMICIZIE, ORDINI, RISCONTRO

from the narrow circles that too often tell the prince only what he already approves, reflecting his image as a mirror – a man who looks at the prince from a far perspective is able to focus on his precise nature, his tasks, and the situation in which he finds himself working. It is a metaphor that draws an overall relation between prince and people in which the former – if he lacks consent, but also popular conflict – will lead the state to corruption, becoming an instrument of the ambition and voracity of the great. This is therefore a relation that is not representative in the modern sense of the term, but instead prospective, because it is founded on the political productivity of difference, duality, and asymmetry, and opposed to the relation of proximity, stasis, and corruption between the prince and his court.[15]

However, it is above all in the *Discourses on Livy* (1520) that Machiavelli's theory of the productivity of conflict is clarified, in its distinction from competition and war. Taking up the theory of humours already espoused in *The Prince*, Machiavelli deepens its meaning and dynamics in light of the history of republican Rome. According to him, this offers two essential teachings, 1) First of all, there is productivity only where there is asymmetry, that is, only when there is a conflict between humours (classes, social classes) and not between sects (courts, clientele, factions). A conflict between humours is an *asymmetrical and materialist conflict*. It takes place between different adversaries for social belonging, available means (economic and political), and above all ends – on one side, the preservation of the political situation as it is, on the other, the transformation of the same situation. Conflict between sects is instead competition, that is, a struggle for identical objectives (such as political offices, for example), in which the competitors are distinguished only by the ways in which they intend to reach those shared ends. For this reason, they are socially anonymous – there is no difference of class among members of different noble families for example – and [they are] similar and homogeneous with regard to the political proposal and the idea of society that they promote. 2) There is productivity of conflict only within an *instituting procedure* for which antagonism does not remain *sciolto* (untied), in Machiavelli's lexicon, but instead is organised through leaders and properly activated through institutional structures. It is indeed this instituting procedure that allows the people to form themselves as a political subject in the proper sense and to influence the current institutional structure through action. This is so to the point that a conflict for the institutions, such as the struggle of the Roman plebs for the tribunate, becomes a struggle between institutions, as when the tribunate itself aligns with the senate, which is traditionally aristocratic.

> I say that to me it appears that those who damn the tumults between the nobles and the plebs blame those things that were the first cause of keeping Rome free, and that they consider the noises and the cries that would arise in such tumults more than the good effects that they engendered. They do not consider that in every republic there are two diverse humors, that of the people and that of the great, and that all the laws that are made in favor of freedom arise from their disunion, as can easily be seen to have occurred in Rome. For from the Tarquins to the Gracchi, which was more than three hundred years, the tumults of Rome rarely engendered exile and very rarely blood.[16]

In the *Discourses*, Machiavelli develops these aspects of his image of political conflict in close contact with the history of Rome, which for centuries had been criticised precisely in light of the clash between orders, that is, between the institutional representations of classes, which characterised it.[17] The title of the

INIMICIZIE, ORDINI, RISCONTRO

fourth chapter of this work, 'That the Disunion of the Plebs and the Roman Senate Made That Republic Free and Powerful',[18] summarises a thesis that represented an authentic break in the Western tradition, becoming a sort of aphorism which was assumed by authors such as Campanella, Alfieri, Montesquieu, Rousseau, Mably, Milton, Sidney, Ferguson, and Adams, among others.[19]

This famous Machiavellian phrase actually has behind it a set of meanings that help to indicate a specific idea of antagonism. While it refers to the fact that the mixed Roman order, composed of monarchic (the consulate), aristocratic (the senate), and democratic (the tribunate) elements, is not too different in this way from examples of aristocratic republics such as Sparta and Venice, it also insists that the Roman order has a conflictual origin that radically separates it from every other experience.[20] In short, it is the struggle to obtain the tribunes by the plebs starting from the first *secessio* that renders the mixed order 'really' mixed. Second, the institutionalisation of conflict represented by the tribunate, whose functioning we will examine further in the next chapter, takes on two meanings. On the one hand, it prevents the violent degeneration of antagonism between the people and the great through the institutional form composed of tools such as the possibility of a veto on laws of the senate and the power to accuse illustrious citizens (patricians and senators in particular). But beyond this work of connection between the institutions, the tribunate allows, through an 'ordinary' form, for the plebs to be united in opposition to the patriciate through non-legal means such as succession, the *detractio militae* (avoiding military obligations), and public demonstrations free of violence.[21] In this sense, institutionalised conflict does not only mean political dialectics but the challenge, struggle, and reciprocal coercion between groups with differentiated interests, as well as the transformation of orders.[22] The tribunes absorb and legalise conflicts, but they also incite and create new ones.

The tumults also animate the political life of the republic within a stable constitutional order, on the one hand by allowing popular resentment towards those in command to 'vent itself',[23] and on the other, by exerting constant pressure on the elites, so as to limit their ambition, moralising their behaviour (Machiavelli associates this power of institutions with religion), and rendering their manners more austere. An institutional pressure can be exerted not only by the popular side, but also, on exceptional occasions and for a limited duration, on the senatorial side through the special magistracy of the dictatorship. However, this non-violent threat is not always effective: this is the case in corrupt republics in which the modes of ordinary conflict (*secessio, detractio militae*, non-violent tumults, targeted exiles, popular trials, struggle between humours) leave room for corrupt modes (violent tumults, military battles, mass exiles, calumnies, struggle between sectors and factions).[24] On these occasions – in which the 'quality' of the 'matter'[25] is compromised – the ordinary ways must leave room for extraordinary ways:[26] the medical metaphor of purging thus gives way to that of surgery, or the violent excision of the evil, according to the widespread Hippocratic practices of the age, from cauterisation to bloodletting.[27]

The asymmetrical and socially characterised nature of Machiavellian conflict emerges with even greater clarity in two further dimensions explained in the *Discourses*. Both refer to what John McCormick has defined as Machiavelli's 'class politics', that is, his distinction of political behaviour on the basis of belonging to a class.[28] The culmination of this attitude is the attribution to the people, in the Roman model and in general,

INIMICIZIE, ORDINI, RISCONTRO

of the role of 'guardian of freedom'[29] – a singular concept, which refers first to the Renaissance and early modern meaning of freedom understood as political independence and absence of domination by an external enemy.

Machiavelli bestows the role of guardian of freedom on the people first of all for their innate desire not to be dominated rather than to dominate, which for him is implicit in all nobility and aristocracy. But secondly, this attribution is the result of a more complex reasoning that suggests how popular interest coincides, in the republics, with the general interest, and how once again the popular subject is constructed in conflict and politico-institutional organisation. By dividing the republic into two large groups, those who place the guarding of freedom with the great and those who delegate it to the people, Machiavelli intends to emphasise the advantages of a typically Roman virtuous circle that unites citizenship, military people, equality, and the duration of the republics. Indeed, Machiavelli argues, Rome is opposed to aristocratic republics such as Sparta and Venice because, unlike them, it exploits the influx of foreigners by easily extending citizenship and involves all of the people in a popular army, which generates a considerable strength of influence on the part of the plebs, caused by the number and the possession of weapons. The result of this is an egalitarian republic, full of tumults (or egalitarian because it is full of tumults) and with a strong popular army, in contrast to the small, peaceful, and oligarchic Sparta and Venice.

However, there is a further advantage of this structure, which concerns a more general context. According to Machiavelli, history is indeed such that every city, however isolated, finds itself invaded or forced to invade, and therefore a strong and large popular army will allow the republic to last over time, addressing

MACHIAVELLIAN ONTOLOGY

these historical needs without being overwhelmed. This is a destiny that separates the long history of republican Rome from the fragility of oligarchic republics:

> But since all things of men are in motion and cannot stay steady, they must either rise or fall, and to many things that reason does not bring you, necessity brings you. So when a republic has been ordered so as to be capable of maintaining itself does not expand, and necessity leads it to expand, this would come to take away its foundations and make it come to ruin sooner. So, on the other hand, if heaven were so kind that it did not have to make war, from that would arise the idleness to either make it effeminate or divided; these two things together, or each by itself, would be the cause of its ruin.[30]

A history of groups and social classes that are constituted in political organisation and in conflict: this is one of the most salient themes of Machiavelli's third great work, *The Florentine Histories* (1525). This is a work that presents an authentic catalogue of conflicts by following the long post-medieval history of the city of Florence, in the continual transformation of its orders and the progressive exclusion of the losing classes within its divisions. More than in any of his other works, Machiavelli further explores here the different behaviours and the different modalities of conflict of the various political actors: from the competition between the magnate families[31] to the properly social antagonism of the Florentines of the Ciompi,[32] up to the use on the part of the Medicis of war against the outside in order to control the city, and the crisis of this family because of the domestic conflicts that afflicted it, the conspiracies that sprang forth from its court and clients.[33] Among these, only a few exceptions, such as the Ciompi tumult, which Machiavelli looked at with suspicion, re-propose the asymmetrical conflict

192

INIMICIZIE, ORDINI, RISCONTRO

between the humours of the Roman model, while more often it is a corrupt conflict between sects and interest groups that prevails, with its endemic antagonism and its incapacity to make the orders last.

The primacy of conflict over concord is unanimously recognised as one of the points of departure for modern politics, and it is on this ground that Machiavelli is often associated with Hobbes, in the common aversion to the Aristotelian model of natural sociability (*zoon politikon*). However, their commonality ends just after this affirmation: Hobbesian conflict, as the natural origin of politics and the constant spectre of its integral juridicisation and pacification, has little to do with the constant interweaving between form and conflict and between order and transformation which characterises Machiavelli's conception of conflict. Roberto Esposito has vividly synthesised this distance in the opposition between the neutralisation of conflict (Hobbes) and its reconversion (Machiavelli):

> there is either politics or conflict. The transition, or rather the leap, from the state of nature to that of society positions the chasms along the temporal axis: when there is conflict there is not yet a politics, when there is politics there is no more conflict [. . .] What distinguishes Machiavelli from Hobbes is not the stark choice between order and conflict: it is the acceptance, or not, of their co-existence at the same time.[34]

In this sense, we can summarise Machiavellian conflict thus:

1. Instituting procedure (activation of conflict through organisation)
   - Transformation of orders: from conflict for institutions to conflict between institutions

- Conflict between institutions: dialectic but also pressure
- Ordinary modes (purge): let the plebs vent, moralise the elite
- Extraordinary modes: excision vs. corruption
2. Conflict between humours: asymmetric and materialist (construction of the people)
   - People guard freedom
   - Inclusive citizenship = armed people = military power and egalitarian republic

2. The Institutions of Conflict

Machiavellian tumults thus develop a close relation with institutions: Neal Wood and Claude Lefort use the term 'institutionalisation' in order to describe this relation,[35] even if these two authors have only identified some of the meanings outlined above. They emphasise only the negative dimension of institutions, understanding them as counterparts that are capable of absorbing and legalising conflict, but seem less interested in their active functioning once the antagonism has been constitutionalised. Machiavelli, on the contrary, insisted at length on the *modes* of conflict, that is, on the instruments and modalities through which to achieve the objectives of political action. Indeed, he agrees with Aristotle and Cicero that the object of political prudence is precisely the means to reach these goals, rather than the ends themselves. However, in disagreement with this political classicism which would bring him closer to a classical humanist, for Machiavelli the ends of politics are not established once and for all (they depend on the *quality of times* and the *matter*,[36] namely the political conjuncture, as we will see in the

INIMICIZIE, ORDINI, RISCONTRO

next chapter), and above all they are not the same for everyone, but differentiated according to the political actors who implement them. The great, in other words, struggle to oppress the people and conserve order, while the people struggle not to be oppressed, and, under certain conditions, in order to transform order.

We have already mentioned two *modes* of conflict which substantially develop outside institutions, as far as they are in contact with them: *secessio* and *detractio militiae*. These are two essentially passive modalities of action, which act by subtraction and negation: on the one hand, the refusal of orders and symbolic exit from the city, on the other, the rejection of contributing to the defence of the political community. Actually, according to Machiavelli, both of these modes have historically played a significant role in the presence of an external threat, that is, the risk of war, through which the Roman plebs were able to exert significant pressure on the senate because of their indispensable military role. However, there is a third mode that Machiavelli focuses on, which is not by chance the most clearly active. This mode leads directly to the relation between conflict and institutions: it is accusation,[37] that is, the possibility that the conduct of illustrious citizens, including members of the senate and patricians, can be submitted to judgement by the tribune of the plebs.

Just as he does with conflict, Machiavelli moves on this terrain in light of the ancient tradition. In particular, with respect to the functioning of Roman institutions, he is confronted by two influential paradigms which are differentiated in many ways: Polybius' *Histories* and Dionysius of Halicarnassus' *Roman Antiquities*.[38] Both are models that valorise the functioning of the mixed constitution of republican Rome, which Polybius distinguishes by static representation (focused on the period of the Punic Wars), whereas Dionysius insists on the historical process that has led Rome to this kind of order. Polybius distinguishes between three forms of healthy government (monarchy, aristocracy, and democracy) and three degenerate forms (tyranny, oligarchy, and ochlocracy), although he maintains that the mixed order is the most preferable.[39] For Dionysius, any non-mixed order is problematic because it will not last over time.[40]

Machiavelli positions himself on Dionysius' side in interpreting the Roman constitution as a whole, as he is important for his treatment of institutions, starting from the accusations and the role of the tribunate. In fact, for Polybius, the popular element of the Roman constitution is given by the right to vote in the assembly,[41] while for Dionysius the Roman model is perfected only with the introduction of the tribunate and the first popular trials that emerged from the tribunal power to accuse the great.[42] Further, according to Polybius, the balance of mixed orders arises from the dialectic (*sunérgein*), which is also antagonistic (*antipráttein*),[43] within the magistracy, which is essentially based on the veto power of the tribunes. For Dionysius, it emerges from the reciprocal thread between institutions (*coercitio*), that is, an authentic conflict between the magistrates moved by accusations, or in an opposite sense, the senatorial instrument of dictatorship.[44]

In the *Discourses*, Machiavelli takes up Dionysius' model, putting it in service of his conception of the relation between conflict and institutions. In particular, there are two theoretical functions covered by institutions in Machiavelli's framework. 1) An *affirmative* element of *structuring* the republic and its people. This is a matter of constructing the people through the work of institutions, since according to Machiavelli, the people can

INIMICIZIE, ORDINI, RISCONTRO

only act as a political agent if they are organised and ordered. For example, the capacity of popular judgement is often far-sighted and lucid if adequately mediated by institutions, whereas without this process of collective discussion and deliberation it risks falling prey to calumnies, false news, and pressure from patricians and ambitious leaders. It is a structuring that is also possible through the construction of assemblies and the practice of drawing lots in order to prevent the prestige and wealth of the great from prevailing. 2) The description of a conflict in form, that is, an antagonism between institutions essentially embodied by the veto power of the plebeian tribunal against the laws of the senate, the power of accusations, and episodes of distributed conflict such as those laws linked to agrarian reform. An affirmative institutional conflict, which is founded on a dynamic that is not only dialectical but of reciprocal threat and coercion within the magistracy.

Finally, as the effect and outcome of this complex articulation, for Machiavelli we have the duration of the republic, whose mixed order allowed the Roman experiment to extend over time. This was possible thanks to the periodic transformation of its constitution (an aspect to which we will return in the next chapter), avoiding stasis and corruption, and in light of its capacity for general inclusion, capable of retaining both the great and the people within the institutional mechanism of the republic.

> It is to be noted [. . .] how detestable calumnies are in free cities [. . .] and that to repress them one should not spare any order that may suit the purpose. Nor can there be a better order for taking them away than to open up very many places for accusations; for as much as accusations help republics, so much do calumnies hurt [. . .] So an orderer of a republic should order

that every citizen in it can accuse without fear or without any respect; and having done this [. . .] he should punish calumniators harshly [. . .] Where this part is not well ordered, great disorders always follow; for calumnies anger and do not punish citizens, and those angered think of getting even, hating rather than fearing the things said against them.[45]

Accusations are primarily an instrument through which Machiavelli suggests organising the republic and the people, institutionally building its capacity for political judgement. In this case, he also separates himself from a tradition that has at times considered the people completely unreliable as political decision makers (Xenophon, Plato), or has relegated their participation to the choice of the best possible elites, that is, the personalities most suitable for a position, and the vote on their proposals (Aristotle, Cicero). Machiavelli, on the contrary, believes that popular will, and with it the people of the republic, is constructed only through the procedure of discussion, as well as deliberation.[46] Indeed, accusations are constructed by passing through an institutional apparatus, and discussion about them allows the people to make substantiated decisions. In these conditions, for Machiavelli, popular judgement is the best possible judgement, because a broad and anonymous will is less conditioned by partisanship and pressures from the accused, above all the rich and powerful. This is the case in the story of Coriolanus told in the *Discourses*,[47] who is accused by the tribunes after proposing to the senate to starve the people in order to induce them to obedience. Machiavelli emphasises how a private revenge of the people provoked a civil war and probably a foreign invasion and the fall of the republic. The *oppression* through *ordinary modes* instead makes it possible to avoid feuds with the friends of the accused, who do not suffer consequences such as lynching by the crowd, but above all to transform the people into a political subject endowed with legal power.[48] As John McCormick has noted:

> a people that is empowered to decide political trials, Machiavelli suggests, cannot be compared to a violent mob; rather it constitutes, on the one hand, a reliable guard against oligarchic or princely usurpations of liberty and, on the other, the surest bulwark against civil instability – not, as critics suggest, the most likely instigator of the latter.[49]

Overall, therefore, according to Machiavelli, the people judge better than nobles, a prince, or individual magistrates. This is so because, on the one hand, they lack a will towards oppression shared by other social groups, and on the other, because a will that is broad, complex, and anonymous resists pressures of all kinds better than singular wills.[50]

Similarly, Machiavelli promotes the methods of Roman assemblies even if he underestimates, or probably does not know, the different weight attributed to the votes of the different classes, such as in the *comitia centuriata*, for example.[51] He describes the functioning of these assemblies according to the principles of Athenian democracy, particularly the *ecclesia*, where there was the rule of one vote for each member and the practice of extensive discussion in addition to the simple vote. Probably referring to the *concilium plebis*, Machiavelli writes that 'a tribune, or any other citizen whatever, could propose a law to the people, on which every citizen was able to speak, either in favor or against, before it was decided'.[52] In this case, the expression 'any citizen whatever' probably refers to the popular citizen, to the exclusion of the patricians, so as to describe a procedure of discussion and deliberation guaranteed by an exclusively plebeian assembly.[53]

MACHIAVELLIAN ONTOLOGY

Machiavelli merges selection according to social class (to which they belong) with the method of drawing lots typical of Greece.[54] The end is twofold: on the one hand, as mentioned, constructing the republican people through an institutional process of participation open to the largest number of citizens (drawing lots is a method that helps the circulation of those elected), but above all trying to circumvent the customary prevalence of the elites in general elections. This is what has been defined as the aristocratic effect of elections, due to which in a broad election, extended to all citizens (include the elite) by a general ballot, the most prominent personalities, the most educated and successful individuals of the city, the members of the richest and most influential families, will always have a competitive advantage over those from lower classes. Machiavelli's Roman (and partially Greek) model fixes inequality, as usual in pre-modern republics, by dividing individual assemblies and even monocratic offices (consuls on the patrician side and tribunes on the plebeian side), but egalitarian effects are proposed in light of the possibility of institutionally creating an otherwise absent people and the conflictual interaction between different institutions. It is not an acceptable model for us, but on the theoretical level it perhaps identifies theoretical needs – the structuring of order and citizenship through the affirmative role of institutions and conflict within political form – as well as political needs – the construction of popular power and pressure over dominant groups – that are not extraneous to our present.

Popular assemblies, however, were widespread in the Italian republics of the Renaissance period, as Machiavelli knew well. What must have seemed to him an authentic exception in the Roman world were the tribunes of the plebs, to the point that he suggests their rediscovery (calling them *proposti*) in the

INIMICIZIE, ORDINI, RISCONTRO

institutional architecture that he hypothesises for Florence in the *Discursus Floentinarum Rerum* (1520). According to Machiavelli, there is no better instrument for exercising institutional conflict capable of containing the ambition and insolence of the great which, over a long period, can undermine the foundations of the republic.[55] The modes typical of the tribunate are divided, in Machiavelli's account, into two large groups: the negative or passive ones, mainly employed to defend the people from the threats of patrician institutions, and the affirmative or active ones, which perform the opposite task, namely to intimidate and threaten the holders of power and wealth.[56]

Among the defensive power of the tribunes, the most important is certainly that of *intercessio*, the possibility of vetoing most acts of the senate, an institution controlled by the nobles. Once challenged by the courts, these measures cannot immediately be implemented by the consuls but must be discussed again. Secondly, the tribunes hold the power of the *auxilium*, thanks to which they can ask for the release of any plebeian who is detained due to accusations by the authorities or the great. Finally, the tribune is a *sacrosanct* person. He cannot be killed, and the plebs undertake to avenge his possible assassination. As regards the affirmative powers of the tribunes, Machiavelli emphasises the possibility, already mentioned, of accusing and prosecuting magistrates and illustrious citizens believed to be the authors of abuses and political crimes,[57] and proposing laws by discussing them in popular assemblies.[58]

However, it is not only about this: in Roman practice, the tribunes, in addition to protecting the people and allowing their active participation, mediate between the great and the plebs[59] and also between the nobles themselves.[60] In this way, the people influence the elites not only by judging in trials or selecting positions,

MACHIAVELLIAN ONTOLOGY

but by mediating their internal conflicts.[61] In conclusion, there is, then, the problematic case of the distributive conflict organised by the tribunes, which Machiavelli discusses with regard to the agrarian reform that the Gracchi proposed. This is a controversial case, traditionally considered the caesura *par excellence* in the history of Rome, between a functioning and expansive republic and its decline towards civil wars and the transformation into empire. Machiavelli, however, believes that when the theme of wealth is touched on, the ambition of the great is so large that if the events of agrarian reform, while failing to achieve a true redistribution, took three hundred years to bring down the republic, it can be said that such an instrument of pressure is useful for the duration and prosperity of its political form.

> Such, thus, were the beginning and the end of the Agrarian law. And although we have shown elsewhere that the enmities in Rome between the Senate and the plebs kept Rome free by giving rise to laws in favor of freedom, and although the end of this Agrarian law appears not to conform to such a conclusion, I say that I do not, because of this, abandon such an opinion. For so great is the ambition of the great that it soon brings that city to its ruin if it is not beaten down in a city by various ways and various modes. So, if the contention over the Agrarian law took three hundred years to make Rome servile, it would perhaps have been led into servitude much sooner if the plebs had not always checked the ambition of the nobles.[62]

For an effective distributive conflict, Machiavelli recalls the example, taken from Plutarch's *Parallel Lives*, of the Spartan legislator Cleomenes, who was capable of reforming corrupt orders by passing through extraordinary modes, that is, through violence and arms. This suggests that the Gracchi, 'whose intention should be more praised than their prudence', were not too

INIMICIZIE, ORDINI, RISCONTRO

bold in their action, but too cautious. Through the story of Cleomenes, Machiavelli suggests that they should probably have waged an open war on the senate, the only way to remove a centralisation of wealth that had become risky for the republic.[63]

In each case, what is most important about these tribunal practices is that through them, what we have defined as an *instituting procedure*[64] is completed. In this procedure, the people first fight for their own magistrates, then are expressed and politically constructed through them, and finally, the people use them in order to fully participate in the governing of the republic. A conflict *outside* and *for* institutions, and later *in* institutions, and finally *through* institutions.

This instituting procedure has several consequences concerning the relation of the republic to historical time. First, the institutional articulation allows a general inclusion of the parties in the republican order: we have already emphasised how the popular institutions construct the people as a political subject through participation and deliberation, but Machiavelli emphasises the fact that apparently domineering and oppressive institutions in relation to the great instead allow inclusion on closer inspection. This is the case for accusations, preferable in comparison to private revenge and lynching, as well as for the mediation of conflicts by the tribunes, for popular participation in the army from which the military power of the republic derives, and for popular judgement which often elects the best possible magistrates, who are not rarely patricians.

Secondly, as the extreme example of Cleomenes suggests, the republic can last if the institutions in it work against corruption. This means, on the one hand, preventing an excessive centralisation of power and wealth, and, on the other, not allowing this eventual control of the great over the republic to slow down to the point of stopping the conflictual dynamic and instituting procedure. Conflict that establishes the relations of force excessively in favour of dominant groups transforms the republic into something different, just as a stasis that excludes the dynamic pressure of the tribunate and the popular assemblies compromises its internal life. The transformation of order which is not permanent but periodic allows Machiavelli to obviate the risk of corruption and dissolution. A specific historicity of the republic immediately follows from the instituting procedure.

In this sense, we can summarise Machiavellian institutions as follows:

1. Structuring: constructing the people and the republic
   - Structured popular judgement vs. immediate judgement
   - Mixing assemblies of class and the drawing of lots in general elections
2. Tribunate, the conflict between institutions (in form): *coercitio* and threat as affirmative modes
   - Veto
   - Accusations, popular trials
   - Proposal of laws, distribution conflict (agrarian reform)
3. Duration of the republic
   - Periodic transformation of order vs. corruption and stasis
   - General inclusion (convenient also for the nobles to remain in the republic)

3. History: *Riscontro* and Return to Beginnings

If there is a moment to which the beginning of Machiavellian political thought can be dated, it is perhaps September 1506.

INIMICIZIE, ORDINI, RISCONTRO

Between the 13th and the 21st, Machiavelli replied to a letter he had received from Giovan Battista Soderini, the start of an accomplished and original meditation on the status of political action and its implications. To conclude our considerations on political conflict and its relation to institutions, it is perhaps useful to grasp how Machiavelli thinks these political instruments in relation to the problem of duration, corruption, and the transformation of republics. This is the theme of *riscontro*, the object of this autumn 1506 letter, which has come down to us as the 'Ghiribizzi al Soderino', owing to Machiavelli's own inscription.

The events that offered this occasion are well known. The letter was sent following a military expedition of Pope Julius II. Machiavelli witnessed his conquest of the city of Perugia through an impetuous act that was extraneous to the usual conduct prescribed by the art of war. The audacity of the warrior Pope is counterbalanced by the timidity of Giampaolo Baglioni, who was the Lord of Perugia. To the glance of a neutral observer, this contrast offers itself as a paradigm. The theoretical problem Machiavelli develops in light of these events starts from the apparent indifference of the forms of political action, that is, the lack of a stable criterion aimed at defining the preference for some specific quality of it. In other words, how should the goodness or otherwise of an audacious action, or on the other hand, a cautious practice, be evaluated, if history shows from time to time that both options lead to success and defeat? Leaving aside a number of implications behind this reasoning,[65] which concern the politics of the time and Machiavelli's specific position in the Florentine republic, what is interesting to emphasise here are some aspects that emerge from his attempt to answer these questions. Machiavelli's problem, as we noted, is the indifference of political action, the result of its consideration in the void, in isolation, which deprives it of a stable criterion of evaluation. His solution is articulated in two successive and concentric moves, the first of which bears the name of the underlying theme that characterises these pages, namely *riscontro*. Machiavelli's thesis is that political action (in its language and the *modes of proceeding*) never moves in a vacuum but must always, and primarily, encounter and clash with the historical conjuncture (the *quality of the times*) in which it finds itself. It is the literal meaning of the term *riscontro*, an encounter/clash, a differential encounter between politics and conjuncture, between conflict and history, which in the last instance decides whether or not the action succeeds, which Machiavelli defines as a *felice riscontro*.

In this way, the question appears to be resolved through the introduction of the lacking parameter: in short, if politics lies in harmony with the times, the predetermined result will be obtained, but otherwise it will be destined for failure. Yet Machiavelli grasps a deterministic trait in this outcome which must be overcome.[66] According to the sensibility of the time, in fact, such a schema would imply the stability of political action, according to a nature of its own or which characterises the agents who embody it. In this sense, there would be no room for the transformation of politics itself in view of an adjustment to the conjuncture.[67] Machiavelli instead seems to postulate a reversal of the tendency through the second theoretical operation that characterises this text: namely the idea that *riscontro* is said in many ways. In other words, in addition to the deterministic option we have just examined, there are two other formulas about the relation between action and the times in Machiavelli's hypothesis. On the one hand, the hypothesis of adaptation, which derives from Aristotle,[68] which says that the wise politician can modify his own nature, allowing his action to correspond to the times. On the other, there is the possibility of a political action aimed at *tentare la fortuna*, that is, forcing the limits of the conjuncture itself, in view of a different structuring of the historical context of reference. This is a modality, in other words, which is oriented towards the transformation of the times.

A 'Machiavellian' perspective carried out in this light would assume a logic capable of overcoming the isolation and autonomy of politics, returning to include its prerogatives within a field whose materiality would be given by the force of the conjuncture, the processes, and the frame of reference. This is a Machiavellian exercise in materialism, therefore, which through the encounter and clash between non-coinciding logics, dictated by the needs and orientations of politics and the social and economic determinisms of a specific moment, shows and guides action in its results and its productivity, aimed both at adaptation and the forcing of the context. The Machiavellian perspective, then, is one aimed at determining the specific historicity of politics, conservative when it assumes the task of adapting and corresponding to the times, and progressive when it contemplates the needs of forcing and non-correspondence to the given framework. Charles S. Singleton has identified a 'modernist' tension towards forcing in Machiavelli's perspective – which he calls the *prospettiva dell'arte*, understood as an artifice of renewal and shaping of the given material – that is capable of thinking the historicity of politics starting from the possibility of a *riscontro* with the quality of the times which is not aimed at adaptation (which owes instead, according to Singleton, to Aristotle and Thomas Aquinas)[69] but at the non-correspondence towards the present – the encounter between a politics measured on the materiality of what exceeds it and the preference for the historicity of a transformation thought as non-correspondence.

Non-correspondence to the origin, to the beginning, to the present, was one of the problems of political modernity from Machiavelli until at least the French Revolution. If, among other things, the modern was the season that set itself the task of rejecting tradition and nature, the figure of the *ritorno all'origine*, or *ai princìpi*, has often been an example of this understanding and the battlefield on which the knot of the past emerged with greater clarity. The image of the *ritorno ai princìpi*, starting from its ancient and Renaissance origins, has in fact given rise to a semantic context capable of meaning both conservation, in its reprise of an archaic origin, as well as newness, through the re-proposition of the founding act and thus the transcendence of given conditions.[70] And Machiavelli did this in the modality of an encounter between different instances, that of the origin, or principles, understood as conditions that have always been given, the ancestral sedimentation of customs and tradition, and the act of reprisal, return, repetition, a figure of the historico-political act in relation to the frame of reference. This is a form, in other words, of *riscontro*, a conflictual encounter aimed at perverting or safeguarding the present, using the past as a function of conservation or innovation, leading towards a future that is either similar to the present or in open rupture with it.

In Machiavelli, the figure of the return to principles shows the breadth of the semantic complex that it helps to frame: on the one hand, it reprises an idea of a tendential identification with the modes and orders of the past, assuming the possibility of their return and their literal reprisal in harmony with so much of Renaissance political literature.[71] On the other, it instead seems to allude to the event of the beginning, to the reprisal of

INIMICIZIE, ORDINI, RISCONTRO

the originary act of the foundation of a city, state, or political community. This is a radical *renovatio* that at the beginning thus re-proposes only the spirit of having begun something new. The most authentically Machiavellian figure of the return to origins is probably something else, however: in his work, the recuperation of principles does not exactly mean either regression or reactivation, but neither does it mean vertical rupture and discontinuity.[72] Rather, the repetition of the founding moment is problematically oriented towards the duration of the political body. In other words, periodically re-founding institutions, according to Machiavelli, allows the aggregate not to become corrupted and to extend its own life. Repetition, renewal, and conservation constitute a complex and non-univocal triangulation.

Modern philosophy has long reasoned along this argumentative chain, sometimes taking up the reference to Machiavelli. This is the case for Spinoza, who, citing the Florentine, recognises the crossroads between renewal and conservation, conflictual encounter and duration, tradition and refoundation. In this, he fully reactivates the entire logic outlined by Machiavelli. Montesquieu's meditation on this ground is also linked to the Spinozist background, indissociable from the question of the corruption of political forms which constitutes the necessary overthrow. To radical corruption, which orients the principles of government beyond the horizon of moderation – the cardinal place of his philosophy – Montesquieu opposes a return to the origin marked by greater caution than the Machiavellian prototype. Here it is a question of reprisal understood as a harmonious encounter between present and past, rather aimed at renewing the correspondence between the nature and principles of a government than at their interference and change. Further,

Montesquieu explicitly rejects the formulation of the authoritarian gesture of change, through which Machiavelli often thinks the return to the origin, in favour of an institutional custom that integrates the needs of renewal. At the same time, Giambattista Vico reflects on the historical outcome of the appeal to the beginning, and on the status of a barbarism whose return has been visible over the course of time. Resolutely rejecting both linear and circular options, Vico identifies the source of a healthy transformation of political systems in the sometimes recursive movement of history, and in the always present risk of barbarism, the historical constant to be overcome through a selective reprisal of the tradition. These are only a few examples, to which we could add the reactivations of the theme in a revolutionary and Marxist key: what is of interest here, however, is the logical structure of this argument.

The return to principles represents a historically determinate example of the relation of differential encounter/clash of political action in general, and conflict in particular, with the given conditions, outside of the isolation and superposition to them. From the beginning, therefore, the concept of non-correspondence seems to elude the rigid alternative between a history understood as linear process, in the multiple forms in which it is possible to conceive its determinism, and the pure simultaneity of a flat space, devoid of historicity, typical of many philosophical perspectives which have intended to avoid, not without reason, the settings of the philosophy of history and its structural concatenations. Non-correspondence, by establishing antagonism at the centre of the structure, configures a conflicting institutionalism, which, as such, is capable of going beyond itself. Its conflictual nucleus is in fact nothing more than a meditation towards the future, in the direction of a historicity not

INIMICIZIE, ORDINI, RISCONTRO

guaranteed by a necessary development, but also not consigned to the eternal repetition of the identical.

Notes

1 See the introduction for further discussion.
2 These authors are also quite diverse, including, for example, Gennaro Sasso, Roberto Esposito, and Antonio Negri in Italy, Maurice Merleau-Ponty, Claude Lefort, and Louis Althusser in France, and John Pocock and Neal Wood in English-speaking debates.
3 For these distinctions, see Marco Geuna, 'Ruolo dei conflitti e ruolo della religione nella riflessione di Machiavelli sulla storia di Roma', in Riccardo Caporali, Vittorio Morfino, and Stefano Visentin (eds), *Machiavelli: tempo e conflitto* (Milan: Mimesis, 2013), pp. 107–40.
4 Neal Wood, 'The Value of Asocial Sociability: Contributions of Machiavelli, Sidney, and Montesquieu', *The Bucknell Review* 3 (1968), p. 1.
5 Aristotle, *Politics*, 1295b–1296a.
6 Ibid., 1302b–1303a.
7 Cf. Aristotle, *Constitution of Athens*.
8 Cf. Loraux, *The Divided City*.
9 Cicero *Republic* II, xlii; Cicero, *Pro Sestio*, XLV–XLVII, LXV–LXVI; Cicero, *De officiis*, I, xxv.
10 Sallust, *Bellum Iugurtinum*, X.
11 See Gabriele Pedullà, *Machiavelli in Tumult: The Discourses on Livy and the Origins of Political Conflictualism* (Cambridge: Cambridge University Press, 2018), pp. 10–26.
12 Niccolò Machiavelli, *The Prince* (Chicago: University of Chicago Press, 1985), p. 39.
13 This is a sort of tribunate of the plebs which Machiavelli conceives for Florence in the *Discourse on Florentine Affairs* (1520).
14 Machiavelli, *The Prince*, p. 4.
15 Cf. at least Roberto Esposito, *La politica e la storia: Machiavelli e Vico* (Naples: Liguori, 1980), p. 32; Fabio Frosini, 'L'aporia del 'principato civile'. Il problema politico del 'forzare' in *Principe, IX*', *Filosofia politica* 2 (2005), pp. 199–218.
16 Niccolò Machiavelli, *Discourses on Livy*, I, 4. All references are *Discourses on Livy* (Chicago: University of Chicago Press, 1998), here p. 16.

MACHIAVELLIAN ONTOLOGY

17 Gennaro Sasso, 'Machiavelli e i detrattori, antichi e nuovi, di Roma', in Gennaro Sasso, *Machiavelli e gli antichi vol. II* (Milan: Ricciardi, 1988), pp. 401–536.

18 Machiavelli, *Discourses on Livy*, I, 4.

19 This is summarised in Pedullà, *Machiavelli in Tumult*.

20 Machiavelli, *Discourses on Livy*, I, 2.

21 Ibid., I, 4.

22 The exponents of the so-called Cambridge School stop at the first part of Machiavelli's description, entirely missing the second. See at least Quentin Skinner, *The Foundations of Modern Political Thought*, 2 vols (Cambridge: Cambridge University Press, 1978); John Pocock, *The Machiavellian Moment: Florentine Thought and the Atlantic Republican Tradition* (Princeton, NJ: Princeton University Press, 1975).

23 Machiavelli, *Discourses on Livy*, I, 4, 7.

24 Ibid., I, 16.

25 Ibid. I, 17.

26 Ibid. I, 17–18.

27 Cf. Anthony Parel, *The Machiavellian Cosmos* (New Haven, CT: Yale University Press, 1992); Nancy A. Siraisi, *Medieval and Early Renaissance Medicine* (Chicago: University of Chicago Press, 1990).

28 Cf. John McCormick, *Machiavellian Democracy* (Cambridge: Cambridge University Press, 2011).

29 Machiavelli, *Discourses on Livy*, I, 5.

30 Machiavelli, *Discourses on Livy*, I, 6.

31 Machiavelli, *The History of Florence*, II, 22–3, 32–7, 42. For an English translation, see Niccolò Machiavelli, *The History of Florence*, in Alan Gilbert (ed. and trans.), *Machiavelli: The Chief Works and Others Volume II* (Durham, NC: Duke University Press, 1989), pp. 1025–435.

32 Ibid., III, 11–17.

33 Ibid., IV, 26–7.

34 Esposito, *Ordine e conflitto*, p. 192. The English translation of this passage is found in Pedullà, *Machiavelli in Tumult*, p. 226. On this set of problems, see Marchesi, *Cartografia politica*.

35 Wood, 'The Value of Asocial Sociability'; Claude Lefort, *Machiavelli in the Making* (Evanston, IL: Northwestern University Press, 2012), p. 173. See Jérémie Barthas, 'Machiavelli e l'istituzione del conflitto', *Rivista Storica Italiana* 127 (2015), pp. 552–66; Mattia Di Pierro, *L'esperienza del mondo. Claude Lefort e la fenomenologia del politico* (Pisa: ETS, 2020).

36 Machiavelli, *The Prince*, XXV; Machiavelli, *Discourses on Livy*, I, 17; III, 9.

INIMICIZIE, ORDINI, RISCONTRO

37 Machiavelli, *Discourses on Livy*, I, 7.

38 Cf. Cary J. Nederman and Mary Elisabeth Sullivan, 'The Polybian Moment: The Transformation of Republican Thought from Ptolemy of Lucca to Machiavelli', *European Legacy* 17 (2012), pp. 867–81; Arnaldo Momigliano, 'Polybius' Reappearance in Western Europe', in *Sesto contributo alla storia degli studi classici e del mondo antico* (Rome: Edizioni di storia e letteratura, 1980), pp. 103–23; Emilio Gabba, *Dionysius and the History of Archaic Rome* (Los Angeles: University of California Press, 1991); and again see Pedullà, *Machiavelli in Tumult*, pp. 181–219.

39 Polybius, *Histories*, VI, 3–4.

40 Dionysius, *Roman Antiquities*, II, 3.

41 Polybius, *Histories*, VI, 17.

42 Dionysus, *Roman Antiquities*, VI, 45–90; VII, 1–67.

43 Polybius, *Histories*, VI, 15–18.

44 Dionysus, *Roman Antiquities*, VII, 55–6, 65–6.

45 Machiavelli, *Discourses on Livy*, I, 8. 27.

46 Machiavelli actually here 'corrects' the Roman model, which did not anticipate discussion but only deliberation.

47 Machiavelli, *Discourses on Livy*, I, 7.

48 Ibid., II, 34.

49 McCormick, *Machiavellian Democracy*, p. 68.

50 Cf. at least Patrick J. Coby, *Machiavelli's Romans: Liberty and Greatness in the Discourses on Livy* (Lanham, MD: Lexington Books, 1999); Fergus Millar, *The Roman Republic in Political Thought* (Boston: Brandeis University Press, 2002); Lily R. Taylor, *Roman Voting Assemblies* (Ann Arbor: University of Michigan Press, 1990).

51 Machiavelli, *Discourses on Livy*, I, 14.

52 Ibid., I, 18.

53 Ibid., I, 58.

54 Cf. Josiah Ober, *Demopolis: Democracy Before Liberalism in Theory and Practice* (Cambridge: Cambridge University Press, 2017).

55 Machiavelli, *Discourses on Livy*, I, 3, 39, 50; III, 11. Cf. at least Andrew Lintott, *The Constitution of the Roman Republic* (Oxford: Oxford University Press, 1999), pp. 11–15, 121–8, 205–11; Claude Nicolet, *The World of the Citizen in Republican Rome* (London: Batsford Academic, 1980), pp. 340–59; Coby, *Machiavelli's Romans*, pp. 25–31.

56 Machiavelli, *Discourses on Livy*, I, 40, 44.

57 Ibid., I, 7–8.

58 Ibid., I, 18.

59 Ibid., I, 3.

60 Ibid., I, 50; III, 8.

61 Cf. Alexander Yakobson, *Popular Power in the Roman Republic* (Oxford: Blackwell, 2006); Cyril Courrier, *La plèbe de Rome et sa culture* (Rome: École Française de Rome, 2014), pp. 427–80; Kurt A. Raaflaub, *Social Struggles in Archaic Rome: New Perspectives on the Conflict of the Orders* (Oxford: Blackwell, 2005).

62 Machiavelli, *Discourses on Livy*, I, 37, 80.

63 Ibid., I, 9, 18.

64 On this, see Esposito, *Pensiero istituente*; Roberto Esposito, *Istituzione* (Bologna: Il Mulino, 2021).

65 Cf. Francesco Marchesi, 'Riscontro: Machiavelli's Art of History', in Prasanta Chakravarty and Sukanta Chaudhuri (eds), *Machiavelli Then and Now: History, Politics, Literature* (Cambridge: Cambridge University Press, 2021), pp. 145–61; Marchesi, *Riscontro. Pratica politica e congiuntura storica in Niccolò Machiavelli*; Carlo Galli, 'Riscontro', in *Enciclopedia Machiavelliana* (Rom: Istituto della Enciclopedia Italiana Treccani, 2014), pp. 427–33; Miguel Vatter, *Between Form and Event: Machiavelli's Theory of Political Freedom* (New York: Fordham University Press, 2014), pp. 137–43.

66 Cf. Jean-Jacques Marchand, 'Machiavelli e il determinismo storico (dai primi scritti al *Principe*)', in Georges Barthouil (ed.), *Machiavelli attuale. Machiavel actuel* (Ravenna: Longo, 1982), pp. 57–64.

67 Cf. Eugenio Garin, *Lo zodiaco della vita* (Bari: Laterza, 1976).

68 Domenico Taranto, *Le virtù della politica: civismo e prudenza tra Machiavelli e gli antichi* (Naples: Bibliopolis, 2003).

69 Charles S. Singleton, 'The Perspective of Art', *The Kenyon Review* 2 (1953), pp. 169–89.

70 Louis Althusser has insisted on this dimension of Machiavellian thought, not without inaccuracies, in *Machiavelli and Us*.

71 Thomas Berns, 'Le retour à l'origine de l'état (Machiavelli, Discorsi sopra la prima deca di Tito Livio, Livre III, ch. I)', *Archives de Philosophie* 59 (1996), pp. 219–48; Francesco Marchesi, *Ritorno ai princìpi. Concezioni della storia da Machiavelli alla Rivoluzione francese* (Rome: Carocci, 2022).

72 Machiavelli, *Discourses on Livy*, III, 1.

8

Neither Monistic, nor Dualistic, nor Pluralistic: A Mixed Ontology

A Machiavellian ontology can perhaps offer a different view on the problems we have examined in earlier chapters: the inertia of pure multiplicity, the repetition of an antagonism thought as competition and war, and the indistinction between order and order, and between conflict and conflict, which is latent in the doctrines of lack and ontological difference. Being in the flow of differences and rejecting every order, repeating the same competition over and over again, assuming order as always positive because it is an alternative to chaos, or conflict because it is irreducible to any structural closure – these are essentially the inertial and unproductive outcomes of these theories.

The static nature of these doctrines rests on the isolation of one of the elements of ontology, or the binary opposition between two of them. The multiple of variety, the duplicity of conflict, and the unity of order – these are particles which must continue communicating, even in antagonistic form: neither isolated and dispersed, nor opposed in a dualism, nor united in a homogeneous whole.

This is probably Machiavelli's main ontological indication: a triadic structure in which conflict can settle itself between one

MACHIAVELLIAN ONTOLOGY

and many. It is a mixed ontology, neither monistic, dualistic, nor simply pluralistic, but triadic in the sense of the conflictual circulation between instances.

This circulation has three immediate effects: 1) using *conflict as an organisation* of multiplicity and not as the nucleus of instability within order; 2) thinking *conflict as a measure of order* and *order as an effect of conflict*; 3) following the historicity of conflict as an *encounter* between politics and economic and social relations, in the alteration of moments of the structuring and deconstruction of order.

In short, it is a question of thinking the Machiavellian ontology of conflict as *non-correspondence*: the conflict in form, the form of conflict, and the historicity of forms and conflicts.

1. Triadic Structure

The mixed order that Machiavelli derives from the ancients and the instituting procedure in which the conflict of the magistracy lives speak of the circulation between one, two, and many. This is not in reference to the structure of classes of classical republics, expressed in the mixed order of monarchic, aristocratic, and democratic elements, and not even in the sense of the Aristotelian just mean, in which a large middle class is the political factor of harmony and balance. If it is possible to derive an ontological structure from Machiavellian thought, it can be done by exploiting the way in which he thinks the coexistence of the free multiplicity of political and social groups, the duality of conflict that organises the relations between them, and the horizon of order that arises from this instituting process and is controlled by the victors of conflict.

A MIXED ONTOLOGY

From this viewpoint, the elements of ontology, if taken as such, appear immobile, condemned to stasis or the indefinite repetition of a pre-established movement. Contemporary philosophy has often concentrated on the critique of inertia in purely monistic structures. The equation between ontological totality and political totalitarianism, which does not lack an ideological accent, has become synonymous with stasis and closure, in relation to its resistance to the unforeseen in the historical dynamic, the search for duration, and the construction of a perimeter to the outside in order to define what is present inside.[1] Yet there is no change except of orders. But even the apologists for an ontological and political monism have often drawn an undifferentiated and anonymous profile of totality and order,[2] simply opposing them to chaos or impersonal processes (technology, the economy) which are considered fraught with risks and not factors of rationalisation.[3] In effect, in order to change, orders cannot all be the same.

It is less obvious to consider pure multiplicity as a factor of stasis rather than movement. In reality, the flow of pure difference, also indistinct, which is theorised by many contemporary authors, does not differ from the limits that have been observed regarding simply monistic ontologies. Without returning to David Hume's theses, there is a part of the European philosophical tradition that has considered plurality as the main instrument of government, precisely because of its conservative character. Indeed, a pure multiplicity cannot change, because there are no relations between elements that can change. At the most, it can follow the horizon outlined by its own internal dynamic. A factor of equilibrium in its purity, the multiple is an element of change only if it is part of a process of structuring.[4]

In the preceding pages, however, we have examined above all the dualistic approaches, typical of several contemporary theories of conflict, which lead to similar outcomes. These approaches isolate conflict in the form of a permanent shift of relations of force within a binary polarity. This is the case with the Foucauldian circle between power and resistance, Schmittian enmity as regulated antagonism, and Arendtian conflict for distinction and memorability. Animated by similar and socially anonymous subjects, this conflict soon takes on the form of competition (in civil or military guise): different actors and means in search of the same end. The result is the stable permanence of a dualism.[5]

Similarly, this inertial effect also invests those theories that stiffen oppositions between these ontological elements. The contrast between order and conflict, for example, is typical of post-dialectical cultural traditions, such as those that characterise so-called Italian Theory. Since its main components – *operaismo*, the discussion of biopolitics, and negative thought – emerged in the Italian horizon of the second half of the twentieth century, characterised by the crisis of Hegelian-Marxist and historicist philosophy, authors such as Mario Tronti and Antonio Negri have tried to think conflict in a dualistic form that avoids a qualitative dialectical leap, which is considered a neutralisation of antagonism.[6] Alternatively, however, some theories have emerged that crystallise the opposition between order and conflict, in a binary choice of one or the other (Tronti),[7] in the preference for the permanence of conflict we just noted (Negri),[8] or in the opposite preference for order on the part of Schmittian authors of negative thought.[9]

The different poststructuralist cultural traditions – taken in a post-Cartesian culture such as France[10] – have tended to oppose the one of order to the multiple. As we have already observed, philosophies of pure difference emerge as hypotheses, albeit divergent ones, of Foucault, Deleuze, and Derrida, but the currents of this framework that have more clearly addressed the problem of conflict are those so-called philosophies of lack which have Lacanian and Althusserian origins.[11] Authors such as Badiou, Laclau, Žižek, and Mouffe have thought antagonism as the element of plurality that traverses institutional order, avoiding the denial of the latter but ending up superimposing every time of order as non-multiple. The effect is still an inertial form of repetition between orders that structure and events/antagonisms that put them in jeopardy.

Machiavelli suggests an entirely different articulation between unity, duality, and multiplicity. First, there is the instituting procedure that he constructs in light of the Roman model, which interprets conflict as an organisation of pure plurality: conflict for institutions and in institutions coordinates the variety of opinions of the Roman people, valorising this variety of perspectives in the framework of a process of discussion and deliberation in popular assemblies. In other words, the number, the extent of individual differences, and the anonymity of the collective will that follows are productive elements only insofar as they are organised in the assemblies by the work of the tribunes. Conflict, secondly, takes place within institutions for the prevalence of the overall order. If antagonism divides plurality into two contrasting instances, the institutions of the senate and the plebs, these struggle among themselves for supremacy over the mixed order, through a complex system of crossing vetoes, reciprocal pressures, and mediations. Finally, the resulting order will not be the same if one or the other contender in the conflict prevails: for Machiavelli, an oligarchic republic and a

MACHIAVELLIAN ONTOLOGY

popular republic cannot be further apart. The quality of order is therefore the effect of the conflictual organisation of multiplicity and the struggle for predominance among the institutions of conflict.

In short, we are in the presence of a triadic system, or a mixed ontology – monistic, dualistic, and pluralistic – at the base of which there is a notion of conflict not understood as the nucleus of instability and irrationality within order, but thought as an instrument of structuring and organisation.

2. Machiavellian Geometry: Conflict as Organisation

Twentieth-century ontologies often went in search of a nucleus of the instability of the real, to the point of describing being itself as the origin of a state of permanent contingency and reversibility of everything that exists. After the Nietzschean rupture, twentieth-century ontologies can be described precisely in these terms: on the one hand, there are those that attempted to renew the rationalist legacy of modernity, while on the other, there are those that are variously anti-modernist which have identified within a nucleus of instability, if not irrationality, an instrument to unhinge any rationalisation of experience.

Michael Foucault already described structuralism as 'the awakened and troubled consciousness of modern thought',[12] and the same could be said in other respects of the historicist tradition, while there are innumerable positions that have at their centre what deconstructs, what renders fragile and contingent, if not what destitutes and revokes, for every possible structuring: Heideggerian ontological difference in all its versions,[13] pluralist scepticism derived from Wittgenstein,[14] and the most varied

A MIXED ONTOLOGY

renewals of the Nietzschean conflict of forces.[15] We could continue. The normative apologia for every possible composition is only an equal and opposite reaction to such a climate. Conflict was precisely conceived as a weapon of this decomposition of forms. In doing so, it was interpreted only on one side of its meaning: as a force for deconstructing the one, leaving aside the possibility that it has of structuring the multiple. It has thus primarily become the irrational nucleus of every form. This is the case in Lacanianism, which describes it as a return of the repressed in psychoanalysis, or Italian *operaismo*, which sees in it the workers' disorder within the capitalist mode of production, and it is also the case in the Nietzschean conflict of forces in Deleuze and Foucault,[16] as authentic nature and constant threat to any moral, social, and political order.

Machiavelli interprets conflict in light of the side that remains more obscure for contemporary philosophy. Rather than a factor of instability, it is an instrument of order and an element of regulated circulation. Machiavellian antagonism produces effects, new orders, as it organises and mediates, and exerts pressure and guarantees inclusion. In its opposition to the rigid and static symmetry of competition and war, its function of mediation between the one and multiplicity emerges. Organising the many and determining the orientation of the one are its tasks.

The established conflict that we have described structures order by including plurality, but above all by outlining the reciprocal pressure within the magistracy: in forming a collective will in the assemblies and opposing this will to the great, the tribunes direct a pressure that structures the mixed order. In the same way, the extraordinary exercise of dictatorship on the part of the senate can exert an equal and opposite pressure. Conflict is here a form of relation. From the Machiavellian viewpoint, conflict is

MACHIAVELLIAN ONTOLOGY

not separateness or scission, but a modality of republican institutional life, a factor of its expansion and growth.

Again, it can be noted how the pressure exerted by one magistracy on the other results in greater social inclusion. In Machiavelli's eyes, popular trials, accusations, and the power of the veto all make it possible to avoid feuds, calumny, and violent tumults. It is in this sense that he also invites the great, who were not least the magnates of his time, to look at the Roman example as a model of inclusive conflict. Pressure within the institutional apparatus is preferable for both the accused and the senatorial class. This is also true in the opposite sense: popular institutions, if not always adequate to the wishes of the plebs, exercise a function of protection, organisation, and promotion of those wills, which in open confrontation would probably not resist the strength and wealth of the nobles.

In this way, the triadic ontology suggested by Machiavelli describes a geometry of conflict: its structuring function, between the one and the multiple, outlines a form of mediation that is different from those in our recent tradition. Conflict actually mediates between plurality and order by organising the former into antagonistic groups, while it orients the latter in light of the prevalence of one over the other in the clash. It is a different meditation from the rationalist order going back to Descartes – reformulated by structuralism and of which Michel Foucault has made history – which in its various guises carried out a passage from multiplicity to unity through the construction of series and logical chains. Structural concepts such as overdetermination (Althusser), the symbolic (Lacan), or the combinatory (Lévi-Strauss)[17] take up the thread of this discourse. Also important is the distance from the qualitative leap of dialectical philosophies in which the conflictual organisation

222

A MIXED ONTOLOGY

of the multiple is reabsorbed by a unity that does not reflect relations of force, instead overcoming them for a new and more inclusive level. Notions such as the non-conceptual (Adorno), non-contemporaneous (Bloch), or the struggle for recognition (Honneth) have tried to renew this heritage without leaving the dialectical enigma of overcoming conflict in a homogeneous totality.[18]

Overall, therefore, the most recent philosophy has rejected any rational mediation, shifting the axis of its interest towards what is placed between one structure and the other, what is attentive to order and constitutes its nucleus of instability: *différance* (Derrida), difference in itself and repetition for itself (Deleuze), inoperativity (Nancy), destitution (Agamben), disagreement (Ranciére), and resistance (Foucault)[19] – figures of the refusal of rational mediation and order. In fact, this is a consolidated but not univocal orientation, since in some contemporary philosophical lines an at least partially affirmative direction can be observed: we can think here of the notions of a truth procedure (Badiou), equivalence (Laclau), and affirmative biopolitics and instituting thought (Esposito).[20]

In Machiavellian ontology, conflict embodies a sort of zero degree of mediation: lacking a high level of rationality, it divides and organises on the basis of the clash. Less ambitious than the structural order and dialectical overcoming, it lets the difference of opposites live within the whole. This is perhaps a modesty that has the advantage of enhancing singular difference, without dispersing but instead organising it, and thinking every order as internally partial, characterised by a relation between forces.

It is what could be defined with conflict as non-correspondence.

MACHIAVELLIAN ONTOLOGY

3. Non-Correspondence:
Conflict from Structure to History

Machiavelli describes an order within which the parts do not correspond. They do not mirror each other, but neither are they separate and isolated. If in the political debate between Hobbes and Spinoza, the transcendence of power or the immanence of horizontal relations, Machiavelli offers, as we have seen, the third option of established conflict, then in the ontological dispute between Hegel and Nietzsche, between homogeneous totality or a dispersion of forces, he proposes a different path.

The parts of order, its institutions, and its social and political groups are never similar, as in the model of competition among the ancients. Neither are they isolated, according to the warning of Dionysius of Halicarnassus, for whom monarchy (consulate), aristocracy (senate), and democracy (tribunate) do not last if they are isolated. These are different, discrete, and even antagonistic elements, but they are always caught in relations of reciprocal coercion and threat, as well as inclusion and mediation. It is what, with a term from the philosophical tradition, it is perhaps possible to call non-correspondence (though Machiavelli does not use this term).

Non-correspondence has often appeared as the negative correlate of correspondence, and therefore as an essentially pathological and negative notion (as the prefix suggests): from Hegel[21] to Balibar,[22] it designates the crisis of a form, whether historical, aesthetic, social, or ontological. On the contrary, it can be positively translated as conflict in form and conflictual form, but also, on the temporal level, as conflict at the origin of form. This is a concept that, interpreted in this way, is opposed to the main characters among contemporary theories

A MIXED ONTOLOGY

of conflict, and also to the main ontological assumptions that support them.

On the one hand, we noted, we have a conflict thought according to the analogy with competition and war, which takes on the appearance of a horizontal line, upon which the centre of gravity of relations of forces can be shifted but never transcended, in an indefinite repetition of the same antagonism. On the other, we saw an antagonism interpreted as the internal fracture of every institutional structure, its structural lack of completeness, or, again according to a vertical axis that unites orders and conflicts, as a potential articulation between high and low, form and chaos, hegemony and dissent, without these polarities, however, effectually distinguishing it. In this context, the latter option tends to be configured as a simple hypothesis of a lack, as the insufficiency of symbolisation. What results is an equivalence of all forms and all conflicts.

This is a double synchronic impossibility, of an order and a conflict that effectively subverts, which produces, as we have tried to show, a specific diachronic failure, that is, the loss of the thinkability of history as such, and of its development, which includes the interruption of time, as well as its reprisal in another form. A hypothesis, characterised by a contemporary absence of matter and history, which is opposed by the perspective of non-correspondence, that is, by the internal relation between matter and history, in the exact sense that the former produces the latter. In fact, a conflict thought according to the Machiavellian model of established conflict – against the competitive/military and psychic models – anticipates different actors for different ends, instruments, and tactics, and necessarily leads to a conservation of the playing field or to its transformation. What follows from this is a historicity thought in the articulation between moments of duration and conflictual events that may or may not lead to a change.

Non-correspondence – which, as we have seen, particularly emerges in the Machiavellian notions of *riscontro* and return to principles – designates the internal nexus between conflict and political form, in the sense that every conflict is judged on the basis of the form it is capable of giving rise to, just as every form harbours a relation between the forces that characterise its orientation. At the same time, on the temporal terrain, every transformation can be thought, and once again judged and measured, as the encounter between action and structural process, between politics and matter, two non-corresponding logics whose encounter can give rise to advances or regressions. The result is sequences of structuration and deconstruction that are external to both the automatisms of the philosophy of history and to the void of opposed autonomies of the social and the political.

In the last instance, non-correspondence represents a method: to exhibit the conflictuality of the real even where it is concealed – for example, in many of our recent philosophies, smashed into a reality without totality or a representation without referent – to observe how phenomena and their representations do not correspond – this is the first condition for activating conflictuality itself. The conflictual nucleus is indeed nothing more than a mediation towards the future, in the direction of a historicity that is not guaranteed by a necessary development nor consigned to an eternal repetition of the identical.

In this sense, we can summarise Machiavellian ontology as follows:

1. A triadic structure (mixed ontology): conflict as mediation between one and multiple

A MIXED ONTOLOGY

2. Machiavellian geometry: conflict as structuring and organisation
3. Non-correspondence 1) conflict in form, conflictual form
4. Non-correspondence 2) history as sequences of structuring and deconstruction

Notes

1 Perhaps the most radical philosophical critique in this sense is Gilles Deleuze and Félix Guattari, *A Thousand Plateaus: Capitalism and Schizophrenia 2* (Minneapolis: University of Minnesota Press, 1987).

2 Recent speculative realism is oriented in this direction. Cf. Levi Bryant, Nick Srnicek, and Graham Harman (eds), *The Speculative Turn: Continental Materialism and Realism* (Melbourne: re.press, 2010).

3 This is the case, for example, in Italian political theology, or the so-called left interpretation of Carl Schmitt, which we analysed in Chapter 2.

4 Whether multiplicity and difference are only thinkable through structuration or within it is a knot that is never clearly resolved by Jacques Derrida (see 'Structure, Sign, and Play in the Discourse of the Human Sciences', in *Writing and Difference* [Chicago: University of Chicago Press, 1978], pp. 278–94) or Gilles Deleuze (*Difference and Repetition* [New York: Columbia University Press, 1994]). This leads both authors to lean towards a flat and undifferentiated pluralism.

5 See Chapters 1, 2, and 3.

6 Cf. at least Dario Gentili, *Italian Theory: Dall'operaismo alla biopolitica* (Bologna: Il Mulino, 2012); Paolo Virno and Michael Hardt (eds), *Radical Thought in Italy: A Potential Politics* (Minneapolis: University of Minnesota Press, 1997); Lorenzo Chiesa and Alberto Toscano (eds), *The Italian Difference: Between Nihilism and Biopolitics*, (Melbourne: re.press, 2009).

7 Mario Tronti, *Workers and Capital* (London: Verso, 2019).

8 Antonio Negri, *Insurgencies: Constituent Power and the Modern State* (Minneapolis: University of Minnesota Press, 1999).

9 Cf., for example, Massimo Cacciari, *The Unpolitical: On the Radical Critique of Political Reason* (New York: Fordham University Press, 2009).

10 We analysed the debate between Derrida and Foucault in Chapter 1.

11 In this regard, see Chapters 4, 5, and 6.

227

MACHIAVELLIAN ONTOLOGY

12 Foucault, *The Order of Things*, p. 226.

13 For a recognition of this, cf. Marchart, *Post-foundational Political Thought*; Dominique Janicaud, *Heidegger in France* (Bloomington: Indiana University Press, 2015).

14 Cf. at least Alice Crary and Rupert Read (eds), *The New Wittgenstein* (London: Routledge, 2000).

15 There were a number of readings which moved in this direction at the height of the so-called 'Nietzsche Renaissance' in France during the 1960s. See Various Authors, *Nietzsche, Cahiers du Royaumont* (Paris: Éditions de Minuit, 1967).

16 See Chapter 1.

17 Cf. François Dosse, *Histoire du Structuralisme* (Minneapolis: University of Minnesota Press, 1998).

18 For a reconstruction, see Martin Jay, *The Dialectical Imagination: A History of the Frankfurt School* (Los Angeles: University of California Press, 1996).

19 See the list proposed in Marchart, *Thinking Antagonism*, p. 219n, which is not unlike this.

20 One area that has thought the affirmative and structuring nature of conflict is modern game theory. For example, it is important in Thomas Schelling's theory of the 'focal point'. Cf. Thomas C. Schelling, *The Strategy of Conflict* (Cambridge, MA: Harvard University Press, 1990).

21 Cf. Georg Wilhelm Friedrich Hegel, *The Science of Logic* (Cambridge: Cambridge University Press, 2015); Georg Wilhelm Friedrich Hegel, *Aesthetics* (Oxford: Clarendon Press, 1988).

22 Cf. Balibar, *Sui concetti fondamentali del materialismo storico*, p. 373.

9

Machiavellian Ontology and Us: Philosophical Lineages of the Twenty-First Century

Contemporary political ontologies do not lack relations with the historical and social framework that surrounds them. The authors we have analysed in this book have been used in order to describe – or are themselves engaged in describing – an idea of the contemporary world that their own theories have contributed to shaping. It is the vicious circle of theory in its ideological guise: it is influenced by the context, but the dominant ideas in that context are also those that it promotes.

The final part of the twentieth century was dominated by two main ideological paradigms. First of all, there is the neoliberal paradigm in the strictly political and political economic field, which has criticised any form of market control and supported a broad deconstruction of the instruments of collective regulation that were developed in the twentieth century (from the welfare state to public planning). Secondly, an idea of globalisation as an open, smooth, and homogeneous space has been affirmed, characterised by a growing equality of opportunity for individual citizens and for each country, and by peaceful coexistence within a global order convenient for all.

MACHIAVELLIAN ONTOLOGY

Both of these models are experiencing a crisis that is the result of a long-lasting decline. The *belle époque* of the twentieth century is over.

1. Conflict Within the Structure

The theoretical assumptions that derive from the neoliberal paradigm appeared for a long period to be widely shared by philosophy. Not only that, but it also seemed in some measure to have anticipated the themes prior to their diffusion on a large scale. The suspicion towards any form of structuring of the real has pervaded philosophy of every orientation since at least the rupture of 1968, and was then accentuated in a conservative sense over the course of the 1980s. In this process, the need for individual freedom and the attention to difference that emerged in the era of the modernisation of advanced societies has progressively supplanted interest in the tools of collective regulation, which had produced that same modernisation after the Second World War, as well as a significant redistribution of wealth. In this sense, the rupture in France between the generation of classical structuralism and that of so-called poststructuralism represented a symbolic moment, just as the transition from the second to the third generation of the Frankfurt School did in Germany, and the crisis of historicism did in Italy, with the emergence of weak thought.

However, it is not by way of these attempts to reform philosophical paradigms considered obsolete in the light of modernisation that neoliberalism has been flanked. At most, it has found in some of these philosophical needs a more favourable ground than the earlier context, linked to collective planning.

Rather, it is in the reorientation of these innovations in a conservative sense that the rupture that led to the contemporary moment emerged: in the 1980s, philosophy separated difference from equality, freedom from society, and criticism of oppression from the search for a different order, using and misrepresenting assumptions that 1968 had unpacked in a progressive, if not revolutionary, key.[1]

The result of these events can perhaps be synthesised in a general philosophical affirmation: every structuring of reality, society, or experience is suspect as such, whereas every deconstruction, whatever it is, is positive.[2] Political ontologies have consequently thought conflict against institutions, isolated the multiple, and rejected every order as innately repressive. Two crises over the course of a decade, the financial shock of 2008 and the pandemic shutdown of 2020, have first eroded and then radically challenged these assumptions. This is so to the point that new forms of collective regulation of capitalism are emerging in the West and perhaps never went away in the East.[3]

A Machiavellian ontology appears useful in order to analyse and, perhaps, fulfil the new tasks of philosophy, completely overturned by the new conjuncture: thinking conflict within institutions in order to understand who commands economic plans and state policies; examining the forms of the organisation of the multiple, which are many and divergent; describing the orders oriented within them by the winners and losers of political conflict.

In short, a Machiavellian ontology can perhaps provide at least some theoretical tools in order to understand the historical process underway and the tasks of philosophy in the twenty-first century. And it might also, in the last instance, be able to observe the change and participate in directing it.

2. Two Images of Globalisation

Behind the philosophical transformations of the late twentieth century, a clear ideological reference stands out. At least in the West, the idea has long dominated that the main historical process that is underway, what we usually call globalisation, can be synthesised by the formula that gives the title to Thomas Friedman's book: *The World is Flat.*[4]

The fall of the Berlin Wall, the spread of the network, the construction of international value chains, the externalisation of production to Asia, and other phenomena have been interpreted as the emergence of a borderless world, unequal but capable of offering opportunity to all, open to relations and the construction of horizontal networks between different people. Even in the radical and conservative variants, this horizon was shared: Michael Hardt and Antonio Negri, reformulating the Deleuzian model of *A Thousand Plateaus* and the legacy of *operaismo*, argued that the process of globalisation offers useful conditions for overcoming capitalism through the reticular and automatic construction of an antagonistic transnational subject, the multitude.[5] Samuel Huntington, from a Spenglerian perspective, hypothesised that the new openings could lead to a clash of civilisations,[6] just as neo-Schmittian sovereignty deemed it necessary to reaffirm Western sovereignty over the world. Radicalising the process, or holding it back and segmenting it, are both tasks that move from the same image of globalisation.

Of course, divergent images of this paradigm do exist, such as that developed by the world-systems theory of Immanuel Wallerstein and Giovanni Arrighi, which emphasised asymmetries and conflicts between centre and periphery.[7] The positions of the philosophies of lack, such as Laclau for example, are formed in a confrontation with this approach, which updates and renews the concept of imperialism.[8]

However, reality also appears different than these critical paradigms. Rather than a symmetrical and flat or asymmetric and unequal space, today globalisation seems to have assumed the guise of a contested space. Different projects of globalisation, between West and East, confront and conflict with one another. On the one hand, there is a project that, far from the pacification of opportunities for all, reaffirms an imperialist, neo-colonialist, and in some cases warlike will. On the other, there is a horizon founded on cooperation and harmony, that is, a compatibility between different people, against the ideology of homogeneity which is actually the rule of some.[9]

A Machiavellian ontology can therefore help to question this new conflictual form of global space, which has at its centre new and different modalities of structuring, that is, of the collective regulation of the market and international relations. But above all, a Machiavellian ontology can carry out a fully philosophical but more difficult task in this framework: how is it possible to pass from a global sphere dominated by conflict to one founded on cooperation and universal compatibility? What is the relation between conflict, competition, and cooperation? Can Machiavellian conflict be a mediation towards cooperation?

Western thought has traditionally contrasted conflict and cooperation, while it has often turned conflict into competition, maintaining its agonistic charge but depriving it of its emancipative and transformative character. More recently, conflict has become the instrument for thinking a conceptual deconstruction and a new subjugation of the world. Thinking conflict as a form of global structuring is in the meantime a way to consider the world as a political subject. A Machiavellian ontology, which is primarily an antagonistic ontology, but also one of inclusion and institution, can contribute to recovering the transformative character of political conflictuality: to move from a world founded on competition to a world built on cooperation.

Notes

1 Cf. Luc Boltanski and Eve Chiapello, *The New Spirit of Capitalism* (London: Verso, 2007).
2 Cf. Bratton, *The Revenge of the Real*.
3 Cf. Gerbaudo, *The Great Recoil*.
4 Cf. Friedman, *The World Is Flat*.
5 Michael Hardt and Antonio Negri, *Empire* (Cambridge, MA: Harvard University Press, 2000).
6 Samuel P. Huntington, *The Clash of Civilizations and the Remaking of World Order* (New York: Simon and Schuster, 2017).
7 Giovanni Arrighi, *The Long Twentieth Century: Money, Power and the Origins of Our Times* (London: Verso, 2009); Giovanni Arrighi, *Adam Smith in Beijing: Lineages of the Twenty-First Century* (London: Verso, 2009); Immanuel Wallerstein, *The Modern World System I: Capitalist Agriculture and the Origins of the European World Economy in the Sixteenth Century* (New York: Academic Press, 1974).
8 Cf. Laclau, *Politics and Ideology in Marxist Theory*.
9 Zhao Tingyang, *Tianxia, tous sous un même ciel. L'ordre du monde dans le passé et pour le futur* (Paris: Les éditions du Cerf, 2018).

Index

absolute enmity, 61, 62, 63–4, 65, 66
absolutes, 1
accusation, 195–8, 201, 203, 204
action, 77–85, 85–6, 87–9, 91
'Action de la structure' (Miller), 106–13, 119–20
Agamben, G., 152, 223
agrarian reform, 201–2
aleatory materialism, 126, 142, 145–6
Althusser, L., 4, 125–46
  conflict in dominance, 134–40
  deviation and genesis, 140–6
  event and determination, 126–34
Annales School, 26, 33
annihilation, 66
antagonism, 114, 162, 163, 164, 165–6, 172–3; *see also* conflict
Arendt, H., 5, 71–93, 218
  action, distinction, competition, 77–85
  ideology and identification, 72–7
  revolutions without history, 85–93
Argentine society, 168

Aristotle, 182, 183, 194, 198, 206, 207
Arrighi, G., 232
assemblies *see* popular assemblies
asymmetrical conflict, 6, 63, 65, 67, 139, 164, 165, 187, 190, 192–3; *see also* psychic model
authoritarianism, 156, 210
authority, 89–90, 91

Bachelard, G., 126
Badiou, A., 6, 8, 102, 113–14, 160, 219, 223
Balibar, É., 127–8
beginning, 88–9, 90, 91
Being and Event (Badiou), 113–14

Cahiers pour l'analyse (journal), 33, 101, 106, 119
Canguilhem, G., 107
Capital (Marx), 131
Cicero, 183–4, 194, 198
class politics, 190
classical Greek thought, 182–3
competition, 5, 9–10, 83–4, 182–3, 187–8

INDEX

conflict, 4–5
  in Althusser, 134–40
  asymmetrical, 6, 63, 65, 67, 139,
    164, 165, 187, 190, 192–3 (*see
    also* psychic model)
  in early Western thought, 182–4
  in Foucault, 18, 24–31
  geometry of, 7–8, 18, 222
  in Italian Theory, 218
  in Laclau, 165–6
  in Machiavellian ontology, 6–8,
    9–10, 184–94, 215–16, 219,
    221–2, 223
  in Schmitt, 51–8
  symmetrical, 5, 82, 83, 162 (*see
    also* military model)
  in twentieth century ontologies,
    220–1
  see also antagonism
conjunctures, 143–5
contingency, 169–71
'Contradiction and
  Overdetermination' (Althusser),
  131, 134, 136, 139
cooperation, 10
corruption, 203–4, 209
courts, 27–8, 29

deconstruction, 1, 17, 18, 24, 161
Deleuze, G., 1, 4, 219, 221, 223,
  232
democracy, 156, 161, 183; *see also*
  liberal democracies
Derrida, J., 17–24, 157–8
Derridean deconstruction, 17, 18
determination, 126–34; *see also*
  overdetermination
development, 74–5
deviation and genesis, 140–6

diachrony, 129–31
diagonal reading, 111
difference, 81, 82, 135, 163–4
Dionysius of Halicarnassus, 185,
  195–6, 224
discontinuity, 32, 33–4, 39, 141,
  143, 170
discourse *see* 'Orders of Discourse,
  The' (Foucault)
Discourses on Livy (Machiavelli),
  187–92, 196–8
Discursus Floentinarum Rerum
  (Machiavelli), 201
disorder, 24–31; *see also* order
distinction, 71, 72, 77–85, 92
dominance, 134–40

economic systems, 168
elections, 200, 204
emergency (*Entstehung*), 58
energy, 46–51
Engels, F., 131, 132
enmity, 53–6, 59–60, 61, 62, 63–6
Epicurean ontology, 141–2
equality, 81
equivalence, 158, 163–6
Esposito, R., 70n45, 193
ethics and politics of the suture,
  113–21
European philosophy, 217
events, 33, 34, 35–6, 39, 129–34,
  158
exception, 46–8
experience, 112

Florentine Histories, The
  (Machiavelli), 192
Folie et déraison (Foucault), 15,
  20–1

INDEX

For Marx (Althusser), 135–6, 138
form, 46–51
Foucault, M., 1, 4, 5, 15–39, 219, 221, 223
  autobiographical reflections, 15–16
  and Derrida, 17–24
  disorder and conflict, 24–31
  neutralising history, 32–9
  structuralism, 220
freedom, 87–9, 90, 91
  guardians of, 191
Freud, S., 104, 122n12

Galli, C., 64
Gasché, R., 17, 24
Gehrke, H.-J., 84
genealogy, 15–16, 36–8, 45
genesis *see* deviation and genesis
geometry of conflict, 7–8, 18, 222
Ginzburg, C., 18
globalisation, 2–3, 229, 232–4
Gracchi brothers, 201–2
Gramsci, A., 4, 157, 158, 174n12
Greek thought, 182–3
guardians of freedom, 191
Gunder-Frank, A., 167

Hardt, M., 232
Hegelian totality, 134–5, 136–7
hegemony, 7, 157, 166, 172
Hegemony and Socialist Strategy (Laclau and Mouffe), 153–4, 167n20, 177–8n37
Heidegger, M., 1, 4
Heideggerianism, 159–60, 220
historicisation, 21
historicity, 131
Histories (Polybius), 195–6

history
  in Arendt, 85–93
  in Foucault, 32–9
  in Laclau, 166–74
  in Machiavellian ontology, 191–2, 204–9
  in Schmitt, 59–67
Hobbes, T., 193
homogeneity, 54, 68n18, 75, 76–7, 136–7, 167–8, 233
Huntington, S., 232

identification, 72–7, 92, 104, 105
identity, 104–5, 131, 135
ideology, 75–6, 80, 84, 137–8, 157
'Ideology and Ideological State Apparatuses' (Althusser), 137
instituting procedures, 203
institutionalised conflict, 188–90
institutions, 194–204, 219, 222
isolation, 76–7
Italian Theory, 218

Julius II (Pope), 205
justice *see* 'On Popular Justice' (Foucault)

labour, 77–80
Lacan, J., 4, 101
'Lacanian left', 102
  action of the structure, 106–13
  ethics and politics of the suture, 113–21
  politics of lack, 103–6
Lacanianism, 221
lack, 109, 110, 115
  politics of, 103–6, 118, 120
  see also void

INDEX

Laclau, E., 6, 101, 152–3
  construction of the void, 153–9
  equivalence and antagonism,
    159–66
  history and contingency, 166–74
Lavoisier, A., 131, 132
law, 49–50
Lefort, C., 160, 194
Lenin, W.I., 61, 62, 63, 136
Leninism, 155–6
Les mots et les choses (Foucault), 32
Lévi-Strauss, C., 4, 158, 222
liberal democracies, 5
linguistics, 107, 130
Loraux, N., 183
Lukács, G., 4
Luporini, C., 135–6

McCormick, J., 190, 199
Machiavellian ontology, 4, 125–6,
    181
  conflict, 6–8, 9–10, 184–94,
    215–16, 219, 221–2, 223
  and globalisation, 233–4
  history, 191–2, 204–9
  institutions of conflict, 194–204
  Machiavellian geometry, 220–3,
    227
  and neoliberalism, 231
  non-correspondence, 224–7
  triadic structure, 216–20, 222,
    226
madness, 15, 18–19, 21–2, 23
manufacturing, 128
Marchart, O., 159, 160
Marx, K., 46, 79, 131, 132; *see also*
    For Marx (Althusser)
Marxian totality, 134
Marxism, 154, 155, 156, 157

military model, 29–31, 56–7; *see also*
  symmetrical conflict
Miller, J.-A., 106–13, 117–20
miscognition, 109–10
mobility, 60, 61
Montesquieu, 209–10
Mouffe, C., 6, 101, 153–9, 160,
    161–2, 164
multiplicity, 7, 77, 216–17, 219–20;
    see also plurality

negation, 58, 70n45, 195
Negri, A., 218, 232
neoliberalism, 1, 2–3, 229, 230–1
Nietzsche, F., 58
'Nietzsche, Genealogy, and History'
    (Foucault), 36–8
non-correspondence, 207–8, 210,
    216, 224–7
non-reason, 17, 20; *see also* madness

'On Popular Justice' (Foucault),
    27–8
'On the Material Dialectic'
    (Althusser), 134, 136
order, 2, 3–4, 4–5, 6
  in Laclau, 161
  in Machiavellian ontology,
    216–17, 218, 219–20
  in Schmitt, 48, 49
  see also disorder
'Orders of Discourse, The'
    (Foucault), 24–6
origin, 36–7
Origins of Totalitarianism, The
    (Arendt), 71, 72–4
overdetermination, 138–9, 140,
    164; *see also* 'Contradiction and
    Overdetermination' (Althusser)

238

INDEX

parole, 133, 143
partisans, 59–63, 65–6
philosophy *see* European philosophy; twentieth century philosophy
Plato, 182, 198
plurality, 7, 81, 83, 217, 219, 221; *see also* multiplicity
'Polanyi moment', 3–4
political agonism, 162
political conflict *see* conflict
politics
   in Althusser, 82–4, 134–40
   in Arendt, 79–81, 92–3
   'Lacanian left': and action of the structure, 111–13; politics of lack, 103–6, 118, 120; politics of the suture, 113–21
   in Laclau, 160, 161–2, 163, 169, 171
   in Machiavellian ontology, 206–11
   in Schmitt, 46–50, 51–7, 60, 62
   see also class politics; Leninism; Marxism; totalitarianism
Polybius, 185, 195–6
popular assemblies, 196, 197, 199–201, 204, 219, 221; *see also* tribunes
popular interest, 191
popular judgement, 197, 198–9
'Poulantzas moment', 4
Prince, The (Machiavelli), 185, 186, 187
production, mode of, 127–8, 134, 168
psychic model, 6, 225; *see also* asymmetrical conflict
psychoanalysis, 103, 104, 105, 107–8, 110

rationalism, 222
Reading Capital (Althusser, Balibar et al.), 127–8, 129, 132, 142, 143
Real, ethics of the, 115–16
reason, 17–23, 25
reflexive reduplication, 108–9
Renaissance, 183–4, 200
republican Rome, 89–90, 187–92, 195–204: *see also* Roman thought
'Returning to History' (Foucault), 33–5
revolutionaries, 59, 60–3, 65–6
revolutions, 85–93
riscontro, 205, 206, 208
Robinson, A., 103
Roman Antiquities (Dionysius of Halicarnassus), 195–6
Roman thought, 183–4; *see also* republican Rome

Saussure, F. de, 126, 130, 142–3
Schmitt, C., 5, 45–67, 218
   form or energy, 46–51
   genealogy, 45
   history and passivity, 59–67
   negation, 70n45
   symmetry of conflict, 51–8
Second International, 155
serial history, 33–5
Singleton, C.S., 207
social antagonism, 162
society, 53, 62, 79, 92–3, 169
   Argentine, 168
Soderini, Giovan Battista, 205
sovereignty, 47–8, 232
Spinoza, B.de, 209
Stavrakakis, Y., 104, 105
structural history *see* serial history

239

INDEX

structuralism, 22, 158, 220, 222, 230
structure
  'Action de la structure' (Miller),
    106–13, 119–20
structuring, 2, 3, 109, 110, 196–7,
    204, 231
struggle, 54, 57
suture, 113–21
symmetrical conflict, 5, 82, 83, 162;
    see also military model
synchrony, 129–30

Theory of the Partisan (Schmitt), 59,
    61
Thrasybulus, 183
time, 34–5
totalitarianism, 72–4, 75–6, 77
transition, 127–8
tribunes, 200–3; *see also* popular
    assemblies
Tronti, M., 218

twentieth century ontologies, 220–1
twentieth century philosophy, 1,
    2–3, 3–4, 8, 9
  and neoliberalism, 230–1

undecidability, 39, 46, 48, 67, 158

Vico, G., 210
violence, 85–6, 189, 202; *see also*
    war
void, 132, 141, 144, 146, 153–9; *see
    also* lack

Wallerstein, I., 167, 232
war, 5, 54, 56, 59, 60
Wittgenstein, L., 1, 4, 220
Wood, N., 182, 194

Xenophon, 198

Zupančič, A., 115–16